GRANDPARENTS AND THE LAW

How ought intergenerational relationships between grandparent, parent and grandchild be regulated? Should grandparents have rights in relation to their grandchildren? If so, what should the content of those rights be, both procedurally and substantively? And what is the appropriate role of the law in providing solutions to problems arising in the context of grandparents' rights?

This book goes beyond family law to draw on a wider range of legal, social and cultural contexts from which to better understand the role of grandparents in the law, specifically exploring issues of rights and relationships between grandparents, their families and the law. The contributors consider a range of issues concerning grandparents and the law, including private and public law proceedings in the family courts, international instruments such as the European Convention on Human Rights and the United Nations Convention on the Rights of the Child, as well as the role of grandparents in other jurisdictions, such as Iran, France and Nepal. The book also engages with key themes including the role and value of kinship, gendered dimensions of the law, procedural versus substantive rights, domestic abuse, and relationality.

The role of grandparents, including their rights and relationships in relation to their families, has received insufficient academic attention. This book is the first of its kind to devote exclusive analysis to the social and legal issues arising in relation to grandparents. The book's intention is to highlight the value of the under-emphasised grandparent/grandchild relationship and explore the tensions which may occur between grandparent and parent, or grandparent and the state. This collection builds on the existing academic contributions in family law, while exploring a rapidly new, exciting and evolving area of law and policy on familial relationships.

Grandparents and the Law

Rights and Relationships

Edited by
Samantha M Davey
and
Jaime Lindsey

·HART·
OXFORD · LONDON · NEW YORK · NEW DELHI · SYDNEY

HART PUBLISHING

Bloomsbury Publishing Plc

Kemp House, Chawley Park, Cumnor Hill, Oxford, OX2 9PH, UK

1385 Broadway, New York, NY 10018, USA

29 Earlsfort Terrace, Dublin 2, Ireland

HART PUBLISHING, the Hart/Stag logo, BLOOMSBURY and the Diana logo are
trademarks of Bloomsbury Publishing Plc

First published in Great Britain 2023

A catalogue record for this book is available from the British Library.

A catalogue record for this book is available from the Library of Congress.

ISBN: HB: 978-1-50995-341-7
       ePDF: 978-1-50995-343-1
       ePub: 978-1-50995-342-4

Typeset by Compuscript Ltd, Shannon

To find out more about our authors and books visit www.hartpublishing.co.uk.
Here you will find extracts, author information, details of forthcoming events
and the option to sign up for our newsletters.

This book is dedicated to grandparents and grandchildren around the globe. As parents, we dedicate this to the grandparents we rely on (Deborah Thirlwell, Raymond Connor and Liz Dowling) and our children who rely on us (Meredith Davey, Bethany Davey and Louis Lindsey-Rexhaj). This book is also dedicated to the late Barbara Davey. A grandmother, a role model and a source of inspiration.

ACKNOWLEDGEMENTS

This collection of essays is the by-product of ideas brought together at a workshop held at the University of Essex. The editors owe their appreciation to Professor Karen Hulme, Professor Joan Hunt, Professor Jean McHale, Professor Sabine Michalowski, Professor Donald Nicolson, Professor Matthew Stone, Professor Maurice Sunkin and Dr Charlotte Bendall for their helpful contributions throughout the project.

We thank Dr Timea Tallodi, Louisa Dickson and Moira Wright for their invaluable expertise on alternative dispute resolution, including mediation, and also Dr Aoife Daly for sharing her research on kinship care.

We would like to note our thanks to Rosie Mearns at Hart Publishing for her helpful assistance from the conception of the book to its publication, as well as to Catherine Minahan for her impressive copy-editing work on the volume. We thank our family and friends for their support throughout this project, including grandparents.

Last, but certainly not least, we would like to thank all the contributors to this volume.

Samantha Davey and Jaime Lindsey
University of Essex
9 December 2022

CONTENTS

LIST OF CONTRIBUTORS

Dr Charlotte Bendall is a Lecturer in Law at Birmingham Law School, University of Birmingham.

Dr Samantha Davey is a Lecturer in Law in the School of Law at the University of Essex.

Ms Liz Fisher-Frank is a solicitor (non-practising) and a Lecturer and Law Clinic Supervisor in family law at the University of Essex.

Dr Joanna Harwood is a Lecturer in Law in the School of Law at the University of Essex.

Professor Joan Hunt OBE has over 30 years of experience as an empirical researcher and is an Honorary Professor in the School of Law and Politics at the University of Cardiff.

Dr Fatemeh Keyhanlou is an Assistant Professor of International Law in Islamic Azad University, Iran.

Dr Jaime Lindsey is an Associate Professor of Law at the University of Reading.

Dr Sahar Maranlou is a Lecturer in Law and Socio-legal Studies at the University of Essex.

Dr Laure Sauvé is a Lecturer in Law at University of Essex and a co-director of the English and French Law Double-Degree.

Ms Sneha Shrestha completed her BPTC at City Law School and is currently a tenant at Holborn Chambers.

1

Introduction

SAMANTHA DAVEY AND JAIME LINDSEY

This collection of essays analyses the vital role of grandparents as caregivers and their relative absence within legal frameworks in England and Wales. We fill a gap within the literature on family law in England and Wales, which has, so far at least, engaged only to a limited extent with intergenerational relationships. The book goes beyond family law, however, to draw on a wider range of legal, social and cultural contexts from which to better understand the role of grandparents in the law, specifically exploring issues of rights and relationships between grandparents, their families and the law. These chapters include perspectives on legal frameworks drawn from human rights (including children's rights), medical law and alternative dispute resolution. The social context is no less important, since many of the chapters speak to the ways in which grandparents navigate social arrangements, with or without suitable legal frameworks. Moreover, these contributions provide insights into how the treatment of the grandparent/grandchild relationship plays out beyond England and Wales in different cultural contexts, including in France, Nepal and Iran.

The book acknowledges that, despite the widespread recognition and advancement of a wider range of parental rights,[1] grandparents have not received similar attention or protection through the law.[2] This edited collection draws out several themes, including: the role and value of kinship; gendered dimensions of the law; procedural versus substantive rights; domestic abuse; and relationality. Several chapters consider the issues from the perspective of English law, while other chapters look at international perspectives.

I. Who Are Grandparents and Why Do They Matter?

A 'traditional' definition would regard grandparents as the parents of a person's mother or father. Biologically, at least, each person has four grandparents. This

---

[1] N Lowe, 'The Allocation of Parental Rights and Responsibilities – The Position in England and Wales' (2005) 39 *Family Law Quarterly* 267.

[2] F Kaganas and C Piper, 'Grandparent Contact: Another Presumption?' (2020) 42 *Journal of Social Welfare and Family Law* 176.

definition, arguably, has the potential for complexity in light of the increased diversity in social relationships arising from new reproductive technology, the increase in gay and lesbian parenting, and remarriage and 'reconstituted' families. Thus, the range of those who are regarded as 'grandparents', or have the potential to be regarded as such, has been widened. A person may have many more, or fewer, grandparental figures in their lives than the biological four.

As the traditional 'nuclear' family has evolved, the need to acknowledge diverse family forms, including the role of grandparents, is similarly challenged in modern societies. Grandparents, in particular, are increasingly relevant in modern-day caring relationships,[3] with over a third providing some form of temporary or permanent form of care for their grandchildren.[4] This is despite the fact that persons from the older generation are typically seen as receivers of care rather than caregivers.[5] The increased lifespan globally, from 66.8 years of age in 2000 to 73.4 years in 2019,[6] means that grandparents are more likely to live for longer than previous generations.[7] The 'flip side' of this, however, is that parents are having children later in life,[8] which, over generations, can have the reverse effect; it means that grandparents will be older and are less likely to be around as their grand-children grow. Moreover, according to Harper and Ruicheva, reduced numbers of siblings means that individuals 'have more vertical than horizontal linkages in the family and spend longer time occupying intergenerational family roles than before'.[9] The picture is therefore rather complex and dependent on a number of social, economic and cultural factors, some of which have confounded predictions about what would happen with kinship care in the twenty-first century.[10]

Grandparents may even be primary caregivers, for example in circum-stances where parents have been deemed unfit to care for their children. In other circumstances, where parents are young or work long hours, grandparents may provide a significant amount of care during a child's lifetime.[11] Moreover, the role

---

[3] C Stelle et al, 'Grandparenting in the 21st Century: Issues of Diversity in Grandparent-Grandchild Relationships' (2010) 53 *Journal of Gerontology and Social Work* 682.

[4] L Spitz 'Grandparents: Their Role in 21st Century Families' (2012) 42 *Family Law* 1254; S Kanji, 'Grandparent Care: A Key Factor in Mothers' Labour Force Participation in the UK' (2018) 47 *Journal of Social Policy* 523; A Gray, 'The Changing Availability of Grandparents as Carers and Its Implications for Childcare Policy in the UK' (2005) 34 *Journal of Social Policy* 557.

[5] SM Neysmith and YR Zhou, 'Mapping Another Dimension of a Feminist Ethics of Care: Family-based Transnational Care' (2013) 6 *International Journal of Feminist Approaches to Bioethics* 141.

[6] World Health Organisation, *WHO Methods and Data Sources for Life Tables 1990–2019* (Geneva, WHO, 2020).

[7] A Buchanan and A Rotkirch, 'Twenty-first Century Grandparents: Global Perspectives on Changing Roles and Consequences' (2018) 13 *Journal of the Academy of Social Sciences* 131.

[8] A Buchanan and A Rotkirch, *No Time For Children? Fertility Rates and Population Decline* (Cham, Palgrave Macmillan, 2013).

[9] S Harper and I Ruicheva, 'Grandmothers as Replacement Parents and Partners: The Role of Grandmotherhood in Single Parent Families' (2010) 8 *Journal of Intergenerational Relationships* 219.

[10] F Chen, G Liu and CA Mair, 'Intergenerational Ties in Context: Grandparents Caring for Grandchildren in China' (2011) 90 *Social Forces* 571.

[11] B Janta, *Caring for Children in Europe* (RAND Europe, 2013) at www.rand.org/pubs/research_reports/RR554.html.

of grandparents may 'evolve' over time, with (potentially) less involvement and significance when children move into their teenage years[12] and beyond. Despite this complexity, we do know that changes in family structures, for example with two parents working or increases in single-parent families,[13] mean that there is the potential for the increased role of grandparents as child carers. Divorce is also said to increase the need for reliance on grandparents' care.[14] This greater diversity in family units in the modern age is not necessarily reflected in the law, which tends to lag behind social change.

In embarking on this edited collection, we recognised that grandparents should be seen as providing a valuable contribution to family life, something widely acknowledged already in the law, the European Court of Human Rights (ECtHR) stating '[t]he Court recalls that the mutual enjoyment by parent and child, as well as by grandparent and child, of each other's company constitutes a fundamental element of family life'.[15] Similarly, Lucy Frazer, Solicitor General for England and Wales, noted in the 2018 Westminster Hall debate:

> Grandparents play a significant role in family life. There is something special about the bond between a grandparent and grandchild. The loving relationship that is formed often enriches family life. Grandparents provide stability when it is needed. They can give a sense of history and show how important it is to belong to a family. They can give familial support when it is needed, such as when it is difficult for more immediate family members to be called on.[16]

The level of involvement that grandparents have in a child's life can be seen on a spectrum though. Many grandparents are heavily involved on a day-to-day or weekly basis, while other grandparents may be less hands-on. Regardless of the extent of grandparental involvement in a child's life, there is strong evidence of the value of kinship ties and how maintaining grandparental relationships has benefits for children. This is especially seen in circumstances where children's parents may be in the middle of a bitter custody battle and children do not feel seen or heard. In other cases there may be safeguarding issues,[17] and it may be necessary to consider alternatives to parental care. In such circumstances, evidence suggests that children in some form of kinship care fare better in terms of behavioural development

---

[12] R Dunifron and A Bajracharya, 'The Role of Grandparents in the Lives of Youth' (2012) 33 *Journal of Family Issues* 1168.

[13] S Harkness, P Gregg and M Fernandez-Salgado, 'The Rise in Single-Mother Families and Children's Cognitive Development: Evidence from Three British Birth Cohorts' (2019) 91 *Child Development* 1762.

[14] SK Westphal, A-R Poortman and T Van der Lippe, 'What About the Grandparents? Children's Postdivorce Residence Arrangements and Contact With Grandparents' (2015) 77 *Journal of Marriage and Family* 424.

[15] *L v Finland* [2000] 2 FLR 118, para 101.

[16] *Hansard*, HC Deb 2 May 2018, vol 640, col 182WH.

[17] *Re N (Children) (Interim Care)* [2020] EWCA Civ 1003.

and mental-health functioning than children in foster care, for example with less educational disruption and greater closeness with siblings.[18]

Such kinship care is, in some cases, formalised via court orders, such as child arrangement orders under the Children Act 1989[19] and special guardianship orders (SGOs) under the Adoption and Children Act 2002. Kinship care, including the use of grandparent care, has generally been welcomed as providing a valuable safety net for children who have been victims of neglect and/or abuse.[20] Even in the absence of such abuse, kinship has been established to have positive effects on a child's development through, for example, facilitating an understanding of their history and identity.[21] This is of particular importance, for instance, in children from ethnic minorities,[22] including those with multi-racial backgrounds.[23] Grandparents can assist with children's mental, emotional and physical development, and often fall within traditional male and female caregiving stereotypes, with grandfathers usually taking on a 'mentoring' role and grandmothers taking on a 'nurturing' role.[24]

Despite the benefits of grandparents as kinship carers outlined above, many of the chapters in the collection highlight that the law in England and Wales has not yet explicitly recognised substantive (or, in many instances, even procedural) legal rights for grandparents, which can affect the recognition of and protection of grandparent/grandchild relationships. Parents act as 'brokers between generations',[25] which means that grandparents are dependent mostly on parents (or the state, where appropriate) to develop relationships with their grandchildren. Such difficulties can be seen most acutely in contact disputes between grandparents and parents in family law proceedings. Our discussion therefore proceeds on the basis that it is important to analyse whether, and how, rights for grandparents might be incorporated into law. This analysis is not one-sided, though. In fact, many of the contributors recognise that there are clear dangers in expanding the role of grandparents to provide them with legal rights, whether in relation to their own children or to their grandchildren. Such dangers include overriding the interests of children and/or parents, reinforcing abusive intergenerational behaviours, and facilitating overreach through the law by creating rights for one group (grandparents) that can, in principle at least, impact negatively upon the rights of

---

[18] M Winokaur, A Holtan and D Valentine, *Kinship Care for the Safety, Permanency and Well-being of Children Removed from the Home for Maltreatment* (Chichester, John Wiley & Sons, 2009); JP Lent and A Otto, 'Grandparents, Grandchildren, and Caregiving: The Impacts of America's Substance Use Crisis' (2018) 42 *Generations: Journal of the American Society on Aging* 15.

[19] As amended by the Children and Families Act 2014.

[20] L Pittman, 'Doing What's Right for the Baby: Parental Responses and Custodial Grandmothers' Institutional Decision Making' (2014) 2 *Women, Gender, and Families of Color* 32.

[21] A Green, 'Grandparents, communicative memory and narrative identity' (2019) 47 *Oral History* 8.

[22] S Nandy and J Selwyn, *Spotlight on Kinship Care* (Bristol, University of Bristol, 2011) 7–9.

[23] ibid.

[24] A Buchanan and A Rotkirch, *Grandfathers: Global Perspectives* (Cham, Palgrave Macmillan, 2016).

[25] Westphal, Poortman and Van der Lippe (n 14) 426.

others (children and/or parents). Furthermore, there is a lack of consensus over the appropriate balance between the 'triad' rights of grandparents, parents and children, and how to resolve conflicts if and when these rights clash. Some of these risks and challenges are particularly explored in chapters 3 and 7 of this volume.

There are practical and social challenges of expanding substantive and procedural legal rights for grandparents too. In an increasingly global society, grandparents may live miles, or even continents, away from their grandchildren. This presents a challenge to any proposed legal reforms that seek to give grandparents substantive rights in relation to their grandchildren, given the variability of the role of grandparents in their grandchildren's lives. Pre-existing close relationships, characterised by strong bonds, may also have been strained because of the separation enforced by legal responses to the Covid-19 pandemic in the United Kingdom (UK) and beyond. Indeed, the twenty-first century has been characterised by greater geographical distances between family members, especially post-parental divorce,[26] but also by greater advances in technology, affording grandparents different ways to connect with their grandchildren.

Regardless of the changing social and emotional landscape, many grandparents play a pivotal role in the lives of their grandchildren. In this collection we provide an original analysis of some of the key questions about the appropriate extent and shape of the law's role in governing relationships between grandparents and grandchildren, and consider this in specific areas of legal practice, including family law, human rights and medical law. Moreover, we explore how the law ought to govern such relationships when they are multi-layered and multi-dimensional, dependent on different family, cultural and social norms.

II. Themes

A. Rights: Procedure versus Substance

Ferguson states it is self-evident that the language of 'rights'[27] has become more prevalent post-Human Rights Act 1998. Although we agree that the discourse of rights is now embedded within law and society, in the UK and global north at least, we suggest that it is premature to conclude that decisions stemming from national courts, or indeed even those, such as *Beccarini and Ridolfi v Italy*[28] and *Terna v Italy*,[29] which have filtered down from the ECtHR, have strengthened the

---

[26] M Thomas, C Mulder and T Cooke, 'Geographical Distances Between Separated Parents: A Longitudinal Analysis' (2018) 34 *European Journal of Population* 463.

[27] N Ferguson, *Grandparenting in Divorced Families* (Bristol, University of Bristol, 2004) 141.

[28] *Beccarini and Ridolfi v Italy* App no 63190/16 (ECtHR, 7 December 2017).

[29] *Terna v Italy* App no 21052/18 (ECtHR, 14 January 2021).

claims of grandparents.[30] This is despite the ECtHR's acknowledgement, as early as 1979 in the case of *Marckx v Belgium*,[31] that grandparents could potentially have rights under Article 8 of the European Convention on Human Rights (ECHR), the right to a private and family life: 'family life … includes at least the ties between near relatives, for instance those between grandparents and grandchildren'; but also and especially that grandparents 'may play a considerable part in family life'.[32]

Fenton-Glynn, for example, expresses optimism about ECtHR jurisprudence, noting that the body of law on grandparents' ECHR rights has grown, representing 'an important acknowledgement by the Court that the protection of Article 8 must stretch further than the nuclear family and reflect the lived reality of children's lives'.[33] It should be noted, though, that although grandparent/grandchild relationships are capable of amounting to 'family life', in circumstances where grandparents have not met their grandchildren this may nonetheless engage the right to a 'private life' under Article 8 ECHR.[34] There are several factors that will be considered by the Strasbourg Court in determining whether 'family life' exists between a child and grandchild, including frequency of contact[35] and whether the child has lived with the grandparent previously.[36] Grandparents who have not met their grandchildren, for instance, tend to have a tenuous foothold. Despite evidence that progress has been made with respect to grandparents' rights, Brown argues that ECtHR decision making is still largely based on 'the idealised image of the traditional nuclear family'.[37] In other words, then, we consider that while the ECtHR has taken important steps in the right direction and has provided greater emphasis on grandparents' rights than, say, the law in England and Wales, more work may be required to protect the grandparent/grandchild relationship. Further exploration of the ways in which such protection may be increased (where appropriate) will be considered in chapters 4, 5, 6 and 9 of this collection.

Our focus is not simply on the grandparent but also on the grandchild(ren), and the importance of the development and maintenance of relationships between them. Although it is less obvious from the United Nations Convention on the Rights of the Child (UNCRC), which focuses on children's rights rather than adults' rights, we argue that the UNCRC does speak to the importance of the wider family unit as being relevant to children's rights. For example, in Article 5 UNCRC, the absence of the paramountcy principle means that interests of adults can be considered; referring to 'extended community family or community', Article 5 provides

---

[30] Ferguson (n 27) 141.

[31] *Marckx v Belgium* App no 6833/74 (ECtHR, 13 June 1979).

[32] ibid para 45.

[33] C Fenton-Glynn, *Children and the European Court of Human Rights* (Oxford, Oxford University Press, 2021) 233.

[34] *Anayo v Germany* App no 20578/07 (ECtHR, 21 December 2010).

[35] *TS and JJ v Norway* App no 15633/15 (ECtHR, 11 October 2016).

[36] *Beccarini and Ridolfi v Italy* App no 63190/16 (ECtHR, 7 December 2017).

[37] A Brown, *What is the Family of Law? The Influence of the Nuclear Family* (Oxford, Hart Publishing, 2019), 40.

that 'States Parties shall respect the responsibilities, rights and duties of parents or, where applicable, the members of the extended family or community … or other persons legally responsible' to provide guidance.[38] Various UNCRC rights, including Article 7, 'the right to know and be cared for by his or her parents' and Article 8, the right to 'preserve his or her identity', place emphasis on the importance of protecting family relationships and the protection of the child's identity, which, in part, stems from genetic connections. The importance of these rights is considered in chapter 6, which explores the significance of grandparents as alternative carers, when birth parents are unable to care for their children safely. We note that domestic case law, while paying some lip service to the value and importance of grandparents via brief 'nods' to the importance of wider family in public law matters,[39] has failed to properly substantiate any legal rights.

In *Re C*,[40] it was emphasised that children have rights to know the truth of their biological and genetic origins, something protected by the UNCRC: 'judges should recognise a greater appreciation that has developed in the law of the value of what grandparents have to offer to a child'. However, the reality is that, in English and Welsh family law proceedings at least, grandparents have few substantive rights in relation to contact, care or residence in respect of their grandchildren. Grandparents lack rights stemming from parental responsibility and are subject to a leave requirement under the Children Act 1989, section 10(9) of which dictates that grandparents must seek leave before applying for a court order such as a child arrangements order for contact or residence, a parental responsibility order or an SGO. Even if leave will be 'sufficiently flexible'[41] in many cases, it is the first in a (potentially) long line of procedural hurdles that make establishing and protecting relationships with children more challenging than for birth parents. Legal aid, for instance, has been reduced drastically, and may mean that grandparents struggle to finance claims to protect their relationships with children unless they have support from Social Services in cases with a public law element. Even if grandparents succeed in being granted leave and can afford to navigate the legal route, the legal framework (as considered in the chapter by Bendall and Davey) does not reflect the diversity of modern family arrangements and is largely set up to support birth parents, rather than other relatives such as grandparents. There is a presumption in favour of parental involvement[42] but no such presumption in

---

[38] S Davey, *A Failure of Proportion: Non-Consensual Adoption in England and Wales* (Oxford, Hart Publishing, 2020) 41.

[39] See, for instance, the Adoption and Children Act 2002, s 1(4)(f), which provides for consideration of 'relatives' in the decision-making process, which may include (although does not explicitly refer to) grandparents.

[40] *Re C (Article 8 Order: Article 10(2): Grandparents' Application for Leave)* [2003] NI Fam 13, para 7.

[41] R Taylor, 'Grandparents and Grandchildren: Relatedness, Relationships and Responsibility' in L Ferguson and E Brake (eds), *Philosophical Foundations of Children's and Family Law* (Abingdon, Routledge, 2018) 230.

[42] Children and Families Act 2014.

favour of grandparents (although, as Kaganas and Piper note, there have been calls to create one[43]). This legal framework can be contrasted to the approach discussed in Sauvé's chapter, which considers the contrasting position of the existence of a grandparent presumption in French law. These frameworks, and the perceived need to 'regulate' the grandparent/grandchild relationship, can also be contrasted to the primacy of grandparental social 'rights' in Nepal despite the absence of prescriptive legal frameworks, considered in chapter 10.

B. Gender, Culture and Grandparents

The interplay between international, multi-cultural and gendered dimensions of the role of grandparents is a recurrent theme in this book. There are, evidently, different cultural practices that influence the extent to which a grandparent is facilitated to be involved in their grandchild's life. In the United States for example, 'African American grandparents raise grandchildren at a higher rate than other racial and ethnic grandparents,'[44] highlighting the complex social factors at play here that make a unified response to the 'grandparents' question deeply challenging. We know that where parents are both in employment, or for a single parent family, there is an increased role for grandparents as caregivers. Yet this points less towards a cultural reason for grandparent care and instead towards an economic motivation. In a study of care provided by Chinese grandparents, 'Care by grandparents may be cheaper, flexible, more reliable, and superficially consistent with cultural expectation; that is, grandparenthood is enacted but filial piety is not.'[45] This challenges the traditional interpretation of the favouring of grandparent care for 'cultural' reasons, because it highlights that grandparents continue to have influence not because of the cultural value attributed to grandparents but due to the economic and social realities that many families face. Although parents are economically reliant on grandparents, they do not necessarily have a strong cultural tie to such kinship care. If this is an accurate depiction of the role of grandparents as carers, in the global north at least, then, as Neysmith and Zhou rightly explain, these economic realities are also affected by the complex relationships of interdependence and (often) transnational connection.[46] Such a complex web means that cultures collide within a particular legal jurisdiction, making the provision of laws to give general rights to grandparents a challenging process. Any changes to the law within England and Wales cannot be assumed based on a homogeneous cultural concept of grandparents and kinship ties. Such reform

---

[43] F Kaganas and C Piper, 'Grandparent contact: another presumption?' (2020) 42 *Journal of Social Welfare and Family Law,* 176.

[44] TL Peterson, 'Grandparents Raising Grandchildren in the African American Community' (2018) 42 *Generations: Journal of the American Society on Aging* 30, 30.

[45] Neysmith and Zhou (n 5) 152.

[46] ibid 154.

would have to take account of the ways that this could play out in different cultures and transnational forms of connection within and beyond that legal system. It is partly for this reason that analysis of the law and culture in three different jurisdictions in addition to England and Wales has been included in this book.

The gender dimension of caregiving choices also materialises in distinct ways, sometimes intersecting with the cultural and economic issues identified above. First, through the distinction between the role of grandmother and grandfather. Second, through the sex of the parent of the grandchild (ie the generation 'in the middle'). Third, through the sex of the grandchild. These gendered dimensions arising from biological sex may influence the landscape of legal practice because different sexes are responded to differently within the family norm. It is argued in chapter 2, for example, that heteronormativity influences the shape of the law's response to grandparents.

Chapters 3 and 10 explain, the law arguably takes a different approach towards grandmothers and their daughters' children, contrasted with grandfathers or grandmothers of their son's children. This is not the case globally, of course, with some jurisdictions prioritising the male kinship line, as can be seen from chapter 8. There is some evidence that paternal grandparents are more likely to be affected by parents' separation/divorce in terms of contact arrangements, with contact likely to increase for maternal grandparents and to decrease for paternal grandparents.[47] In addition, maternal grandparents (particularly grandmothers) are more likely to care for grandchildren.[48] Grandparent involvement (of both genders) is of particular importance in child protection cases,[49] or through the provision of practical and moral support for single parents.[50] As shown by Lindsey's chapter, grandmothers may be of particular importance in child-protection cases concerning the future placement of unborn children. Moreover, in single parent families, grandmothers may, in fact, become 'replacement parents and partners',[51] taking on responsibilities that would traditionally be undertaken by a father or shared between both parents (such as listener, teacher and provider of discipline).[52] All of this means that there is a gendered dimension

---

[47] K Fingerman, 'The Role of Offspring and In-Laws in Grandparents' Ties to Their Grandchildren' (2004) 25 *Journal of Family Issues* 1026; PG Coleman and A Hanlon, *Aging and Development: Social and Emotional Perspectives*, 2nd edn (Abingdon, Routledge, 2017) 117; Westphal, Poortman and Van der Lippe (n 14); L Jamieson, E Ribe and P Warner, 'Outdated Assumptions About Maternal Grandmothers? Gender and Lineage in Grandparent-Grandchild Relationships' (2018) 13 *Contemporary Social Science* 261; L Dickson, 'Grandparents and Contact – What's the Solution?' (2019) 49 *Family Law* 1091.

[48] Peterson (n 44).

[49] S Gair and I Zuchowski, 'Grandparent Carers, Child Protection Practice and the Best Interests of Children: A Case Study' (2019) 72 *Australian Social Work* 299.

[50] R Dunifon and L Kowaleski-Jones, 'The Influence of Grandparents in Single-Mother Families' (2007) 69 *Journal of Marriage and Family* 465; JL Thomas, 'The Grandparent Role: A Double Bind' (1990) 31 *International Journal of Aging and Human Development* 169.

[51] Harper and Ruicheva (n 9).

[52] S Harper, *The Demographic Implications of Ageing Societies for Families in Ageing Societies: A Multidisciplinary Approach* (Oxford, Oxford University Press, 2004).

to this area of practice, even though, on the face of it at least, 'grandparents' is otherwise a gender-neutral term. The impact of gender on the use of grandparent care is not linear, though. Evidence suggests that mothers benefit from the provision of care by grandparents,[53] for example, through a statistically significant increase in labour supply.[54] Therefore, females may gain the benefits of grandparent connection and care while also bearing the 'burden', with the grandmother typically being the primary care-provider.[55] These gendered dimensions need to be addressed in any analysis of an expansion of grandparents rights, which, if enacted, is likely to play out in differential ways for different cultural, racial, gender and social identities.

C. Relationality

Relationality is a theme that emerges explicitly in chapters 2 and 3 and as a more general undercurrent in others. Relationality is essentially about relationships, that is, that humans live their lives with, in and through relationships with others.[56] It is an acknowledgement of the 'nested'[57] nature of relations through which people exist. Relationality recognises that we all live in a relative position within our social worlds, that we cannot exist without interdependence and connectedness with others – it is not a choice but a fundamental feature of human existence.[58] It is immediately obvious, then, why the concept is a theme throughout this book.

What is it about the relationship between grandparents and their kin that matters, though? Jeske argues that what is valuable is 'intimate' or 'close' relationships.[59] She argues for moving away from a focus on blood relations towards relationships that have a degree of social closeness or bonding. While that is certainly an important factor, in the context of intergenerational relationships it

---

[53] Kanji (n 3).

[54] Chen, Liu and Mair (n 10); B Arpino, CD Pronzato and LP Tavares, 'The Effect of Grandparental Support on Mothers' Labour Market Participation: An Instrumental Variable Approach' (2014) 30 *European Journal of Population/Revue Européenne de Démographie* 369.

[55] L Spitz, 'Grandparents: Their Role in 21st Century Families' (2012) 42 *Family Law* 1254.

[56] C Mackenzie and N Stoljar (eds), *Relational Autonomy: Feminist Perspectives on Autonomy, Agency, and the Social Self* (Oxford, Oxford University Press 2000); J Nedelsky, *Law's Relations: A Relational Theory of Self, Autonomy, and Law* (Oxford, Oxford University Press, 2011); J Herring, *Law and the Relational Self* (Cambridge, Cambridge University Press, 2019).

[57] Nedelsky (n 56).

[58] J Nedelsky, 'Law, Boundaries, and the Bounded Self' (1990) 30 *Representations* 162; S Sherwin, 'A Relational Approach to Autonomy in Health Care' in S Sherwin (ed), *The Politics of Women's Health: Exploring Agency and Autonomy* (Temple University Press, 1998) 19; Mackenzie and Stoljar (eds) (n 56); J Christman, 'Relational Autonomy, Liberal Individualism, and the Social Constitution of Selves' (2004) 117 *Philosophical Studies: An International Journal for Philosophy in the Analytic Tradition* 143; AC Westlund 'Rethinking Relational Autonomy' (2009) 24 *Hypatia* 26; Nedelsky (n 56); C Mackenzie, 'The Importance of Relational Autonomy and Capabilities for an Ethics of Vulnerability' in C Mackenzie, W Rogers and S Dodds (eds), *Vulnerability: New essays in ethics and feminist philosophy* (Oxford, Oxford University Press, 2014) 33.

[59] D Jeske, 'Moral and Legal Obligations to Support "Family"' in Brake and Ferguson (eds), *Philosophical Foundations of Children's and Family Law* (Oxford, Oxford University Press, 2018).

is not always an effective starting point of analysis. That is because if grandchildren are not given the opportunity to develop relationships with their grandparents, closeness may well never occur. Furthermore, grandparents may seek closeness in their relationships but be prevented from achieving that, through the force of law that prioritises other rights and relationships. One of the key questions to which this book contributes, then, is how to deal with the importance of relationality in situations where the closeness element has not been able to seed sufficiently within the lives of those involved? It therefore grapples with the fundamental question of how legal obligations ought to be structured[60] to effectively address this particular *type of relationship*.

As noted in the following section, relationships can be damaging and distant as well as supportive and close. Conceptualising all grandparental relationships as purely positive and wholesome would be naive. Rather, we argue that such relationships can be seen on a spectrum and may fluctuate over time, due to the shifting needs of grandparents, parents and children. In section II.D we highlight how a conflict of rights between children and their parents has been criticised and risks leaving children exposed to abuse. This is also a risk in over-valuing grandparents' relationships with their grandchildren, at least through formal legal mechanisms. Relationships are essential to understanding this area of law and practice, and giving grandparents legal rights in relation to their grandchildren will always involve a relational analysis of their respective positions. We think this collection of essays contributes to relational thinking in the context of a particular type of relationship, one that is significant to many children and under-researched in law.

D. Domestic Abuse

Another theme in this book is the appropriateness of protecting and promoting the grandparent/grandchild relationship where abuse or exploitation might be present – either at the hands of parents towards children, or at the hands of grandparents towards their adult children or grandchildren. The role of power dynamics within relationships is well established as potentially undermining autonomy-enhancing conditions.[61] Therefore, in considering any expanded legal rights for grandparents, this book acknowledges the risks that can arise where parental or intergenerational abuse is alleged (or established). As Harwood outlines in chapter 7, this abuse issue has arguably materialised in relation to the role of the statutory presumption for parental involvement with their children under section 1(2A) of the Children Act 1989, which presumes that it is in a child's best

---

[60] Drawing on Jeske's work, who argues that there is a moral obligation that stems from such relationships, and the question then is how ought the law to respond. See ibid.

[61] M Oshana, *Personal Autonomy in Society* (Aldershot, Ashgate, 2006).

interests to have contact with both parents.[62] The Ministry of Justice commissioned a review into private family law cases and noted:

> Since its introduction, PD12J has been updated twice to reflect the developing understanding of the impact of domestic abuse on children and parents, and relevant changes in the law … It was further updated in 2017 to make clear its mandatory nature; to change the terminology from domestic 'violence' to 'abuse'; to widen the definition of domestic abuse to include culturally specific forms of abuse; to place greater emphasis on the safety of the non-abusive parent as well as the child; and to require the court to consider carefully whether the presumption of parental involvement applies in each case.[63]

Despite this doctrinal position, according to academic commentary,[64] courts have ordered and do still order contact between parents and their children even where there has been evidence of domestic abuse.[65] The power of a statutory presumption should therefore not be underestimated, and any argument for such an approach for grandparents needs careful consideration in the light of issues that have arisen elsewhere. This can be seen strongly in relation to the conflict between parents' rights and children's rights, highlighted by one participant in a Family Justice Young People's Board focus group:

> The presumption of contact, it's not helpful at all. I mean it's putting parents' rights above children. At the end of the day unless children can look after themselves and defend themselves, it's putting them in a situation where they are at risk of harm, emotional and physical.[66]

A statutory presumption has the force of law and the power to change legal practice, which has implications for the lives of real people, including adults and children at risk of abuse, either directly from their grandparents, or via the grandparents as intermediaries or facilitators of contact with abusive others. While there is enormous value in protecting and promoting grandparents' relationships with their grandchildren, this ought not be viewed through a 'rose-tinted' lens without consideration of the unintended consequences of law reform in this area. At one end of the spectrum, there may be circumstances where grandparents would use

---

[62] See also Practice Direction 12J, Part 3A Family Procedure Rules 2010, Practice Direction 3AA.

[63] Ministry of Justice (2020), *Assessing Risk of Harm to Children and Parents in Private Law Children Cases*, Final Report, at https://assets.publishing.service.gov.uk/government/uploads/system/uploads/attachment_data/file/895173/assessing-risk-harm-children-parents-pl-childrens-cases-report_.pdf, 28.

[64] ibid.

[65] Ministry of Justice, *Domestic Abuse and Private Law Children Cases* (London, OGL, 2020); J Harwood, Presuming the Status Quo? The Impact of the Statutory Presumption of Parental Involvement' (2021) 43 *Journal of Social Welfare and Family Law* 119.

[66] Ministry of Justice (n 65) 77.

such a presumption to circumvent a prohibition on contact between a child and his or her abusive non-resident parent. This could, in turn, cause a resident parent to be subjected to further domestic abuse and put children at risk of significant harm. In that sense, then, the replication of a presumption in favour of parental involvement could cause a replication of the problems created by a presumption of parental involvement. At the other end of the spectrum, grandparents might behave in a manner that is not in a child's best interests and makes it difficult for a parent to 'parent' effectively, for example due to disagreements about discipline, education, religion and other matters that are largely within the parents' remit.

III. Chapter Outlines

A. 'The "Grandparent" Problem: Encouraging a More Relational Approach Towards Child Arrangements via Mediation'

Chapter 2 of this volume, by Charlotte Bendall and Samantha Davey, focuses on the relationships between grandparents and their grandchildren, and on the ways in which those might best be preserved. Many grandparents are involved in tasks such as collecting their grandchildren from school and keeping them occupied until their parents finish work, or even looking after them for the day whilst their parents are out at their paid employment. However, in the event of family network fragmentation, the courts and legal frameworks have minimised, and in many cases ignored, the practical involvement that grandparents can have on an everyday basis. Grandparents have no specific legal rights that are recognised in the law of England and Wales, with a blanket preference instead being shown towards parents. Private law matters concerning children have, in this way, failed to accommodate more diverse family arrangements.

The authors seek to argue that, during dispute resolution, it is important to focus on the child's wider relationships, rather than to view the family in such a restrictive way. This helps to recognise not only that we, as people, are interconnected and interdependent, but also the importance of multi-generational bonds for children's well-being and support. The authors identify how stepping outside of the legal frameworks, via mediation, can more effectively foster greater 'relationality', reinforcing the connections not only between grandparents and grandchildren, but also with the parents themselves. This is in the sense that mediation can be less confrontational than the court system, and it enables parties to reach outcomes that break away the more 'heteronormative' conclusions that the law might draw. Mediation offers important opportunities to 'write in' those that are 'other' to the 'nuclear' family, and who are virtually unseen by the 'formal' law, and yet who perform crucial caring work.

B. 'Best Interests and Relationality in Reproductive Healthcare'

Chapter 3 of this volume by Jaime Lindsey explores the role of grandmothers – or, more accurately, prospective grandmothers – in influencing decisions about best interests under the Mental Capacity Act (MCA) 2005. In particular, it focuses on the role of prospective grandmothers in influencing decisions about medical treatment of their daughters, particularly caesarean sections, termination of pregnancy, contraception and sterilisation. Cases in the Court of Protection (CoP) – the court that deals with disputes under the MCA 2005 – often involve challenging questions relating to vulnerable pregnant women's ability to make their own decisions regarding whether to access particular healthcare treatments. Drawing on relational theory and autonomy theory throughout, this chapter argues that the courts have, in some instances, adopted a relational autonomy approach that uses the wishes of the grandmother to override the wishes of the daughter. This approach is criticised, including by reference to the wider risks in incorporating a relational approach through the law, via analysis of the broader context in which best interests decisions are made in healthcare and family law.

C. 'On the Sidelines? Grandparents and Care Proceedings'

In chapter 4 of this volume, Joan Hunt notes that the Children Act 1989 placed a duty on local authorities in England and Wales to consider placing a child requiring substitute care with a member of their extended family or social network, an arrangement known as kinship or family and friend care. Subsequent legislation has strengthened that duty, and there has been increased emphasis on this form of care in policy, practice and case law. This potentially enhances the capacity of grandparents to keep the child in their family, without giving them a right to do so. However, where care proceedings are involved, grandparents can face significant obstacles in securing the child's future with them. As the chapter shows, since the enactment of the Children Act, they no longer have automatic party status in the proceedings, and may struggle to have their voice heard either because they cannot fully participate in decision-making processes or because they are unable to afford legal representation to put their case.

D. 'Special Guardianship Orders – Love is Not Enough'

When family circumstances dictate that parents are unable to care for their child, a grandparent often intervenes to undertake the role of primary carer. Grandparents can opt to legally secure this relationship via means of an SGO. These orders were introduced to provide 'greater security' whilst aiming to encourage the continuation of the child's relationship with parents. In chapter 5 of this volume, Liz Fisher-Frank considers that 'greater security', with a particular focus on the impact on the family and child of the special guardians' enhanced parental responsibility. The discussion considers the importance of the child's voice in proceedings because of this, especially since SGOs are often made in relation to older children. This chapter also assesses other legal options available to a grandparent and the viability of grandparents' taking the special guardianship route as opposed to the 'lives with' child arrangement order options. A particular consideration that might, surprisingly, have an impact on the legal route undertaken is the grandparent's status as a litigant in person. The chapter considers the role of the SGO in both private and public law proceedings, challenges that may affect these placements, including parental conflict, finances and the support needs of the grandparent special guardian. From the use of real and fictitious case studies, this chapter demonstrates that in navigating highly complex family dynamics, love is not enough.

E. 'Grandparents through the Lens of Family Constellation Theory: Anchors in Uncertain Times and Alternatives to Adoption?'

Chapter 6 of this volume, by Samantha Davey, is concerned with circumstances in which non-consensual adoption might be considered by the state when parents are no longer capable of caring for their children. Alternative care might be appropriate when parents are unable to look after their children for a plethora of reasons, including drug and/or alcohol abuse, learning disability, mental illness or domestic abuse. It is suggested that, in many cases, children might receive equally effective – or superior – care from grandparents to that which can be provided by the state via adoption orders. This is because grandparents are powerful 'anchors', linking children to their memories and identities. If children can be cared for without endangering their welfare, it is proposed that grandparent care may provide the best protection to children's identity rights under the UNCRC and Article 8 ECHR.

The UNCRC is an important (albeit non-binding) legal document that ought to be considered when determining the best measure of long-term care for a child (such as non-consensual adoption or kinship care). It is also the most authoritative legal document on children's rights, and serves as an interpretative tool to key concepts, including identity and the collective rights of families. It is argued that emphasis ought to be placed on how the 'family relations' aspect of identity under Article 8 UNCRC is crucial to children's well-being and how kinship carers, such as grandparents, may contribute towards and support a child's sense of identity. The UNCRC, viewed from the lens of 'family constellation' theory, would provide greater protection of the relationship between children and their extended kinship networks, including grandparents.

F. 'Symbolic and Expedient "Solutions", Grandparents and the Private Family Justice System: The Risk of Unintended Consequences'

In chapter 7 of this volume, Joanna Harwood reveals that debates on the legal status of grandparents have existed for many years, with the law often viewed both as the problem and the solution to the challenges faced by grandparents in spending time with their grandchildren. Calls for reform have repeatedly included the removal of the requirement for grandparents to seek leave from the court before applying for child arrangements orders and, more recently, calls to extend the existing statutory presumption of parental involvement, currently housed within the Children Act 1989, to include grandparents. Weighing against claims that grandparents are neglected within the current legal system is evidence that grandparents are being called upon in some cases to perform a protective role in child arrangements disputes involving domestic abuse. For the first time, this chapter applies autopoietic theory to these key debates and argues that there are significant risks in framing the law as both the problem and solution in this context, and that the inherent challenge of the uncertainty within family law cannot be resolved by symbolic and expedient solutions. It is argued that neither the removal of the leave requirement nor the extension of the statutory presumption to include grandparents would bring significant benefits to grandparents, and that introducing such changes for symbolic purposes would be more likely to pose significant risks of harm to children. By the same token, it is argued that the expedient use of grandparents in cases involving domestic abuse to perform a protective role is risk-laden and ought not to be an outcome easily reached.

G. 'An Iranian Socio-Legal Analysis of Grandparents' Rights'

Chapter 8 of this volume, by Sahar Maranlou and Fatemeh Keyhanlou, recognises that grandparents are, culturally, considered important resources in times of family crises such as divorce and the death of parents. Islamic Law also offers the power of guardianship (*Wilayah*) to paternal grandfathers, to establish and execute contracts and other legal conducts on behalf of their grandchildren. Little is written, however, about the socio-legal relation between cultural norms, gender, and rights and duties of grandparents in the best interests of children after parental death or divorce. The chapter seeks to examine the current position in Iranian law and legislation regarding the rights and duties of grandparents concerning the best interests of their grandchildren, enshrined in the UNCRC. It considers the gap between the modern concept of the best interests of the child and Islamic law approaches to child welfare about grandparents, which is also framed as a largely gendered legal concept.

H. 'A French Perspective on Grandparents and Private Law: The Right of the Child to Maintain Personal Relationships'

In England and Wales, there are no specific provisions for grandparents who want to maintain personal relationships with their grandchildren, while, as Laure Sauvé shows in chapter 9, the French Civil Code contains a specific provision related to the right of children to maintain personal relationships with their grandparents. This chapter aims to analyse in detail the French provision, to provide the English reader with some comparative elements of reflection within the context of a potential reform of grandparents' rights under English and Welsh laws. The chapter explains the justifications behind the French statutory presumption in favour of children's right to maintain personal relations with their grandparents. It considers critically how French courts apply this presumption in practice, and argues that the 'child's right' to maintain personal relations is rather a reciprocal right of the grandparents and the child, based on what the judge would consider as being in the interest of the child. The chapter considers that the French system offers satisfactory solutions, as the existence of a statutory presumption offers some clear 'guidelines' for the courts but confers at the same time some important discretionary powers of appreciation to the courts. As such, the author concludes that despite the existing statutory presumption, French law may not differ much from English law in practice.

I. 'The Impact of Culture on Grandparents' Rights: Laws and Social Practices in Nepal'

Chapter 10 of this volume, by Sneha Shrestha, examines the impact of cultural and social practices in Nepal vis-à-vis the availability, or indeed lack, of legal protection afforded to grandparents in relation to contact with their grandchildren. The imbalance of power between maternal and paternal grandparents is a theme that runs through this chapter, which is reflected by the relevant sections of the Act Relating to Children 2075 (2018), Civil Code 2074 (2017) and the Senior Citizens' Act 2063 (2006). Patriarchal traditions and gender bias lead to prospective grandparenthood in Nepal, adding an additional layer to the grandparents' rights conversation. This chapter highlights the wide gap between the current law and contemporary Nepali families. The legal concept of grandparents' rights is novel idea to the Nepalese public, and indeed policy-makers, which has yet to be explored. This contribution aims to bring grandparents' rights to Nepalese consciousness so that Nepal can prepare before it becomes a problem without a remedy, due to the tension between historical traditions and contemporary modern Nepali families. It is suggested that a more effective family-law structure is needed in Nepal. This would take place via the creation of 'Family Law Procedure', which would facilitate a focused and specialist approach towards family law in Nepal. Further, given Nepal's context (social stigma, shame/disgrace surrounding divorce), the introduction of family-law mediation within the legal system would assist many women and their maternal families in accessing justice when the traditional joint families fall apart. This chapter concludes that the law needs to catch up with the social trends by taking steps forward with grass-root studies, interdisciplinary research and dialogue among key actors and other stakeholders (formal consultation). Ultimately, if amendment or creation of laws is considered necessary, it must be sensitive to cultural norms and the history of Nepal if such changes are to be effective and meaningful.

IV. Future Agenda for Grandparents and the Law

The various essays in this collection emphasise the potential rights and responsibilities that grandparents might have or acquire, as well as the clear potential benefits to children of relationships with their grandparents. Such rights touch on key provisions under the ECHR (such as Article 6, the right to a fair hearing, and Article 8, the right to respect for private and family life), as well as on a range of provisions under the UNCRC (such as Articles 5, 7, 8, 12 and 18). The specific benefits of expanding the role of grandparents include: providing an alternative to foster care or adoption outside of the family; enabling children to maintain important connections with identity and cultural heritage;[67] preserving neutral territory during parental disputes;[68] providing a role model for children; providing emotional and practical support, or supporting grandchildren through an otherwise stressful period of parental separation.[69] This collection balances the potential benefits of recognising the role of grandparents through procedural or even substantive legal rights, against the need to protect the child's welfare and the rights of the primary caregiver(s).

First, there is a real lack of reliable data about the role of grandparents in the law. This is apparent in family law, where no statistics are maintained on, for example, the numbers of grandparents who seek to apply for care of their grandchildren in either private or public proceedings. We can deduce, however, from a recent study by Cusworth et al,[70] that approximately 10 per cent of private law court orders are applied for by a non-parent (ie a grandparent or other family member). It is, however, also a wider issue in respect of judicial practice. For example, as chapter 3 highlights, the subtle effects of a more relational approach can risk giving

---

[67] Green (n 21).
[68] I Butler et al, *Divorcing Children: Children's Experience of Their Parents' Divorce* (London, Jessica Kingsley, 2003) 151.
[69] Lent and Otto (n 18).
[70] L Cusworth et al, *Uncovering Private Family Law: Who's Coming to Court in England?* (London, Nuffield Family Justice Observatory, 2021).

grandparents rights 'through the back door'. If data are difficult to collect in relation to formal court applications made by grandparents, then data of this more subtle effect of a change in legal practice are likely to be even more difficult to adduce.

Another key challenge in taking this agenda forward is the role of funding for grandparents who want to intervene in cases affecting their grandchildren, whether via a formal application for contact or residence, or more generally to participate in the proceedings and contribute to the body of evidence before the court. Chapter 5, for instance, considers the types of court orders that can be applied for by grandparents, and the challenges that grandparents may face in applying for them.

As well as some of the specific challenges noted throughout this book, there is, perhaps, a wider challenge posed by the subject matter of this collection, that is, whether law is, in fact, the right mechanism through which to establish the role of grandparents in the lives of their grandchildren. Chapter 2 in particular shows how more creative 'solutions' might be necessary to facilitate grandparents' relationships with their children without recourse to judicial enforcement. Mediation is certainly one option the authors recommend, albeit that its use needs to be carefully delineated.[71] Another potential solution might include giving grandparents procedural rights in relation to proceedings, for example, which can be seen from chapter 9, which shows how French law provides procedural protection to the grandparent/grandchild relationship.

The grandparent/parent/grandchild dynamic can be supportive or adversarial, depending on the family circumstances, including whether or not state intervention is necessary, and may also vary over time. Families are unique and relationships are complex. Our intention with this collection is to both highlight the value of the under-emphasised grandparent/grandchild relationship and explore the tensions that may occur between grandparent and parent or grandparent and the state. This collection therefore builds on the existing academic contributions in family law, while exploring a rapidly new, exciting and evolving area of law and policy on familial relationships.

---

[71] R Blakey, 'Cracking the Code: The Role of Mediators and Flexibility Post-LASPO' (2020) 53 *Child and Family Law Quarterly*; C Irvine, 'What Do "Lay" People Know About Justice? An Empirical Enquiry' (2020) 16 *International Journal of Law in Context* 146.

2

The 'Grandparent' Problem: Encouraging a More Relational Approach Towards Child Arrangements via Mediation

CHARLOTTE BENDALL AND SAMANTHA DAVEY

I. Introduction: A 'Nuclear' Norm

This chapter focuses on the relationships between grandparents and their grandchildren, and on the ways in which these might best be preserved in the event of family network fragmentation. It identifies how the 'traditional' legal frameworks around private children matters have failed to accommodate more diverse family arrangements due to 'dominant, orthodox'[1] understandings of the family. A recent poll found that as many as 40 per cent of grandparents over the age of 50 in the United Kingdom (UK) had provided regular care for their grandchildren, highlighting the prevalence of what has been termed 'grannannying'.[2] This is in a context of a rise in lone-parent employment, and in the number of dual-earning households,[3] combined with the significant cost of childcare.[4] Grandparents have increasingly undertaken caregiving, particularly within 'working-class' families across Europe,[5] where both parents are in full-time employment.[6] Many grandparents are involved in tasks such as collecting children from school and keeping

---

[1] A Brown, *What is the Family of Law? The Influence of the Nuclear Family* (Oxford, Hart Publishing, 2019) 3.

[2] Age UK (2017) *5 Million Grandparents take on Childcare Responsibilities* at www.ageuk.org.uk/latest-news/articles/2017/september/five-million-grandparents-take-on-childcare-responsibilities.

[3] Office for National Statistics (2018), *Families and the Labour Market, England: 2018* at www.ons.gov.uk/employmentandlabourmarket/peopleinwork/employmentandemployeetypes/articles/familiesandthelabourmarketengland/2018.

[4] J Herring, *Law and The Relational Self* (Cambridge, Cambridge University Press, 2019).

[5] Grandparents Plus, *Grandparenting in Europe* (London, Grandparents Plus, 2010).

[6] T Leonce, 'The Inevitable Rise in Dual-Income Households and the Intertemporal Effects on Labor Markets' (2020) 52 *Compensation and Benefits Review* 64.

them occupied until their parents finish work, or even looking after them for the day while their parents are out at their paid employment. Yet the courts and legal frameworks have ignored the practical involvement that grandparents can have on an everyday basis, with a blanket preference being shown towards parents instead. We identify how stepping outside of the legal frameworks, vis-à-vis mediation, can more effectively foster greater 'relationality', reinforcing the connections not only between grandparents and grandchildren, but also with the parents themselves.

The 'nuclear' family, comprising (generally two) parents and their biological, dependent children, has traditionally held greater 'legal legitimacy'[7] in England and Wales than other family units. The twenty-first century has, however, been a 'game changer', characterised by a 'kaleidoscope of family forms'.[8] Altered familial social norms have led to corresponding changes in legislation and judicial decision making. Unmarried fathers have enjoyed the establishment of their legal status as parents with parental responsibility,[9] transsexuals' rights to recognition have been protected by the law,[10] and same-sex relationships have attained formal legal status through the development of a regime on civil partnership[11] and the subsequent introduction of same-sex marriage.[12]

Legislators and the courts have also had to contend with challenges in defining 'parent', 'parentage' and 'parenthood',[13] in the light of advances in medical treatment vis-à-vis assisted reproduction,[14] including surrogacy arrangements.[15] The focus, though, in the modernisation of the concept of family within medical law has been on the legal recognition and protection of *parental* interests, rather than the recognition of the interests and involvement of extended family, including grandparents. Thus, one stone has been left unturned: the recognition and protection of grandparents' rights in legal proceedings – especially in private law matters. The omission continues despite research by Cusworth et al, based on a sample of 546,000 private law applications between 2007 and 2020, which found that approximately 10 per cent of private law applications were made by non-parents, including grandparents.[16] This high number of applications suggests a significant issue for many grandparents, who have felt the need to commence litigation.

---

[7] C Huntington, *Failure to Flourish: How Law Undermines Family Relationships* (Oxford, Oxford University Press, 2014) xv.

[8] D Orchard, 'Family and Family Law' in E Brake and L Ferguson, *The Philosophical Foundations of Children's and Family Law* (Oxford, Oxford University Press, 2018) 59, 59.

[9] Under s 111 of the Adoption and Children Act 2002, unmarried fathers can acquire parental responsibility if paternity is registered on the child's birth certificate.

[10] Gender Recognition Act 2004.

[11] Civil Partnership Act 2004. See also A Rolfe and E Peel, 'It's a double-edged thing: The paradox of civil partnership and why some couples are choosing not to have one' (2011) 3 *Feminism and Psychology* 317.

[12] Marriage (Same Sex Couples) Act 2013.

[13] A Bainham, 'Arguments About Parentage' (2008) 67 *CLJ* 322.

[14] Human Fertilisation and Embryology Acts 1990 and 2008.

[15] *Z (Surrogacy agreements: Child arrangement orders)* [2016] EWFC 34.

[16] L Cusworth et al, *Uncovering Private Family Law: Who's Coming to Court in England?* (London, Nuffield Family Justice Observatory, 2021) 19.

In other words, despite all of the challenges to the deeply embedded social norm of the 'nuclear' family, and the superior courts' insistence that there is no natural parent 'presumption',[17] there is a tendency 'to marginalise, to exclude, and to deny equal protection to relationships and families who do not come close to the normative ideal'.[18] Grandparents have no specific legal rights that are recognised in English law, and family law has remained 'heteronormative', declining to opt for a more 'relational' route. In suggesting that the law in this area has operated 'heteronormatively', we mean that it has worked to privilege those behaviours and relationships that closely replicate the heterosexual 'binary' familial norm, whilst attaching less value to those that deviate. In this respect, it is both reflecting and ultimately sustaining patterns of social 'normality'.[19] The law has failed to promote the various caring relationships that can exist between the child and those connected to the child, such as grandparents.[20]

This chapter begins by interrogating what 'relationality' means, and why adopting a more connected approach is so important in private law children matters. It then discusses the various legal routes through which grandparents can secure contact, and how these, in contrast to operating 'relationally', have encouraged 'heteronormativity'. It considers the practical challenges faced in accommodating grandparents within the existing legal frameworks, and argues that they are, in fact, ill-equipped to meet those. Ultimately, the chapter asserts that mediation offers greater prospects for adopting a 'relational' approach, and thereby for protecting children's relationships with extended family members. This is not only in the sense that mediation can be less confrontational than the court system, but also in that it enables parties to reach outcomes that differ from the 'heteronormative' conclusions that the law might draw. Mediation should consequently be promoted through, for example, greater public education and judicial encouragement.

II. 'Relationality': A Preferred Approach Towards Private Children Disputes

When it comes to dispute resolution in this context, we argue that it is important to focus on the child's wider relationships, rather than to view the family in a restrictive way. This would help to recognise that we, as people, are 'constitutively interconnected and interdependent'.[21] The notion behind the 'relational' approach is that the 'very nature' of our selves is to be in 'interaction' with others,

---

[17] *W (A Child)* [2016] EWCA Civ 793; *Re B (A Child)* [2009] EWCA Civ 545.

[18] A Margaria, *The Construction of Fatherhood* (Cambridge, Cambridge University Press, 2019) 5.

[19] M Davies, 'Legal Pluralism' in P Cane and H Kritzer (eds), *The Oxford Handbook of Empirical Legal Research* (Oxford, Oxford University Press, 2010) 805.

[20] Herring (n 4).

[21] M Friedman, 'Relational Autonomy and Individuality' (2013) 63 *University of Toronto Law Journal* 327, 327.

with the relationships that we have operating to 'shape' our lives.[22] As Naffine puts it, 'human beings are inseparable from their relations ... within [these] relations we become what we are as persons'.[23] We live in the context of a 'web', or network, of interconnection, within which our relationships are central to our identities and to the capacities that we can develop.[24] Our social connections influence our well-being, with close, 'strong, stable' relationships being essential for human growth.[25] The very possibility of our 'flourishing' is created through the relationships that we have established, with 'flourishing' being defined here as including 'the development, and exercise, of cognitive, social, [and] affective ... skills'.[26]

Children, like all of us, are connected and 'live in the context of relationships',[27] with 'no child [being] an island unto itself'.[28] Even just genetically, each child is a product not only of their parents, but also of their grandparents before them.[29] In this respect, Kornhaber stresses that 'the child in the womb already possesses instincts, temperament, and emotions that are not his or hers alone', with the child developing 'not only in the world of [their] parents, but within the larger world of [their] grandparents'.[30] It is, Liebermeister suggests, an 'illusion' to imagine that we are 'unconnected to the generations that preceded us', with those generations playing 'an important part in affecting the lives of [the following] generations'.[31] Moreover, when first beginning to interact with the world, children do so through the relationships that they have with their caregivers.[32] In this sense, the 'collectivity' of family helps to 'form' us and 'explain much of [our] behaviour'.[33]

Familial caregivers provide not only the language that children use, and the development of their ideas, but further offer them a sense of 'who [they] are and where [they] belong'.[34] As Herring suggests, even from this early stage, 'we think, live, and establish our identity through [these] relationships'.[35] They supply us with our belief systems, values and world view.[36] Where caring is conducted by a grandparent, previous generations 'leave their mark' on the current one, impacting the child's 'ways of knowing and seeing'.[37] Especially as children grow older,

---

[22] ibid.

[23] N Naffine, 'The Liberal Legal Individual Accused: The relational case' (2013) 29 *Canadian Journal of Law and Society* 123, 123.

[24] J Nedelsky, *Law's Relations* (Oxford, Oxford University Press, 2011).

[25] Huntington (n 7) 6.

[26] J Herring and C Foster, 'Welfare Means Relationality, Virtue and Altruism' (2012) 32 *Legal Studies* 480, 487.

[27] Herring (n 4) 162.

[28] Herring and Foster (n 26) 497.

[29] J Herring, *Older People in Law and Society* (Oxford, Oxford Publishing, 2009).

[30] A Kornhaber, quoted in E LeShan, *Grandparenting in a Changing World* (New York, Newmarket, 1993) 268.

[31] S Liebermeister, *The Roots of Love* (Cambridge, Perfect Publishers Ltd, 2006) 8, 87.

[32] Herring (n 4).

[33] Liebermeister (n 31) 295.

[34] Herring (n 4) 196.

[35] ibid.

[36] Liebermeister (n 31).

[37] C Smart, *Personal Life* (Cambridge, Polity Press, 2007) 45, 87.

grandparents can offer 'knowledge of family ... roots [and] a sense of [their] origins or heritage, as well as emotional support'.[38] This is important, given that Article 8 of the United Nations Convention on the Rights of the Child (UNCRC) states that the child has a right 'to preserve his or her identity including nationality, name and family relations'. Those 'family relations' arguably extend further than parent and child to those between the child and other relatives, including grandparents.[39] Children who enjoy strong bonds with their grandparents have been found, within empirical studies, to be more secure emotionally.[40] Eekelaar argues that the 'maintenance and development'[41] of relationships between children and grandparents can be in children's best interests, particularly in the aftermath of parental separation, where grandparents can offer 'safe' or 'neutral' territory.[42] It is clear that such relationships can be central to children's lives, well-being and sense of self, and a similar observation might be made about grandparents too. Given that 'every time a child is born, a grandparent is born',[43] grandparents' understandings of themselves can emerge from the relationships that they have with their extended families. It is accordingly unsurprising that qualitative research identifies that grandparents who have experienced a loss of contact with their grandchildren suffer emotional and physical health problems related to that loss.[44]

We focus particularly on the grandparent/grandchild relationship, because grandparents so frequently assume a caring role. Many of the arguments that we are making could, though, be carried across to other 'caring' relatives, such as aunts or uncles. It is also recognised that whilst some grandparents have significant relationships with their grandchildren, others play only a peripheral role; the extent and nature of their involvement can vary greatly (and can be financial, as well as practical and emotional).[45] Therefore, for the law to adopt a blanket 'presumption' in favour of contact with grandparents, as has been previously suggested as a potential reform, may seem inappropriate.[46]

Indeed, to encourage a 'relational' approach is not to suggest that all relationships are good, or should necessarily be maintained.[47] There may, for instance, be difficulties in terms of contact with paternal grandparents where there are safeguarding concerns based on domestic abuse perpetrated by the father against

---

[38] Grandparents' Association, quoted in Herring (n 29) 255.

[39] R Hodgkin and P Newell, *Implementation Handbook for the Convention on the Rights of the Child*, 3rd edn (Geneva, UNICEF, 2007) 114.

[40] M Purnell and B Bagby, 'Grandparents' Rights: Implications for family specialists' (1993) 42 *Family Relations* 173.

[41] J Eekelaar, *Family Law and Personal Life* (Oxford, Oxford University Publishing, 2006) 70.

[42] M Murch, *Supporting Children When Parents Separate* (Bristol, Policy Press, 2018) 60.

[43] Kornhaber, quoted in LeShan (n 30).

[44] L Drew and P Smith, 'The impact of parental separation/divorce on grandparents-grandchild relationships', (1999) 48 *International Journal of Aging & Human Development*, 191.

[45] Herring (n 29).

[46] F Kaganas and C Piper, 'Grandparent Contact: Another Presumption?' (2020) 42 *Journal of Social Welfare and Family Law* 176.

[47] Herring (n 4).

the mother and/or child (see chapter 7 in this volume). It is crucial to distinguish between cases where communication has simply broken down and those where grandparents have placed, or have the potential to place, children at risk of significant emotional or physical harm, for reasons that may include the level of ongoing conflict and disagreement between grandparent and parent. If such relationships put children at risk of significant harm, the state is obliged to take the steps required to 'protect the child from all forms of physical or mental violence, injury or abuse, neglect or negligent treatment' under Article 19 UNCRC. Moreover, under Article 5 UNCRC, the state must 'respect the responsibilities, rights and duties of parents', which can be construed to include decisions to exclude influences that may be harmful to children. We do not argue that contact is always in the child's best interests. Parents and grandparents may also disagree over important decisions such as religious beliefs, medical treatment or schooling. Nevertheless, particularly where a grandparent has performed some sort of caring role within a child's life, it is argued here that this should be given recognition, and that an ongoing relationship should be facilitated wherever possible. Attempts should be made to 'write-in' those 'others' who conduct caring work, to reflect the complexity of family life.[48] An expansive vision of 'family' needs to be adopted, which acknowledges the varying contributions and responsibilities of wider family members, and the significance of intergenerational relationships.[49] This is not, though, what is taking place within the existing frameworks for child arrangements, which, as we will move on to discuss, instead work 'heteronormatively'.

III. Making and Enforcing Contact Orders in a 'Heteronormative' Framework

A. Defining Heteronormativity

The courts have expressed a preference towards applying the welfare principle,[50] in private law proceedings concerning children, in a way that is 'free from generalisations'.[51] However, we assert that they tend to favour the interests of parents over the claims of others, such as grandparents, in private law proceedings. We do not, in this chapter, necessarily dispute the preferred status enjoyed by parents. We do, however, believe that this prioritisation means that the law operates 'heteronormatively', and that the vital importance of family members such as grandparents is, at times, overlooked.

---

[48] M Kavanagh, 'Rewriting the legal family: Beyond exclusivity to a care-based standard' (2004) 16 *Yale Journal of Law & Feminism* 83.

[49] ibid.

[50] Children Act 1989, s 1(1).

[51] J Herring, 'The welfare principle and the Children Act: presumably it's about welfare?' (2014) 36 *Journal of Social Welfare and Family Law* 14, 14.

We argue that, through this prioritisation, the legal system within England and Wales has reproduced the traditional ('heteronormative') 'nuclear' family, comprising two parents only and their biological, dependent children. The law, in so operating, is not recognising the full diversity of parenting arrangements, or the nexus of relationships within which children can exist. Bendall has identified (albeit in the context of financial relief) that family law sometimes entails the application by legal actors of familiar, existing 'scripts' that can be 'mismatched with the parties' realities'.[52] In the case of less 'normative' forms of family living, relatively little consideration may be given to the ways in which the parties' lives diverge from those 'scripts'. It is arguable that we can see this happening in private law children matters too, in that the law struggles with how to acknowledge and protect the grandparent/grandchild relationship (given that it strays from the 'nuclear' norm). This is despite the fact that some children are raised by their grandparents, and others have close, loving bonds with their grandparents due to the frequency of contact.

Whilst 'heteronormativity' is a contested term, we use it to refer to the ways in which heterosexual identity and practices are 'expected, demanded and always presupposed by society'.[53] 'Heteronormativity' assumes that heterosexual relationship behaviour is 'self-evident ... and necessary',[54] and works to privilege those relationships that closely replicate the heterosexual norm, while disregarding and ignoring (or even condemning) those that deviate. It has entailed a focus on procreation, and on conjugality and romance,[55] as well as the assumption that there are only two genders, the 'masculine' male (who engages in the production and circulation of commodities and operates as the family 'provider') and the 'feminine' female (who performs the domestic work). In fact, the assumption that the family should centre around gender complementarity has played out within family law to such an extent that attempts have been made to apply 'binary' norms to the context of same-sex relationships.[56] 'Heteronormativity' has been used as a term to describe practices that 'derive from and reinforce a set of taken-for-granted presumptions', including around the idea that 'marriage and the family are appropriately organised around different-sex pairings'.[57] 'Heteronormativity', in encouraging this exclusively 'binary' form of family living, links up with notions

---

[52] C Bendall, 'A 'divorce blueprint'? The use of heteronormative strategies in addressing economic inequalities on civil partnership dissolution' (2016) 31 *Canadian Journal of Law and Society* 268, 278.

[53] S Chambers, '"An incalculable effect": Subversions of heteronormativity' (2007) 55 *Political Studies* 656, 662.

[54] D Cameron and D Kulick, *Language and Sexuality* (Cambridge, Cambridge University Press, 2003) 55.

[55] N Palazzo, *Legal Recognition of Non-conjugal Families: New Frontiers in Family Law in the US, Canada and Europe* (Bloomsbury, London, 2021).

[56] C Bendall, 'A break away from the (hetero)norm? Lawrence v Gallagher' [2012] 1 FCR 557; [2012] EWCA Civ 394' (2013) 21 *Feminist Legal Studies* 303.

[57] C Kitzinger, 'Heteronormativity in action: Reproducing the heterosexual nuclear family in after-hours medical calls' (2005) 52 *Social Problems* 477, 478.

such as 'mononormativity' (under which assumptions of the 'normalcy and natu-
ralness of monogamy' are 'dominant').[58]

Butler's concept of 'performativity' suggests that norms (such as 'heteronormativity') are reproduced and perpetuated, ultimately coming to be seen as natural,
via continued repetition through social and institutional structures and practices.[59]
The law in this area, having placed more importance on the relationship between
a child and their mother and father than on the child's other relationships, has
largely operated to bolster this dichotomous, 'heteronormative' parenting model.
Notably, developments within family law, such as the Human Fertilisation and
Embryology Act 2008, have moved somewhat away from the gender 'binary' in
recognising parents of the same sex. That said, such developments have continued
to adhere to a maximum of a 'two-parent model [where] the couple must be (at least
potentially) in a sexual relationship'.[60] As a result, the radical potential of multiple
parenting models (including parties such as known sperm donors), which have
been regarded as a 'point of difference in lesbian parenting practices',[61] has been
blunted. Of course, same-sex relationships are not the only context within which
multiple people are performing a key role in children's lives. Importantly, the law,
as it stands, also neglects to provide sufficient recognition of the increase in close
relationships between grandparents and grandchildren, with grandparents often
taking on the role of part-time or full-time caregivers (as considered in chapter 6).

Having set out the key theoretical frameworks on 'relationality' and 'heteronormativity', we now consider how these connect to legal frameworks on the
leave requirement and the making of child arrangements and enforcement orders
under the Children Act 1989.

B. Leave Requirement

The focus of this subsection is on a grandparent's ability to obtain leave (ie the
court's permission) for the purposes of obtaining contact with a grandchild.
Unlike mothers and fathers, grandparents do not enjoy automatic leave to
commence legal proceedings[62] (see chapter 4 and chapter 5 for more detail on
the leave requirement). This means that, in some cases, the courts will not even
consider the merits of making a child arrangements order for contact between a
grandparent and their grandchild. At present, the leave requirement is viewed as

---

[58] M Pieper and R Bauer, quoted in M Barker and D Langdridge, 'Whatever happened to non-
monogamies? Critical reflections on recent research and theory' (2010) 13 *Sexualities* 748, 750.

[59] J Butler, 'Critically Queer' (1993) 1 *GLQ: A Journal of Lesbian and Gay Studies* 17.

[60] J McCandless and S Sheldon, 'The Human Fertilisation and Embryology Act (2008) and the tenac-
ity of the sexual family form' (2010) 73 *MLR* 175, 188.

[61] L Smith, 'Tangling the web of legal parenthood: Legal responses to the use of known donors in
lesbian parenting arrangements' (2013) 33 *Legal Studies* 355, 375.

[62] Grandparents must apply for leave under s 10(9) of the Children Act 1989.

necessary by the Government and the judiciary alike, because it is perceived that some grandparents' claims may be 'vexatious'.[63] Currently, the courts are guided by explicit considerations under section 10(9) of the Children Act 1989 when deciding whether to grant leave, such as risk of harm to the child and the wishes and feelings of the child's parents. Within England and Wales, grandparents are treated unequally to parents, since parents do not have to satisfy a leave requirement in private law matters, and discord between a primary caregiver and a non-resident will rarely prevent a contact order from being made in a parent's favour.[64] It could be said that the leave requirement itself may reflect a 'binary' 'heteronormative' approach emphasising the primacy of the 'nuclear' family.

Despite the existence of this 'hurdle', Herring has observed that serious reasons would need to be given for the refusal to grant leave to grandparents.[65] Otherwise, such a refusal could be a potential violation of procedural and substantive rights under the European Convention on Human Rights (ECHR), specifically, Article 6 (the right to a fair hearing) and Article 8 (the right to respect for private and family life).[66] In fact, leave is not an insurmountable 'hurdle',[67] nor a blanket 'hurdle' applied to all grandparents, since those who fall within the special category of persons under section 34(1) of the Children Act 1989 are exempt and need not apply.[68] Even so, given that leave is required for most grandparents, this is a literal, and symbolic, example of the preferential status provided to parents and the 'subsidiary'[69] status of grandparents. Again, this reflects the law's tendency to embed 'heteronormativity', and failure to acknowledge the importance of the 'relationality' between children and grandparents.

Some legal scholars and non-governmental organisations have argued that greater emphasis needs to be placed on multi-generational bonds[70] via the removal of the leave requirement for grandparents,[71] a presumption in favour of contact[72] or more rigorous enforcement of child arrangement orders against uncooperative parents.[73] Others, such as Taylor, argue the law is sufficiently flexible to support

---

[63] Ministry of Justice, *Family Justice Review: Final Report* (London, Ministry of Justice, 2011) 21.

[64] See J Hunt and A Macleod, *Outcomes of Applications to Court for Contact Orders after Parental Separation or divorce* (London, Ministry of Justice, 2008) 36. According to this research, 86% of applications for staying contact were successful in obtaining face-to-face contact.

[65] Herring (n 29) 246.

[66] ibid.

[67] Ministry of Justice (n 63). Also, generally, see R Taylor, 'Grandparents and Grandchildren: Relatedness, relationships and responsibility' in B Clough and J Herring (eds), *Ageing, Gender and Family Law* (Abingdon, Routledge, 2018) 230.

[68] *Re M (Minors in Care) (Contact: Grandmother's Application)* [1995] 2 FLR 86. For more detail on these exceptions, see ch 1 of this volume.

[69] L Spitz, 'Grandparents: their role in 21st century families' (2012) 42 *Family Law* 1254.

[70] V Bengtson, 'Beyond the Nuclear Family: The Increasing Importance of Multigenerational Bonds' (2001) 63 *Journal of Marriage and Family* 1.

[71] Kaganas and Piper (n 46).

[72] Grandparents Apart (2006) *Grandparents Speak Out for Vulnerable Children* at http://grandparentsapart.co.uk/wp-content/uploads/2018/08/Grandparents-Book.pdf 28.

[73] For a general overview on the arguments, see Kaganas and Piper (n 46).

grandparents when it is for the child's benefit.[74] Although such options for legal reform exist,[75] we contend that these changes would not adequately tackle the underlying 'heteronormativity', and lack of 'relationality', inherent within the family justice system. This is due to the preference, in law, for supporting the interests of parents over those of grandparents. We will move on to examine in greater detail how this preference manifests.

C. Child Arrangements Orders with 'Contact'

Contact can take place in a myriad of forms. Whilst direct 'face-to-face' contact may be the most welcome format, especially post-Covid-19, we acknowledge that indirect contact (via telephone, e-mail and video conference) may alternatively be beneficial. Regardless of this increase in 'unconventional'[76] non-binary family relationships, there is still a 'hierarchy' within this area of the law,[77] and the grandparent/grandchild relationship is not prioritised in contact matters. Brown suggests that, in natural reproduction, the genetic connection is favoured over social parenting, and that the opposite is true for assisted reproduction.[78] Grandparents and their relationships with their grandchildren sit uneasily within the current legal framework, which emphasises parental genetic connections but not necessarily grandparental genetic connections. Despite the increased emphasis on grandparents' rights to relationships with their grandchildren under Article 8 ECHR,[79] the domestic courts have tended to differ in their treatment of grandparents when compared with non-resident parents (usually fathers).

The courts appear to have been more willing to grant contact in favour of fathers, whether married or unmarried, and mothers (where appropriate). They have taken the perspective that parental contact is almost always in the child's best interests,[80] whereas contact with grandparents is not. In many cases, grandparents will see their grandchildren during contact visits between children and their fathers (for example, assuming the father is the non-resident parent). Although this creates a practical way for such grandparents, there are circumstances where this is not possible (for example, in cases where fathers are not permitted to have direct contact, do not seek contact, have acted as sperm donors but are not regarded as a child's 'legal' parent, or are deceased). Moreover, this reliance on the parental route is still indicative of a symbolic legal hierarchy that may not reflect the strength

---

[74] Taylor (n 67) 230.

[75] For discussion, see Kaganas and Piper (n 46).

[76] Margaria (n 18) 27.

[77] ibid.

[78] Brown (n 1) 3.

[79] *L v Finland* App no 25651/94 (ECtHR, 27 April 2000); *Mitovi v The Former Yugoslav Republic of Macedonia* App no 53565/13 (ECtHR, 16 April 2015); *Beccarini and Ridolfi v Italy* App no 63190 (ECtHR, 7 December 2017).

[80] *Re O (Contact: Imposition of Conditions)* [1995] 2 FLR 124.

of the relationship between grandparents and their grandchildren. In circumstances such as those outlined above, it is submitted, children may well have much closer relationships with the non-resident grandparents (typically the paternal grandparents) than with their fathers.

Grandparents are, however, granted some, albeit limited, rights to contact under Article 8 ECHR (the right to respect for private and family life) where a de facto relationship is established.[81] The stance of the European Court of Human Rights (ECtHR) is important, since it marks a less 'traditional' approach that more readily encompasses the need to protect different types of familial relationships. Moreover, the ECtHR undertakes a more 'relational' approach that values the connections between children and wider familial networks, including the grandparent/grandchild relationship. Fenton-Glynn observes that the jurisprudence of the ECtHR on grandparents 'represents an important acknowledgement by the Court that the protection of Article 8 must stretch further than the nuclear family and reflect the lived reality of children's lives'.[82]

Whilst we agree that these developments are a step in the right direction, the ECtHR has not been critical of the tentative approach taken towards the grandparent/grandchild relationship in the legal frameworks and judicial decision making in countries such as England and Wales. This may, in part, be due to the state's wide margin of appreciation. As Brown has identified, however, ECtHR decision making is still primarily based on 'the idealised image of the traditional nuclear family'.[83] It is apparent to us that much more work needs to be undertaken to improve the recognition of diverse parenting arrangements and to move away from the 'nuclear norm'. Moreover, change is necessary (via soft law guidance, legislation or judicial decision making) to adopt a more 'relational' approach as concerns disputes between grandparents and parents.

The courts have tended to take the position that contact with parents will be in a child's best interests, save in 'exceptional circumstances'.[84] In contrast, the common law and statutory legal frameworks provide no grandparent 'preference' or 'presumption'. Instead, the grandparent appears to bear the burden of proving that contact is in the child's best interests. This can be seen in the cases of *Re A (A Minor) (Contact Application: Grandparent)*[85] and *Re K (Mother's Hostility to Grandmother's Contact)*.[86] Again, in contrast to situations of hostility between a mother and a non-resident father, where the courts appear willing to order contact between children and non-resident fathers and express 'vehement disapproval'[87]

---

[81] *Re H (A Child)* [2014] EWCA Civ 271. For further detail, see ch 1 of this volume.
[82] C Fenton-Glynn, *Children and the European Court of Human Rights* (Cambridge, Cambridge University Press, 2021) 233.
[83] Brown (n 1) 40.
[84] *Re W (A Minor) (Contact)* [1994] 2 FLR 441 CA at 447.
[85] *Re A (A Minor) (Contact Application: Grandparent)* [1995] 2 FLR 153.
[86] *Re K (Mother's Hostility to Grandmother's Contact)* [1996] CLY 565.
[87] J Wallbank, 'Castigating Mothers: The Judicial Response to "Wilful" Women in Disputes over Parental Contact in English Law' (1998) 20 *Journal of Social Welfare and Family Law* 357, 558.

of mothers seen as wilfully obstructing such contact, the courts have refused to take the same approach with a non-resident grandparent.[88] Indeed, in *Re K*,[89] not only was the grandmother's application refused, but a prohibited steps order was made, preventing the non-resident father from allowing contact between the child and the grandparent. This was because it was considered that the mother's hostility towards the grandparents would risk causing emotional harm to the child. Unfortunately, even if grandparents can assert that their interests (and, of course, the best interests of children) ought to be protected legally vis-à-vis a contact order, this is not necessarily the end of the matter, as we will now consider.

D. Enforcement of Court Orders

Research has shown that, for the most part, loss of contact with grandparents can be explained by the residential arrangements made after divorce.[90] In that sense, then, there is the potential for a 'mirroring' effect in that, if contact with a non-resident parent decreases or ceases (whether due to limited contact via court order or difficulties in enforcing contact), so will the grandparental contact. Often, primary caregivers may refuse to comply with court orders, and grandparents who have contact orders in place (like non-resident parents) must then decide whether to 'give up' or seek enforcement of contact through further court proceedings. Primary caregivers who obstruct contact may, in 'high-conflict' cases, be regarded as 'implacably hostile',[91] or as exhibiting 'parental alienation'[92] towards the non-resident parent.[93] This hostility and alienating behaviour may be directed against grandparents too, thereby exacerbating interpersonal conflict. This means that grandparents may seek to enforce court orders to counter the failure of parents themselves to recognise the 'relationality' between grandparents and grandchildren. While we recognise that non-resident parents and grandparents both face challenges in the enforcement of court orders, we submit that the challenges faced by grandparents may be greater because of the more tentative approach taken by the judiciary, and also due to the 'heteronormative' legal frameworks that, for grandparents, exacerbate the challenges they may face.

The enactment of sections 2–5 of the Children and Adoption Act 2006 sought to broaden the range of remedies available for breaches of court orders, rather

---

[88] See also a study that shows that, in most cases, contact will be ordered in favour of fathers (whether indirect or direct) despite such hostility: Hunt and Macleod (n 64) 192–94.

[89] *Re K* (n 86).

[90] M Albertini and M Tosi, 'Grandparenting after parental divorce: The association between non-resident parent-child meetings and grandparenting in Italy' (2018) 15 *European Journal of Ageing* 277.

[91] See eg *Re A (A Child)* [2015] EWCA Civ 910.

[92] See eg *Re A (Children) (Parental alienation)* [2019] EWFC B56. For further discussion and analysis of parental alienation, see J Doughty, N Maxwell and T Slater, *Review of Research and Case Law on Parental Alienation* (London, OGL, 2018).

[93] *MFS (Appeal: Transfer of Primary Care)* [2019] EWHC 768 (Fam); *Re H (Parental Alienation)* [2019] EWHC 2723.

than to simply fine or imprison parents. The Act provided powers that encouraged the courts to promote and enforce contact orders via the attachment of 'warning notices' stating the consequences of the failure to comply, which could include imprisonment for contempt of court.[94] Alternatively, enforcement orders[95] can include less serious consequences, such as unpaid work, the ongoing monitoring of contact[96] by the Children and Family Court Advisory and Support Service (CAFCASS) or compensation for financial loss[97] caused by non-compliance. The difficulty is that although research has been undertaken into enforcement applications,[98] the data do not yet disaggregate grandparents from other 'nonparental' figures in determining how many grandparents have applied for enforcement proceedings and been successful in the enforcement of contact.

In terms of the measures of enforcement, imprisonment is the most draconian measure that the courts have in their toolkit. In practice, the courts have been hesitant to commit a parent to prison for non-compliance with a court order in general, but perhaps especially when a grandparent seeks enforcement of contact. In *CH v CT*,[99] the grandmother successfully applied for an enforcement order and requested the making of a suspended committal order against the mother. The mother's appeal was permitted on the basis that committal to prison should be a last resort, and that sufficient consideration had not been afforded to less draconian alternatives. This approach is broadly in line with the jurisprudence of the ECtHR, which emphasises that committal to prison ought to apply only as an exceptional measure.[100]

Comparatively, the transfer of residence has become a popular sanction against primary caregivers who fail to make children available for contact.[101] Judges may, however, be less inclined to use this tool to enforce contact for grandparents, because the grandparent/grandchild relationship is not viewed as being of the same value as that of the parent/child. This approach serves to emphasise the lack of 'equal footing'[102] between grandparents and parents. In *Re B (Transfer of Residence to Grandmother)*,[103] Thorpe LJ considered whether to transfer residence to a grandmother and stated that 'I know of no case in which such a dire sanction has been exercised against an obdurate parent'.[104] He also expressed concern that '[i]nevitably there are disbenefits for a child to be brought up by an adult of a different generation to either of her parents'.[105] This latter comment, in particular,

---

[94] Children and Adoption Act 2006, s 3.
[95] ibid s 4.
[96] ibid s 2.
[97] ibid s 5.
[98] Cusworth et al (n 16).
[99] *CH v CT* [2018] EWHC 1310 (Fam).
[100] *Fourkiotis v Greece* App no 74758/11 (ECtHR, 16 June 2016).
[101] *V v V* [2004] EWHC 1215 (Fam).
[102] *Re B (A Child)* [2012] EWCA Civ 858 [13].
[103] *Re B (Transfer of Residence to Grandmother)* ibid.
[104] ibid [13].
[105] ibid.

demonstrates a potentially outdated and traditional approach towards parenting and 'grandparenting'. This is especially the case since the age of first-time parenting is consistently getting higher,[106] due to changes in lifestyle and developments in assisted reproduction.[107]

Current legal frameworks, which can be used to 'make contact happen', have favoured the 'nuclear' family. This is due to the existence of legal 'presumptions' and 'preferences', past and present, which affect court applications and the likelihood of success in obtaining court orders and enforcing them. We suggest that the need for (and corresponding increase in) the enforcement of court orders[108] shows that the system is not working as well as it should to protect familial relationships. Thus, mediation is a preferred route, which may save the parties expense in the long term, and agreements could be included in a 'consent order' to highlight a symbolic (as well as a legally binding) commitment to making contact happen. We argue that if parties have reached the stage where enforcement proceedings are necessary, this will only serve to cause further damage to tenuous relationships between parents and grandparents. We consider in section III.E how the existence of a 'parental preference' interacts with the existing legal frameworks aimed (in part) at facilitating contact, and how the relationship between legal frameworks and a 'parental' preference have served to favour the 'divided' 'nuclear' family.

E. A Broader 'Dyadic' Parental Preference

We have argued, up to this point, that a 'heteronormative' approach, which favours the traditional 'nuclear' family, can be seen via the process of obtaining leave, and of making and enforcing contact orders. In this respect, the law has not operated 'relationally', recognising the wider nexus of relationships within which children can exist. Specifically, we submit this because parents have a 'preferred position'[109] in law, which usually (but not always) stems from a genetic connection.[110] They also derive the benefits and burdens that accompany automatic parental responsibility,[111] provided for within section 3 of the Children Act 1989, which states 'all the rights, duties, powers, responsibilities and authority which by law a

---

[106] Office for National Statistics, *Birth characteristics in England and Wales: 2019* at www.ons.gov.uk/peoplepopulationandcommunity/birthsdeathsandmarriages/livebirths/bulletins/birthcharacteristicsinenglandandwales/2019.

[107] S Sharma and N Aggarwal, 'In vitro fertilization in older mothers: By choice or by law?' (2016) 7 *Journal of Mid-life Health* 103.

[108] Cusworth et al (n 16).

[109] Eekelaar (n 41).

[110] Under the Human Embryology and Fertilisation Act 2008, s 33, the legal mother is the gestational mother, regardless of whether she is the biological parent. Under pt 2 of the Act, circumstances in which a man or woman can be regarded as the child's legal parent are provided for.

[111] Children Act 1989, s 3(1).

parent of a child has in relation to the child and his property'. Grandparents do not enjoy the same protected status, despite the existence of a genetic connection.[112] The Court of Appeal has observed that 'manifestly grandparents are not on equal footing with parents'.[113] This highlights the fact that, during the court process, parents' interests will usually be afforded more weight than grandparents' interests.

The weight that should be attached to the relative interests of natural parents versus others, such as grandparents, has, according to Everett and Yeatman, 'vexed' the courts for years.[114] Historically, the courts applied the natural parent presumption, which assumed that children would be better off with their parents.[115] In the oft-quoted Court of Appeal decision of *Re D (Care: Natural Parent Presumption)*,[116] rather than grant residence to the grandparent, the court favoured the father, despite his having a questionable background, including a history of drug abuse. In the House of Lords[117] decision in *Re G (Children)*,[118] Baroness Hale also placed a strong emphasis on the biological tie between the children and their mother, although the importance of 'relationality' is implicit within her observations about wider familial connections beyond the traditional 'nuclear' networks:

> The knowledge of that genetic link may also be an important (although certainly not essential) component in the love and commitment felt by the wider family, perhaps especially grandparents, from which the child has so much to gain.[119]

In fact, both the common law and statutory frameworks are weighted heavily in favour of parents. The importance of parental status is also reflected in the statutory presumption in favour of parental involvement in the Children and Families Act 2014, section 11 of which states that the court is 'to presume, unless the contrary is shown, that involvement of that parent in the life of the child concerned will further the child's welfare'. However, doubt has been shed on the weight to be placed on the interests of parents. The courts have lately indicated that there is no 'broad natural parent presumption'[120] that children will always be better off living with their parents; nor is there a presumption for a child to be brought up by a member of the natural family,[121] such as a grandparent. There are those, such

---

[112] *Re B (A Child)* (n 102).
[113] ibid [13].
[114] K Everett and L Yeatman, 'Are Some Parents More Natural than Others?' (2010) 22 *Child and Family Law Quarterly* 290.
[115] *Re KD (A Minor) (Ward: Termination of Access)* [1988] 1 All ER 577.
[116] *Re D (Care: Natural Parent Presumption)* [1999] 1 FLR 134. For further discussion of this case and the natural parent presumption, see J Fortin, 'Re D (Care: Natural Parent Presumption) Is blood really thicker than water?' (1999) 11 *Child and Family Law Quarterly* 435.
[117] The final court of appeal in the UK is now the Supreme Court.
[118] *Re G (Children)* [2006] UKHL 43.
[119] ibid [33].
[120] *Re E-R (A Child)* [2015] EWCA Civ 405 [31]. See also *Re B (A Child)* [2009] UKSC 5.
[121] *Re H (A Child)* [2015] EWCA Civ 1284; *Re W (A Child)* [2016] EWCA Civ 793; *A v B and C* [2018] EWHC 3834 (Fam).

as Fortin, who have questioned the emphasis placed on genetic (or at least 'legal') parents over others.[122] Taylor has argued that it can be problematic to emphasise biological connections, stating that '[s]uch presumptions risk distorting children's welfare by emphasising biology over practical care'.[123] Indeed, according to Taylor, the law takes an 'ambivalent'[124] and 'outdated'[125] approach towards grandparents, despite their importance in children's lives.

Grandchildren typically have stronger relationships with grandparents related to the resident parent.[126] In many cases, it is the mother who will impede and restrict contact with the father and/or the (typically) paternal grandparents.[127] The situation can potentially be reversed in situations where fathers act as the primary carers.[128] It can also vary due to the rising numbers of gay and lesbian households.[129] In 2019, there were 212,000 same-sex families in the UK, having increased by 40 per cent since 2015.[130] This increase may mean that, in time, the balance of maternal versus paternal grandparents losing contact with the children changes, with the incidence of two maternal or two paternal grandparents also increasing. Furthermore, the increasing number of gay and lesbian parents may mean that the usual dispute 'framework' is complicated by additional matters, such as whether grandparents whose son has acted as a 'sperm donor'[131] for lesbian couples, or grandparents who are not 'genetic', have a claim equal to that of grandparents in 'divided' 'nuclear' family disputes. This could include, for instance, 'step-grandparents'.

There are, indeed, cases where the grandparent/grandchild relationship has been put before parents' interests, in furtherance of a child's welfare. The legal framework is largely geared towards prioritising the protection and promotion of the 'nuclear' family – whether 'united' or 'divided'. Bendall and Harding note, for example, that the legal framework on civil partnership was based on the marriage legal framework.[132] The legal framework on parenthood is likewise

---

[122] Fortin (n 116). See, also L Yeatman, 'Lesbian Co-Parents: Still Not Real Mothers' (2013) 43 *Family Law* 1581, 1587.

[123] Taylor (n 67) 230.

[124] ibid.

[125] ibid 231.

[126] S Westphal, A Poortman and T Van Der Lippe 'What About Grandparents? Children's Post-divorce Residence Arrangements and Contact with Grandparents' (2015) 77 *Journal of Marriage and Family* 424.

[127] L Dickson, 'Grandparents and contact – what's the solution?' (2019) 49 *Family Law* 1091. See, eg, *Re B (Transfer of Residence to Grandmother)* (n 103).

[128] A Tavares, C Crespo and MT Ribeiro, 'What Does it Mean to be a Targeted Parent? Parents' Experiences in the Context of Parental Alienation' (2021) 30 *Journal of Child and Family Studies* 1370.

[129] Office for National Statistics, *Families and Households in the UK: 2019* at www.ons.gov.uk/peoplepopulationandcommunity/birthsdeathsandmarriages/families/bulletins/familiesandhouseholds/2019.

[130] ibid.

[131] *Re G (A Child)* [2018] EWCA Civ 305.

[132] C Bendall and R Harding, 'Heteronormativity in Dissolution Proceedings: Exploring the Impact of Recourse to Legal Advice in Same-Sex Relationship Breakdown' in E Brake and L Ferguson (eds), *Philosophical Foundations of Children's and Family Law* (Oxford, Oxford University Press, 2018) 134.

based on the norm of a heterosexual 'nuclear' family. Consequently, the notion of 'grandparenthood' has been largely ignored. Herring states the present position succinctly:

> The current approach of the law (on parenthood) is based on the heterosexual married model. The requirement that a child has one father and one mother reinforces that as a norm for parenthood.[133]

Herring advocates departing from the 'nuclear' norm to improve the recognition of a network of people who play roles in a child's family.[134] We support this type of 'relational' approach, albeit that we are less optimistic than Herring about the law's capacity to achieve it.

F. What Prospects Does the Legal System Hold for Accommodating 'Relationality'?

We submit that it is difficult to conceive of this kind of more connected approach being adequately accommodated within the legal structures of England and Wales. In any event, there has been little appetite to do so. The UNCRC (through, for example, the 'best interests' principle in Article 3) recognises the importance of parents and the wider community, and the possibility that parental, and even grandparental, interests might conflict with those of the child.[135] Although ratified by the UK in 1989, the Convention has still not been incorporated into English legislation, and there has been 'pessimism' around the possibility of this happening in the foreseeable future.[136] Turning to the Children Act, in terms of the assessment of what is within the concept of the 'welfare' of the child under section 1, Herring and Foster have claimed that the courts will 'typically follow the course of action which best promotes the interests of the child, viewed as an atomistic entity'.[137] Regardless, they argue that it is not desirable, nor even possible, to view children's interests in isolation from those of their parents, any other children, or even the wider community.[138] This is particularly the case if we take the perspective that all our lives are inherently interconnected and interdependent, and that the rights and interests of children and their carers are intertwined.[139] Herring and Foster suggest it to be 'absurd' to imagine it as feasible to break off the interests of one family member from another due to that interconnection: 'In family life, and

---

[133] Herring (n 4) 157.
[134] ibid.
[135] C Henrikson and A Bainham, *The Child and Family Policy Divide: Tensions, Convergence and Rights* (York, Joseph Rowntree Foundation, 2005).
[136] S Davey, *A Failure of Proportion: Non-consensual adoption in England and Wales* (Oxford, Hart Publishing, 2020) 28.
[137] Herring and Foster (n 26) 491.
[138] ibid 480.
[139] J Herring, *Caring and the Law* (Oxford, Hart Publishing, 2014).

particularly in caring for those who lack capacity, "I" and "you" become so inter-mingled that it is impossible to force them apart.'[140]

To follow this line of thinking, within intimate relationships, 'the boundaries between selves break down'.[141] A judge who conducts an assessment by taking a person outside of their social context will reach an incorrect conclusion, because that context is 'inextricably bound up' with what that person is.[142] It is arguable, therefore, that the courts should adopt a broader approach towards the 'welfare' principle, given that it is only possible to properly consider a child's well-being by also acknowledging the network of relationships within which that child lives.[143]

The focus of Herring's work here, though, is predominantly on the parent–child relationship (and so, how to account for the rights and interests of parents), and we argue that it would be challenging to extend this approach to include grandparents too. In this sense, the legal process is inadequately equipped to account for the intricacies of parenting/caring arrangements. A dilemma is posed particularly in terms of the fact that litigation requires that matters ultimately be adjudicated one way or another. Were the courts to try to 'balance out' the independent interests of both parents and grandparents, they would be faced with difficulties around weighing up interests that point in different directions. Under the UNCRC, in the case of conflict, decision makers are to analyse and weigh the rights of all of those concerned, bearing in mind that the right of the child to have their 'best interests' taken as a primary consideration means that those interests have high priority.[144] This entails that more weight is attached to what actions serve the child best. Yet in many cases it would be problematic were the interests of a grandparent, in relation to their grandchild, to outweigh those of the resident parent, as this would present a risk that they might overstep boundaries. Chapter 3 speaks to similar issues with respect to reproductive health decisions. Lindsey concludes that the courts should draw on prospective grandmothers' evidence simply to contextualise the deci-sions of prospective mothers, rather than taking into account the interests of the prospective grandmothers in themselves. However, of course, that kind of decision making can be contrasted with the present context, where the application made will relate directly to the grandparent.

Consequently, it might be possible to somehow attribute less weight to grandparents' interests than to those of the parents. Still, it would perhaps seem inappropriate to suggest that, for example, a father who has hitherto not been involved in his child's upbringing, and who suddenly shows an interest in contact, should be in a more advantageous position than a grandparent who has seen that child regularly and formed strong bonds with them. An issue would also be posed

---

[140] Herring and Foster (n 26) 489.
[141] ibid 487.
[142] ibid 494.
[143] ibid 481.
[144] Committee on the Rights of Children (2013) General Comment No 14 (2013) on the right of the child to have his or her best interests taken as a primary consideration (Art 3, para 1).

in terms of quantification. A key problem is that, in practice, 'parental responsibility', as defined in section 3(1) of the Children Act 1989, involves a variety of different tasks and has been criticised as being 'vague'.[145] In the absence of an agreed list, these tasks would seem to include, but not be limited to: bringing up the child on a day-to-day basis; having contact with them; determining and providing for their education and religion; and consenting to their medical treatment.[146] These tasks are often allocated in a fragmented way. Different people take on different responsibilities within different families, with some of the de facto tasks being performed by grandparents. Were the courts required to decide how much significance to allocate to each of these tasks to determine a grandparent's 'level' of interest, this would prove complex, time-consuming and potentially expensive. Accordingly, we make the case that the legal system is not the most suitable forum for preserving positive relationships between children and their grandparents.

IV. Mediation: A More Promising Option for Furthering Grandparents' Claims

We argue that relationships between children and their grandparents can be better promoted and protected outside of the court system, using mediation. Notably, within England and Wales (unlike in some jurisdictions), mediation is not court-based. Mediation can incorporate various functions, including those that are 'evaluative' and 'facilitative'.[147] Whereas 'evaluation' and 'facilitation' have been seen as binary opposites, Blakey has instead conceived of them as forming part of a 'continuum', in the sense that aspects of both may be present.[148] In their 'evaluative' capacity, mediators are themselves more likely to express opinions and to assist the parties in assessing the merits of the arguments. They adopt techniques that 'direct some or all of the outcome' of the matters before them.[149] It is recognised that, given the absence of publicly funded legal advice as a result of the Legal Aid, Sentencing and Punishment of Offenders Act (LASPO) 2012, mediators now behave more 'evaluatively'.[150] Maclean and Eekelaar, for instance, have found that mediators frequently give information that moves parties towards a particular action.[151] However, in this section we are concentrating less on mediation's

---

[145] Brown (n 1) 137.

[146] N Lowe and G Douglas, *Bromley's Family Law*, 11th edn (Oxford, Oxford University Press, 2015).

[147] L Riskin 'Understanding mediators' orientations, strategies, and techniques: A grid for the perplexed' (1996) 1 *Harvard Negotiation Law Review* 7.

[148] R Blakey, 'Cracking the code: The role of mediators and flexibility post-LASPO' (2020) 32 *Child and Family Law Quarterly* 53.

[149] Riskin (n 147) 24.

[150] Blakey (n 148).

[151] M Maclean and J Eekelaar, *Lawyers and Mediators: The Brave New World of Services for Separating Families* (Oxford, Hart Publishing, 2016).

'evaluative' possibilities and more on its 'facilitative' role, as a way of encouraging greater 'relationality'. 'Facilitation' refers to the more traditional understanding of mediation, entailing a voluntary, confidential process within which participants seek to decide amongst themselves to resolve their disagreement with the help of a 'facilitator' – a mediator. In addition, we see promise in mediation's 'transformative' capacity, through which it can bring about an 'internal move in participants from an individualistic orientation to a balanced concern for self and others'.[152]

We identify two broad advantages to mediation, from a 'relational' perspective, when it operates in these ways. These are in terms of its less adversarial and confrontational nature, fostering greater cooperation between the parties, and also in terms of its capacity to depart from the 'heteronormativity' of the legal system. First, Huntington has emphasised that the court system is

> [b]ased on the same ... system that was developed to address commercial disputes and the like. When this ... approach is overlaid on families, [it] creates a win-lose dynamic that pits one family member against the other.[153]

Likewise, courts 'impose' a 'solution' upon the parties from 'above', adopting a 'one-size-fits-all approach' that does not account for important differences between family disputes and other types of legal matter.[154] These include the intense emotions that can be involved, and the potential need for the parties to continue to relate to one another after their dispute has concluded.[155] As against the court-based approach towards dispute resolution, mediation can instead 'support the parties to find their own solutions',[156] conferring flexibility and 'outcome control' on them.[157] Both sides are encouraged to negotiate and compromise to find an arrangement that everyone can live with, presenting the greatest chance that no one walks away feeling injustice and loss. The emphasis is more on reaching a position that the parties find 'acceptable', and on all parties getting something from the process.[158] This is rather than strictly adhering to notions of 'fairness' and 'justice' as they have been conceived of from a legal perspective, that is, as 'objectively pre-determined (and pre-determinable) and based on precedent and comparison with like for like cases'.[159] That aspect of mediation has been criticised,[160] not least in

---

[152] P Franz, 'Habits of a highly effective transformative mediation programme' (1998) 13 *Ohio Journal on Dispute Resolution* 1039, 1042.

[153] Huntington (n 7) 82.

[154] ibid.

[155] ibid.

[156] K Salminem, 'Mediation and the best interests of the child from the child law perspective' in A Nylund, K Ervasti and L Adrian (eds), *Nordic Mediation Research* (Cham, Springer, 2018) 209, 215.

[157] J Lindsey, *Reimagining the Court of Protection: Access to Justice in Mental Capacity Law* (Cambridge University Press, Cambridge, 2022).

[158] www.familymediationhelpline.co.uk, quoted in C Irvine 'ADR Professional: Mediation and social norms: A response to Dame Hazel Genn' (2009) 39 *Family Law* 351.

[159] Lindsey (n 157).

[160] H Genn, 'Civil Justice and ADR', Hamlyn Lecture, Edinburgh, December 2008.

the sense that at least one party might find themselves in a worse position having attended mediation than they might have done had they litigated.[161] There is, moreover, some debate as to how reflective this kind of understanding is of how mediation operates in 'reality'.[162] Nevertheless, it is arguable that, where adopting such an approach, mediation presents more opportunity for healing rifts and promoting better ongoing relationships between the disputing parties as well as with the child.

For grandparents, the potentially 'heated', divisive nature of legal proceedings is unlikely to improve, and may well exacerbate, already strained relationships with (and between) parents. This is important, because the relationship between grandparent and grandchild is itself interdependent on the relationship between child and parent, and cannot be viewed in isolation. As Herring highlights, 'the grandparent-grandchild relationship must ... be seen as part of the network of interlocking family relationships'.[163] Where one or both of the parents object to a child's contact with their grandparent, that will impact the role that a grandparent will be able to perform (in much the same way as grandparents can themselves help to either strengthen or weaken the relationship between parent and child).[164] Equally, in the context of a more collaborative environment, there is a possibility of tackling those objections, which can result in greater involvement by grandparents in their grandchildren's lives.

It is appreciated that where the parties are determined not to engage with the process, mediation will not work. Getting parties into the same room may present a challenge in itself (although, notably, mediation can operate in separate physical spaces, via telephone calls, online meetings or in separate rooms within the same building).[165] However, in contrast to the 'nastiness and aggravating effects'[166] of the court system, mediation attempts to 'orient the parties towards reasonableness and compromise, rather than ... vindication'.[167] Given that outcomes must be consensual, the 'punitive urge' that is often a feature of disputes could be 'tempered by pragmatism'.[168] Within court proceedings, participants can become combative and adopt a more individualistic view of the scenario at hand. They can be emboldened by their legal advice, seeing their way as the only way. In contrast, mediation encourages the parties to listen to, and appreciate, the other's viewpoint. This means that, ultimately, choices can be made based not just on one's own needs

---

[161] Lindsey (n 157).

[162] Irvine (n 158).

[163] Herring (n 29) 236.

[164] ibid.

[165] Family Solutions Group, '"What about me?" Reframing Support for Families following Parental Separation' (Family Solutions Group, 2020) 73.

[166] L Riskin, 'Mediation and lawyers' (1982) 43 *Ohio State Law Journal* 29, 33.

[167] T Grillo, 'The mediation alternative: Process dangers for women' (1991) 100 *Yale Law Journal* 1545, 1560.

[168] C Irvine, 'What do "lay" people know about justice? An empirical enquiry' (2020) 16 *International Journal of Law in Context* 146.

but also in light of what others have said.[169] It is in this respect that we argue that mediation can helpfully act 'transformatively', urging people to recognise other people's interests.[170] Mediation engages the 'neuroplasticity'[171] of the brain, helping to encourage rationality and communication, in addition to active listening and reflection on one's actions. This is in stark contrast to the adversarial process, which draws on the more primitive limbic system,[172] meaning that participants' responses are based on instinct rather than on thoughtful reflection.

The participants' discussions are particularly aided by the fact that lesser restrictions are imposed on the parties to mediation than in the legal context. A strict approach is adopted, in the context of legal proceedings, to what is relevant and 'sayable'. As Rosenberg has expressed it, 'the message that comes from the court is: "your wants and needs are irrelevant, except to the extent that we say otherwise"'.[173] Parties in court may also talk to each other through legal counsel (where instructed), becoming even further apart emotionally and often losing sight of the other's humanity in the process. In comparison, while mediation does not offer an alternative to counselling,[174] and while the focus is largely on problem solving, the parties are not 'silenced' in the way that they can be by the court process.[175] They are offered a more empowering opportunity to 'tell their stories'[176] and to have some validation of their perceptions and feelings.[177] Their defensive barriers, which obstruct agreement, can be lowered through the satisfaction of their 'natural need to be heard and understood'.[178] The participants are able to speak to one another directly in a 'safe space'[179] and, often for the first time, discuss the 'root' of the issue at hand. Mediation, where operating 'facilitatively', can '[f]acilitate … communication between the parties and empower … them … to articulate their own interests, concerns, needs and solutions, and to genuinely listen to and understand each other's'.[180] This enables the parties to have conversations around what has gone wrong in the past, and what might be improved in the future.

---

[169] Franz (n 152).

[170] R Baruch Bush and J Folger, *The Promise of Mediation: The Transformative Approach to Conflict* (San Francisco, CA, Jossey-Bass, 2004).

[171] This refers to 'the brain's ability to modify, change, and adapt both structure and function throughout life and in response to experience'. See P Voss et al, 'Dynamic Brains and the Changing Rules of Neuroplasticity: Implications for Learning and Recovery' (2017) 8 *Frontiers in Psychology* 1657.

[172] This is the part of the brain that processes emotions and memories. See V Rajmohan and E Mohandas, 'The limbic system' (2017) 49 *Indian Journal of Psychiatry* 132.

[173] J Rosenberg, 'In defence of mediation' (1991) 33 *Arizona Law Review* 467, 484.

[174] Gingerbread (2020) *Help When you Can't Agree* at www.gingerbread.org.uk/information/legal-help-and-responsibilities/help-when-you-cant-agree.

[175] J Nolan-Haley, 'Court mediation and the search for justice through law' (1996) 74 *Washington University Law Review* 47.

[176] A Davis and J Rifkin, quoted in J Nolan-Haley, 'Court mediation and the search for justice through law' (1996) 74 *Washington University Law Review* 47, 56.

[177] Rosenberg (n 173).

[178] Franz (n 152) 1051.

[179] T Tallodi, *How Parties Experience Mediation: An Interview Study on Relationship Changes in Workplace Mediation* (Dordrecht, Springer, 2019) p51.

[180] Salminem (n 156) 215.

The mediation process can also be used to protect and promote the 'voice' of the child, a right recognised and protected under Article 12 UNCRC. This can be done either directly or indirectly. Although still relatively uncommon,[181] it is possible to engage in 'child-inclusive' mediation, where the mediator speaks to the child alone and confidentially. Children are able to speak honestly about what they want, how they feel, who they want to spend time with and with whom they wish to live. This provides for a greater voice for children in a context where a child's 'right to be heard' has 'not sufficiently benefited children'.[182] The Family Solutions Group has advocated the wider use of 'child-inclusive' mediation, including the introduction of funding for it,[183] and a presumption in favour of listening to the voice of a child over the age of 10 in 'mediation and solicitor-led processes'.[184]

Whilst we would broadly support the more widespread use of a more 'child-centred' approach towards mediation, it is not a central purpose of this chapter to argue in its favour. Indeed, it is recognised that there is also a debate to be had as to whether the burden of responsibility for children to be involved in family decision making may be too onerous (although, of course, there is a distinction between giving the child a 'voice' and giving them a 'choice').[185] Even in the absence of the direct involvement of the child, though, where the parties are able to reach an agreement between themselves, mediation holds the capacity to '[r]eorient parties toward each other ... by helping them to achieve a new perception of their relationship ... that will redirect their attitudes and dispositions towards one another'.[186]

The focus is on establishing 'a degree of harmony through a resolution that will work best'[187] for all parties concerned. Where an agreement has been reached between, and accepted by, the parties, this will, in itself, be advantageous to the child. This is on the basis that it is beneficial for children to be raised in families whose members respect, and are able to cooperate with, one another. As is stated in the preamble to the UNCRC, 'the child ... should grow up ... in an atmosphere of happiness, love and understanding'. Enabling the parties to reach their own 'solution' to their dispute, on the basis of what they (rather than the law) perceive to be 'fair' and what is most congruent with their lives, offers a greater chance of success in the long run, with a higher likelihood of compliance.[188] This helps to put the dispute to rest once and for all, removing the need for enforcement (which, as is identified in section III, has frequently proved problematic for grandparents). Through the process of mediation, the parties can gain the skills to 'manage their

---

[181] J Smithson et al, 'The "child's best interests" as an argumentative resource in family mediation sessions' (2015) 17 *Discourse Studies* 609.

[182] For detailed discussion see A Daly, *Children, Autonomy and the Courts* (Leiden, Brill, 2017) 115.

[183] Family Solutions Group (n 165) 95.

[184] ibid 94.

[185] A Smith and N Taylor, 'Rethinking children's involvement in decision-making after parental separation' (2003) 10 *Childhood* 201.

[186] L Fuller, 'Mediation – Its forms and functions' (1971) 44 *Southern California Law Review* 305, 325.

[187] Riskin (n 166) 34.

[188] See, for instance, The Scottish Government, *An International Evidence Review of Mediation in Civil Justice* (Social Research Series, Edinburgh, 2019).

relationships in such a way as to lessen their future dependence upon lawyers'.[189] It can therefore help to 'induce learning and build bridges between parties'.[190] Mediation carries an additional benefit of potentially reducing the amount of time and cost involved in resolving disputes, in comparison to pursuing those disputes through the court process.[191] This takes some of the strain off the parties (which can have a knock-on impact on the children involved as well) and keeps the length of any interruptions in the relationship between grandparent and grandchild to a minimum. 'Strength and stability' are promoted in enabling the child to develop 'a secure attachment with a caregiver, [which] requires repeated, ongoing contact'.[192]

Moving on to the second broad advantage of mediation from a 'relational' perspective, it offers opportunities to break away from problematic norms that underpin family law. We do, of course, recognise that research has not supported the 'mythical' notion of the mediator as a completely 'neutral' entity, with it possible for mediators to 'actively influence' the sessions that they oversee.[193] This can pose difficulties in the sense that participants may 'mirror' any talk that is not neutral in nature.[194] Mediators with a legal background may particularly be more likely to adopt an approach driven by the law than those without one.[195] We have noted as well that, in the era post-LASPO, mediators are required to perform more of an assessment role (predicting court outcomes and 'reality testing' proposals), which requires greater awareness of the law.[196] However, the substantive law is at least conventionally viewed as not being dispositive in the process of mediation. Instead, it operates simply as a 'template' to show what might happen in a more formal legalistic setting.[197] As Nolan-Haley describes it, relatively 'free-standing normative standards govern' in the mediation context.[198] Where the parties order their affairs through the more private route of mediation, it is possible for them, to a greater extent, to 'opt out' of legal norms. This is because, for example, parties can use mediation to focus solely on resolving their problems, rather than concentrating on asserting their legal rights. This approach has been criticised by Genn[199] but, given the lack of legal rights that grandparents have in the context of the law,

---

[189] Riskin (n 166) 49.

[190] Tallodi (n 179) 4.

[191] S Bahr, 'Mediation is the answer: Why couples are so positive about this route to divorce' (1981) 3 *Family Advocate* 32.

[192] Huntington (n 7) 18.

[193] See, eg, D Kolb and K Kressel, 'The realities of making talk work' in D Kolb & Associates (eds), *When Talk Works: Profiles of Mediators* (New York, John Wiley & Son Inc, 1994); S Silbey, 'Mediation mythology' (1993) 9 *Negotiation Journal* 349.

[194] Smithson et al (n 181).

[195] J Lewis, *The Role of Mediation in Family Disputes* (Edinburgh, Scottish Office Central Research Unit, 1993).

[196] Blakey (n 148).

[197] Nolan-Haley (n 175) 56.

[198] ibid.

[199] H Genn, 'What is civil justice for? Reform, ADR, and Access to Justice' (2012) 24 *Yale Journal of the Law & Humanities* 397.

we argue it serves to level the playing field. Participants within mediation can determine their own outcomes in a less constrained, pre-determined way. They are able to reach outcomes that would be unlikely to be favoured, or may not even be possible, were the matter to be decided by a court.[200] Agreements can be reached that are simply beyond the law's scope.[201] As Irvine emphasises, self-determination is a 'driving value', and the parties are ultimately able to ignore any guidance from the mediator.[202]

Mediation, as is emphasised by Riskin, is less 'hemmed-in by … assumptions that dominate the adversarial process'[203] in this area, such as 'heteronormativity'. This 'heteronormativity' can be seen, as previously explained, in the plethora of legislative provisions that protect and promote the interests of parents over others (such as on 'parental responsibility' and the 'presumption of parental involvement'). A 'heteronormative' approach is also evident from the 'hurdle' of leave, which applies to grandparents but does not apply to parents in private law proceedings,[204] as well as in the reluctance to apply remedies (such as a change of residence) to protect the grandparent/grandchild relationship. The fact that parties can resolve their own matters within mediation, and prioritise what they, rather than the law, see as important, means that mediation presents a real chance to break away from the dyadic parenting norm that has been evident within the law and to accommodate greater diversity in family forms. It enables the protection of devalued and de-emphasised relationships that fall outside of the 'nuclear' model and yet which form an important part of children's identity. Having the ability to do this is particularly important in the context of enormously varying familial relationships and roles, which are, in any event, better suited to a more individualised form of decision making than the court process can offer.

We therefore argue that mediation offers greater prospects for promoting ongoing relationships between grandparents and grandchildren. This is in the sense that it allows greater significance to be placed on the caring roles that grandparents can perform (in addition to others who similarly do not fit neatly into the 'heteronormative' binary parenting model). In other words, mediation allows for greater emphasis on contemporary, and often complex, de facto relationships, rather than on the narrow range of relationships upon which the law has tended to focus.

---

[200] R Field and A Lynch, 'Hearing parties' voices in Coordinated Family Dispute Resolution (CFDR): An Australian pilot of a family mediation model designed for matters involving a history of domestic violence' (2014) 36 *Journal of Social Welfare and Family Law* 392.

[201] Lindsey (n 157).

[202] Irvine (n 162).

[203] Riskin (n 166) 34.

[204] Unless placement orders have been made under the Adoption and Children Act 2002, s 21. If so, a parent needs to apply for leave to apply for the revocation of the placement order and to oppose the making of an adoption order.

V. Conclusion

We have stressed in this chapter the central importance of grandparents in the lives of many children. Grandparents may have lived with, or have had substantial contact with, their grandchildren prior to separation or divorce. Research demonstrates that multi-generational bonds can, in fact, be more important than 'nuclear' ties for well-being and support over the course of children's lives.[205] Grandparents' importance may even extend onwards, becoming significant figures once their grandchildren reach adulthood.[206] Yet the law in this area has performed a significant role in minimising grandparents. In focusing on the 'heteronormative' binary model of the family, the legal system has not recognised or accommodated key societal developments, and we have expressed concern over its capacity to do so. This is not least given the adversarial nature of this system, and the difficulty of balancing interests in a context where 'a' decision is ultimately required to be produced. Mediation, in helping to break away from the norms of the law, offers some prospect of hope for those who are virtually unseen by the legal process. Mediation helps parties to identify all issues and needs, legal and non-legal, and to find a mutually satisfactory resolution. Given its possibilities for fostering a more 'relational' approach, we submit that mediation needs to be encouraged wherever possible in disputes involving grandparents. Empirical investigation is needed into grandparents' experiences of mediation 'on the ground', although currently data from family mediation outcomes tend not to be collected routinely. Nonetheless, the 2019 Family Mediation Council (FMC) statistics compiled from 122 participating mediators across 2,161 mediation sessions demonstrated full or partial agreement in approximately 70 per cent of these disputes.[207]

Whilst we recognise that mediation is already promoted via the compulsory attendance of a Mediation Information and Assessment Meeting (MIAM), this appears to have been insufficient, with uptake still being relatively low. A recent freedom of information request by the authors has revealed that, of the 1,916 child arrangement order applications made in 2019, a MIAM session was attended in only 622 cases,[208] and it is unknown how many of these were attended by the grandparents themselves.

More recently, the Ministry of Justice has introduced a scheme, to be administered by the FMC via individual mediators, that will provide a £500 voucher towards mediation for up to 2,000 eligible families, to be distributed on a

---

[205] Bengtson (n 70); D Coall et al, 'Interdisciplinary perspectives on grandparental investment: A journey towards causality' (2018) 13 *Contemporary Social Science* 159, 162.

[206] R Giarusso et al, 'Grandparent-adult grandchild affection and consensus. Cross-generational and cross-ethnic comparisons' (2001) 22 *Journal of Family Issues* 456.

[207] Family Mediation Council, *Family Mediation Survey Autumn 2019 Results* at www.familymediationcouncil.org.uk/2020/01/20/survey-shows-mediation-is-successful-in-over-70-of-cases.

[208] Ministry of Justice, freedom of information request, on 'child arrangements orders' (13 April 2021).

first-come-first-served basis. This, it is hoped, will encourage greater uptake, and will help to address the further difficulties in facilitating and enforcing contact that exist in the wake of the coronavirus.[209] We also hope that the introduction of 'no fault' divorce via the Divorce, Dissolution and Separation Act 2020 may help to reduce conflict between parents and make them more likely to engage with mediation, whether with each other or with grandparents. Time will tell.

We acknowledge that mediation is not the answer in every case. It can be unsuitable where there have been issues of domestic abuse, or where there is significant power imbalance between the parties (albeit that those with the least power and resources are also unlikely to fare well in the courts[210]). There may be issues outside of developing and maintaining relationships, such as decision making over religious beliefs, education or medical treatment, that are not appropriate matters for grandparental interference. We also appreciate that many see the aspect of 'choice', and people's ability to come 'voluntarily' to the process, as being one of mediation's key strengths.[211] Consequently, we are not suggesting that mediation should become compulsory. We are mindful, too, that there can be variation amongst mediators, and would support a move towards greater consistency in training programmes. We do, however, assert that there should be an even stronger steer towards mediation in private law children matters, especially when involving parties who fall outside of the 'nuclear' family. This makes sense in the context of the significant court backlog caused by the pandemic,[212] with the resultant delays potentially leading to parties' relationships deteriorating further.[213]

The challenge is to determine how to promote the use of mediation more effectively. We favour continuing to educate the public about the benefits of mediation via workshops mandated by court, such as the 'Separated Parents Information Programme',[214] as well as promoting its usage via the extension of initiatives such as the voucher scheme. We also support the exploration of funding for packages of mediation, legal advice and counselling,[215] where appropriate. Further consideration as to whether to make mediation agreements legally binding, as proposed by the Family Solutions Group,[216] may have the benefit of strengthening the status of mediation agreements. While significant sums are currently being channelled into CAFCASS and the high-conflict pathway,[217] resources would be better utilised on

---

[209] E Neil, R Copson and P Sorensen, *Contact During Lockdown: How are children and their birth families keeping in touch?* (London, Nuffield Family Justice Observatory/University of East Anglia, 2020).

[210] A Sarat, 'The law is all over: Power, resistance and the legal consciousness of the welfare poor' (1990) 2 *Yale Journal of Law & the Humanities* 343.

[211] E Richardson, 'The role of mediation in family disputes' *Law Gazette* (2021) at www.lawgazette. co.uk/practice-points/the-role-of-mediation-in-family-disputes/5107078.article.

[212] J Robey, 'It's time to consider making family mediation compulsory' *Family Law* at familylaw. co.uk/news_and_comment/it-s-time-to-consider-making-family mediation-compulsory.

[213] *Bergman v The Czech Republic* App no 8857/08 (ECtHR, 27 October 2011).

[214] CAFCASS, *Separated Parents Information Programme* (London, CAFCASS, 2017).

[215] Family Solutions Group (n 165) 70.

[216] ibid 83.

[217] CAFCASS, *High Conflict Child Arrangements Disputes Handbook* (London, CAFCASS, 2016).

these sorts of more proactive, rather than reactive, solutions. The judiciary could also use their powers to order mediation with greater frequency. Were judges encouraged by law to order mediation at an early stage in the process, this might serve to halt further court processes such as CAFCASS reports, expert reports and the provision of further evidence from parties, which tend to promulgate an unhelpful, adversarial mindset. Although the removal of the leave requirement is widely conceived of as the most effective way of assisting grandparents in private law children matters, it is merely a small symbolic step that still sets them onto a conflict-ridden path. We argue that, instead, a legal steer towards early judicial intervention could help steer the parties onto a more 'relational' route towards resolution. Such incremental steps would help to 'level the playing field' between parents and grandparents, serving to sidestep (and thereby challenge) the current approach within the law, which perpetuates the norm of the 'nuclear' family.

3

Best Interests and Relationality in Reproductive Health Care

JAIME LINDSEY

I. Introduction

Choices about health care are some of the most important, challenging and emotive decisions we make. For many, decisions about reproductive health care specifically can be life-changing, for example deciding to terminate a pregnancy[1] or refusing interventions during childbirth. In making healthcare decisions, many of us draw on our familial relationships and wider networks for advice, support and guidance. As many other chapters in this edited collection have identified, a mother is often instrumental in steering her daughter through pregnancy and childbirth, as well as wider reproductive decisions. In this way, one of the prospective grandparent's roles is to draw on their own experience to support their child in this process. However, as other chapters also demonstrate, a grandparent's relationship with their grandchild may, in some instances, create legal rights and duties of its own, which leapfrog the parent or at least come into conflict with the parent's rights. While some in this collection are supportive of giving grandparents procedural or even substantive rights in relation to their grandchildren, I express some caution about how this could play out in healthcare law, an area with links to, but distinct from, family law. The complex and interwoven relationship between grandchild, child and grandparent requires careful consideration before we permit any expansion of legal rights for the grandparent.

This chapter explores these intergenerational relationships in a particular social context. It specifically focuses on relationships between women and their own mothers as they become, respectively, mothers and grandmothers. This gender dimension of the social aspect of parenthood and grandparenthood is important, partly because reproduction remains a gendered phenomenon that impacts upon mothers to a greater extent than fathers due to the biological realities of pregnancy

---

[1] That is in no way to suggest that decisions about terminations are necessarily exceptional or distressing, merely that they can change the direction of a person's life.

and childbirth. The evidence is overwhelming that women most often turn to their mothers for support, rather than to their fathers or other family members, during pregnancy and following childbirth, and so the special and particular nature of the relationship between child, mother and grandmother is worthy of focus in this chapter.[2] However, the gender dimension is also a relevant factor in the cases that arise in both the disciplines of healthcare law and family law.[3] For example, we know that maternal grandmothers are more likely to be involved in kinship care, whether informally or formally through care proceedings.[4] Therefore, under both a social and legal analysis, the focus on child, mother and grandmother is justified.

In addition to the gender dimension, the substantive scenarios I consider in this chapter concern cases where the daughter has a disability or impairment, and therefore raise issues of mental capacity. Sometimes these women are referred to as 'vulnerable',[5] which can be hugely stigmatising, notwithstanding attempts by feminists to adopt a more nuanced and inclusive conception of it.[6] In light of this, the chapter draws on the jurisprudence of the Court of Protection (CoP), the court that deals with cases that arise under the Mental Capacity Act (MCA) 2005. Where a person is found to lack the capacity to make a decision for themselves, the decision must be taken in accordance with the person's best interests. For the purposes of this chapter, I focus on decisions about reproductive health care, most typically caesarean sections, termination of pregnancy, contraception and sterilisation. These cases explicitly, and almost exclusively, concern women. The chapter further concerns cases either where a child has not yet been born, or where there is a desire to prevent pregnancy. In this respect I am discussing the appropriate role

---

[2] S Winterburn, M Jiwa and J Thompson, 'Maternal Grandmothers and Support for Breastfeeding' (2003) 17 *Journal of Community Nursing* 4; R Negron et al, 'Social Support During the Postpartum Period: Mothers' Views on Needs, Expectations, and Mobilization of Support' (2013) 17 *Maternal Child Health Journal* 616; I Nenko et al, 'Will Granny Save Me? Birth Status, Survival, and the Role of Grandmothers in Historical Finland' (2021) 42 *Evolution and Human Behavior* 239.

[3] For further analysis of the gendered dimension of these areas of law, see L Pittman, 'Doing What's Right for the Baby: Parental Responses and Custodial Grandmothers' Institutional Decision Making' (2014) 2 *Women, Gender, and Families of Color* 32; K Cook and K Natalier, 'Gender and Evidence in Family Law Reform: A Case Study of Quantification and Anecdote in Framing and Legitimising the "Problems" with Child Support in Australia' (2016) 24 *Feminist Legal Studies* 147; S Halliday, *Autonomy and Pregnancy: A Comparative Analysis of Compelled Obstetric Intervention* (Abingdon, Routledge, 2016).

[4] P McGrath and L Ashley, *Kinship Care: State of the Nation Survey 2021* at https://kinship.org.uk/kinship-annual-survey-2021/, 14, 16.

[5] J Herring and J Wall, 'Autonomy, Capacity and Vulnerable Adults: Filling the Gaps in the Mental Capacity Act' (2015) 35 *Legal Studies* 698; J Lindsey, 'Developing Vulnerability: A Situational Response to the Abuse of Women with Mental Disabilities' (2016) 24 *Feminist Legal Studies* 295; B Clough, 'Disability and Vulnerability: Challenging the Capacity/Incapacity Binary' (2017) 16 *Social Policy and Society* 469; L Pritchard-Jones, 'The Good, the Bad, and the "Vulnerable Older Adult"' (2016) 38 *Journal of Social Welfare and Family Law* 51; J Herring, *Vulnerable Adults and the Law* (Oxford, Oxford University Press, 2016).

[6] Lindsey (n 5); Clough (n 5); C Mackenzie et al, 'Introduction: What Is Vulnerability and Why Does It Matter for Moral Theory?' in C Mackenzie et al (eds), *Vulnerability: New Essays in Ethics and Feminist Philosophy* (Oxford, Oxford University Press, 2014) 1.

of *prospective* grandmothers in influencing legal determinations that impact upon their daughters and unborn grandchildren.

The context of intergenerational relationships in reproductive decision making is used to illustrate a wider concern about the adoption of a relational approach to the concept of best interests, something that has wider implications beyond mental capacity law, for example in family law too. This contributes to academic and practitioner interest in the concept of best interests, as it is applied across legal jurisdictions.[7] Drawing on autonomy theory in the chapter, I show how the courts have trodden a delicate balance between the competing interests of the grandchild, daughter and (prospective) grandmother in their analysis of best interests; acknowledging the primacy of the daughter's autonomy while accepting the relational value of the intergenerational network. The value of drawing on theoretical insights into autonomy throughout the chapter is twofold. First, I highlight that, on a relational autonomy[8] approach, the courts could use the wishes of the grandmother to override the wishes of the daughter, which raises concerns about whose interests are really being protected. Second, I highlight the wider risk in incorporating a strong relational approach through the law, through analysis of the wider context in which best-interests decisions are made in family law. The relational nature of human interaction certainly requires that a wider network is drawn upon for evidence in any weighing up of best interests. However, I argue that the courts should draw on the prospective grandmother's evidence to contextualise the person at the heart of the case, rather than considering the wishes and/ or interests of the prospective grandmother herself. That is, to understand what the *woman's own* wishes and feelings are. This is an important distinction, which, I argue, is blurred by various relational approaches to law.

I start with an overview of the relevant legal frameworks governing mental capacity law, specifically in the domain of reproductive decision making. I then move on to my focus on the concept of autonomy, comparing liberal and relational interpretations. The chapter shows how both liberal and relational conceptions of autonomy are implicitly invoked in judgments to balance best interests, as well as highlighting links with the best-interests concept in family law. Finally, I show how the courts must be careful in incorporating relational autonomy-based reasoning into their judgments, because it risks placing primacy on the wishes of the wider family network rather than prioritising the wishes of the individual.

---

[7] M Donnelly, 'Best Interests, Patient Participation and The Mental Capacity Act 2005' (2009) 17 *Medical Law Review* 1; J Herring, 'Forging a Relational Approach: Best Interests or Human Rights?' (2013) 13 *Medical Law International* 32; HJ Taylor, 'What are "Best Interests"? A Critical Evaluation of "Best Interests" Decision-Making in Clinical Practice' (2016) 24 *Medical Law Review* 176; C Kong, *Mental Capacity in Relationship: Decision-Making, Dialogue, and Autonomy* (Cambridge, Cambridge University Press, 2017); C Kong et al, 'An Aide Memoire for a Balancing Act? Critiquing The "Balance Sheet" Approach to Best Interests Decision-Making' (2020) 28 *Medical Law Review* 753.

[8] C Mackenzie and N Stoljar (eds), *Relational Autonomy: Feminist Perspectives on Autonomy, Agency, and the Social Self* (Oxford, Oxford University Press, 2000); SJ Khader, 'The Feminist Case Against Relational Autonomy' (2020) 17 *Journal of Moral Philosophy* 499; J Nedelsky, *Law's Relations: A Relational Theory of Self, Autonomy, and Law* (Oxford, Oxford University Press, 2011).

II. The Legal Context

Not all adults are permitted by law to make their own decisions in life. For example, where they are found to lack the mental capacity to make certain decisions, those decisions can be made on the person's behalf in their best interests.[9] In those cases, the views of a person's wider network can be hugely influential, notwithstanding that the concept of 'next of kin' has no legal effect because the application of the MCA 2005 means that the person with capacity, or the relevant best-interests decision maker where the person lacks capacity, has decision-making authority.[10] As other chapters have identified, many cultures and societies would see the influence of family and wider networks as both inevitable and positive. However, the appropriate role that grandmothers ought to play is contested, with concerns about them overstepping the boundaries and taking a malignly maternalistic approach towards their children and grandchildren.

Turning to the requirements for decision-making under the MCA 2005, the legislation requires that unwise decisions are not treated as incapacitous decisions. Simply because a prospective grandmother views her daughter's wishes as unwise, for example by refusing a caesarean section and putting the unborn grandchild at risk, that does not mean that the grandmother has any legal recourse to override her daughter's wishes. The legal test under the MCA 2005 for whether a person has the mental capacity to make decisions about health care has two stages. It requires that the person has an impairment or disturbance in the functioning of their mind or brain[11] and that, as a result, they are unable to make a decision because they cannot understand information relevant to that decision; cannot retain that relevant information; cannot use or weight it; or cannot communicate their decision.[12] Further, it requires that a person understands the reasonably foreseeable consequences of the decision.[13] In the context of medical treatment, the issue typically turns on what information is relevant to the decision. For example, whether it extends to the impact of the treatment decision on one's family or friends, or the impact on the foetus. The case law on these points is well established; the information relevant to medical treatment decisions is narrowly drawn to include a 'broad, general understanding'[14] of the risks and benefits of the treatment in question. This may include some general understanding of the availability of alternative options and their comparative risks and benefits, but the person need not understand all

---

[9] MCA 2005, s 4. See also discussions of legal personhood, which can impact upon decision making, in N Naffine, *Law's Meaning of Life: Philosophy, Religion, Darwin and the Legal Person* (Oxford, Hart Publishing, 2009).

[10] Note that there are exceptions to this, for example where a family member (or another person) has been granted a power of attorney or deputy to deal with the incapacitated adult's affairs; see MCA 2005, ss 5, 9, 14 and 24 in particular.

[11] MCA 2005, s 2.

[12] ibid s 3(1).

[13] ibid s 3(4).

[14] *Heart of England NHS Foundation Trust v JB* [2014] EWCOP 342.

options available to them in detail. The more complex the healthcare decision, the more likely it is that incapacity will be proved. For example, a decision to consent to a sterilisation procedure is likely to be more complex than a decision to consent to contraception, with the latter having fewer long-term consequences than an irreversible procedure such as sterilisation.

The CoP has, mostly successfully, emphasised that it is a capacitous person's right to make any decision they like, for any reason at all, and the importance of respecting unwise decisions through a clear statutory statement within the MCA 2005 should not be underestimated.[15] However, once a person is found to lack the mental capacity to make a decision, a decision can be made on that person's behalf only if it is in their best interests to do so.[16] What is in a person's best interests extends beyond their medical interests to include a much wider range of factors.[17] This is set out in the legislation, which states that in determining best interests the following must be considered:

(a) the person's past and present wishes and feelings (and, in particular, any relevant written statement made by him when he had capacity),
(b) the beliefs and values that would be likely to influence his decision if he had capacity, and
(c) the other factors that he would be likely to consider if he were able to do so.[18]

The factors considered under the best-interests test are subject to analysis throughout this chapter. In particular, I argue that some CoP decisions demonstrate a very fine line between the best interests of the person themselves and the interests of their wider network. For example, anyone involved in caring for the person must also be consulted on their best interests.[19] Of course, the statutory legal position is clear that others are to be consulted to help determine the best interests of the person themselves. Yet, on a deeper analysis, it is not always clear that it is how the law is interpreted in practice.

III. Liberal or Relational Autonomy: Competing for Best Interests

Analysis of relevant CoP case law shows that the courts have, in some instances, tried to uphold the concept of autonomy as self-determination, even where the

---

[15] ibid.
[16] There is also the more challenging scenario where a person may be found to have capacity to make the decision but is subjected to the inherent jurisdiction of the High Court instead to justify intervention; for further analysis in this context, see Halliday (n 3).
[17] See, eg, *Re Y (Mental Patient: Bone Marrow Donation)* [1996] 2 FLR 787.
[18] MCA 2005, s 4(6).
[19] ibid, s 4(7).

person at the centre of the decision has been found to lack the capacity to make the relevant decision. They have mainly done this by prioritising the wishes of the person through interpretation of the best-interests test. Autonomy is a complex concept, which is not always used or applied consistently through this or other areas of law, meaning that the courts invoke different ideals of autonomy, and not always overtly, depending on the case before them. There are various interpretations of it, ranging from individualist/liberal, to relational understandings.[20] In very general terms, use of the word 'autonomy' connotes an ideal of self-determination: people can and should be able to make their own decisions about their own lives. This is often not the form of autonomy that is upheld in the CoP, as a person's express wishes can be, and often are, overridden.[21] Skowron explains that, in the CoP,

> [j]udges tend to use whatever ideas about personal 'autonomy', a word that is not legally defined, best suit their rhetorical needs in the immediate case, whether or not their usage can coherently account for the law as a whole.[22]

I agree and take his analysis further in this section by contrasting how the liberal and relational interpretations of autonomy can both be seen in CoP judgments. For the most part, the CoP has balanced the competing intergenerational interests in these cases to respect the primacy of the woman's autonomy while acknowledging the importance of relationships to achieving autonomy. However, there is emerging evidence that the best interests of the person at the heart of the decision are unjustifiably displaced by the wishes of her relational network. For the purposes of this chapter, I focus on the wishes of the (prospective) grandmother and her views in relation to best interests. I suggest that analysing the best-interests test through a lens of relational autonomy can result in the person's own interests being relegated to those of their wider network, something that may only increase if the rights of grandmothers (or grandparents more generally) are expanded. I further consider how this problem might develop in family law cases too, with the aim of showing how the difficulty arises when we interpret the best-interests concept relationally beyond the specific context of this edited collection.

---

[20] For an overview of the different approaches to autonomy as relevant to the healthcare context and that I draw on here, see J Coggon and J Miola, 'Autonomy, Liberty, and Medical Decision-Making' (2011) 70 *The Cambridge Law Journal*; Khader (n 8); J Warriner, 'Gender Oppression and Weak Substantive Theories of Autonomy' in M Oshana (ed), *Personal Autonomy and Social Oppression: Philosophical Perspectives* (Abingdon, Routledge 2015) 25; Nedelsky (n 8); M Oshana, *Personal Autonomy in Society* (Aldershot, Ashgate 2006); S Sherwin, 'A Relational Approach to Autonomy in Health Care' in S Sherwin (ed), *The Politics of Women's Health: Exploring Agency and Autonomy* (Philadelphia, PA, Temple University Press, 1998) 19; Mackenzie and Stoljar (eds) (n 8).

[21] P Skowron, 'The Relationship Between Autonomy and Adult Mental Capacity in the Law of England and Wales' (2019) 27 *Medical Law Review* 32.

[22] ibid 33.

A. Liberal Autonomy

Traditionally, English law has adopted a liberal interpretation and application of autonomy. This typically means that people should be free to make their own choices about their own lives without unjustified interference. The liberal approach to autonomy reflects an endorsement of John Stuart Mill's 'harm principle', that a person's choices can only be interfered with to the extent that it protects another from harm.[23] Debates have been extensive in the literature, with particularly interesting issues being raised by feminist legal scholars as to precisely what harm entails in scope and specificity.[24] It is not necessary for the purposes of this chapter to engage in those debates about harm, although the issue could arise where the daughter's wishes are seen by the grandmother as harmful to the grandchild. However, in broad terms, this approach reflects that people should be allowed to make any decisions about their lives unless or until those decisions are harmful to others, at which point some evaluation of the respective value of their decisions/ actions may be weighed up.

The law's endorsement of the liberal approach to autonomy reflects a wider concern about freedom and state interference in individual choices. This defence of freedom has been particularly important from a feminist perspective as women have, historically at least, struggled to have their choices respected by the law.[25] While there has been a movement within feminist scholarship in this area away from liberal notions of autonomy, a more circumspect analysis may be helpful to remind us of the extent to which a woman's wishes were previously sidelined in the interests of her child or wider network. For example, *St George's Healthcare NHS Trust v S*[26] represented an important re-statement of the liberal conception of autonomy. The case was an appeal against an out-of-hours declaration that it would be lawful to carry out a caesarean section on a 28-year-old pregnant woman, S, without her consent. In the period following the initial declaration and the subsequent appeal, S gave birth to the baby by caesarean section against her wishes. The case before the Court of Appeal centred on whether the hospital had acted lawfully in treating her without consent. It was held that S had the requisite mental capacity to refuse a caesarean section and, therefore, the medical procedure was unlawful.

---

[23] JS Mill, *On Liberty* (1909) at https://ebookcentral.proquest.com/lib/bham/detail.action?docID= 435870 (downloaded 3 January 2018).

[24] C Fabre, *Whose Body is it Anyway?: Justice and the Integrity of the Person* (Oxford, Oxford University Press, 2006); M Fox and Thomson, 'Bodily Integrity, Embodiment, and the Regulation of Parental Choice' (2017) 44 *Journal of Law and Society* 501; R Fletcher et al, 'Legal Embodiment: Analysing the Body of Healthcare Law' (2008) 16 *Medical Law Review* 321; Naffine (n 9).

[25] Z Eisenstein, *The Female Body and the Law* (Berkeley, CA, University of California Press 1988); Fletcher et al (n 24); M Fox and K Moreton, '*Re MB (An Adult: Medical Treatment)* [1997] and *St George's Healthcare NHS Trust v S* [1998]: The Dilemma of the "Court Ordered" Caesarean' in J Herring and J Wall (eds), *Landmark Cases in Medical Law* (Oxford, Hart Publishing, 2015) ch 8.

[26] *St George's Healthcare NHS Trust v S* [1999] Fam 26.

This ruling was enormously important for reinforcing the rights of all adults with capacity, particularly women going through childbirth, to refuse any medical treatment for any reason, even where it puts the life of their unborn child at risk.[27] Halliday makes an important and persuasive case that, despite this ruling, women continue to struggle to have their healthcare decisions respected, particularly in the context of pregnancy and childbirth,[28] because this and other rulings turn on the question of capacity. That is, the right to non-interference is not absolute and depends on the individual's internal decision-making abilities.

While the liberal approach to autonomy is often posited as respecting, in absolute terms, an individual's freedom to make their own choices, on some interpretations individuals who are unable to make their own decisions, by whatever criteria adopted, can have those decisions overruled against their wishes.[29] The difficulty with such an approach, then, is, first, how we determine whether or not a person is able to make their own decision. More importantly for this discussion, though, is whether or not the person still has a degree of autonomy even where they are found to lack capacity. For example, should the person's wishes and conception of the good life still be relevant once they have been found to lack capacity to make the decision? Eldergill J's comments in the case of *Manuela Sykes* are an important reminder that even incapacitated persons still enjoy autonomy, on some accounts at least:

> The importance of individual liberty is of the same fundamental importance to incapacitated people who still have clear wishes and preferences … This desire to determine one's own interests is common to almost all human beings.[30]

In *GSTT & SLAM v R*,[31] Hayden J similarly remarked that 'The right of all individuals to respect for their bodily integrity is a fundamental one. It is every bit the right of the incapacitous as well as the capacitous.'[32] This is clearly a facet of the liberal conception of autonomy and its underpinning conceptual justification of non-interference. That all of us have some right to determine whether or not our liberty or bodily integrity can be compromised is an important backstop against the state, professionals and others with the power to override our wishes, something that has been brought into stark reality and not always fully protected against during the Covid-19 pandemic.[33] The values of bodily integrity and liberty are

---

[27] Moreton and Fox (n 25).

[28] Halliday at n 16.

[29] For further discussion on who counts as law's persons, see Naffine (n 9).

[30] *Westminster City Council v Manuela Sykes* [2014] EWHC B9, §10.

[31] *GSTT & SLAM v R* [2020] EWCOP 4.

[32] ibid [48].

[33] See, eg, T Hickman, E Dixon and R Jones (2020) 'Coronavirus and civil liberties in the UK' at www.ucl.ac.uk/laws/news/2020/apr/dr-tom-hickman-qc-co-authors-report-coronavirus-restrictions-law; D Studdert and MA Hall, 'Disease Control, Civil Liberties, and Mass Testing – Calibrating Restrictions during the Covid-19 Pandemic' (2020) 383 *New England Journal of Medicine* 102.

intimately linked, something that has been particularly emphasised by feminist scholars highlighting, for example, the medical profession's power over women's bodies.[34] A similar argument can be made in respect of kinship power, with the complexities of liberty and bodily freedom within controlling family dynamics.[35] However, it is still the case that adults can have both their liberty and bodily integrity lawfully compromised if they are found to lack the mental capacity to make a decision for themselves, if it is in their best interests to do so, despite Hayden J's comments.

For example, in many cases women have been found to lack the mental capacity to make a decision about childbirth and have had caesarean sections forced on them, even against their express wishes.[36] Hayden J's point is, of course, more subtle. It alludes to the importance that we place on bodily integrity in our social, legal and moral world.[37] Such that just because a person lacks the mental capacity to make a particular decision, that does not mean that they can have their bodily integrity interfered with against their wishes. Even where infringing their bodily integrity would benefit them in some way, for example medically, there is no automatic entitlement to interfere with their bodily integrity, as doing so must be in the person's best interests. Case law suggests that for bodily integrity to be interfered with under the best-interests test, there must be a proportionate level of justification to the interference.

Returning to the issue of grandparents and the law, the strong wishes of a prospective grandmother in relation to her prospective grandchild must still be couched in terms of the person's own best interests for healthcare decisions. For example, the grandmother cannot simply insert her own wishes to persuade a judge that her daughter's views should be overridden. This is the case even where the daughter is a child, provided that she is *Gillick* competent[38] to make the decision herself or, where she is not, the daughter's best interests still prevail over those of the grandmother or grandchild. By way of example, in *A Local Authority v K*[39] Cobb J was unwilling to authorise a request from parents for the sterilisation of their daughter, K, on the basis that it was not the least restrictive option at that point in time. K was a 21-year-old woman with Down's Syndrome and a learning disability. She lived with her parents and there was a perception that

---

[34] Lord Woolf, 'Are the Courts Excessively Deferential to the Medical Profession?' (2001) 9 *Medical Law Review* 1; Fletcher et al (n 24); M Fox and J Lindsey, 'Health Law, Medicine and Ethics' in R Auchmuty (ed), *Great Debates in Gender and Law* (London, Palgrave, 2018) 121; J Lindsey, 'Psychiatric injury claims and pregnancy: *Re (a Minor) and Others v Calderdale & Huddersfield NHS Foundation Trust* [2017] EWHC 824' (2018) 26 *Medical Law Review* 117.

[35] V Bell, *Interrogating Incest: Feminism, Foucault and the Law* (Abingdon, Routledge, 1993); J Miles, 'Family Abuse, Privacy and State Intervention' (2011) 70 *Cambridge Law Journal* 31.

[36] Halliday at n 16.

[37] Naffine (n 9).

[38] See *Gillick v West Norfolk & Wisbech Area Health Authority* [1986] AC 112.

[39] *A Local Authority v K* [2013] EWHC 242.

the relationship was generally positive. However, as K was maturing and gaining more independence, her parents believed that there was a risk of pregnancy. They attempted contraception via K's general practitioner, but the hormone implant procedure was distressing for K and, according to her parents, over the following months, while on contraception, K became 'difficult to manage'.[40] Following this, K was referred to a consultant gynaecologist and obstetrician who recommended sterilisation, with the support of K's parents. The sterilisation, had it been authorised, would have been non-therapeutic, meaning that it provided no particular health benefits to K; she was not experiencing any pre-menstrual difficulties nor any other specific health difficulties that would be alleviated by sterilisation. Following expert evidence on the issue, which was unsupportive of sterilisation, the court held that, at that point in time, the sterilisation procedure was not in her best interests because it was not the least restrictive option, but it was an issue to which the court was willing to return in the future. This approach, while reflecting that K lacked capacity and, therefore, did not have full autonomy to make her own healthcare decisions, did at least show some respect to her autonomy conceived as freedom from interference, in that she was not forcibly treated against her wishes, showing that any interference at the request of others has to be limited by what is in the best interests of the person themselves.

This approach, I suggest, reflects an invocation of the liberal conception of autonomy; that even where a person, here K, is unable to meet the criteria for making their own decisions, their wishes should still be given weight and should not be replaced with the wishes of the prospective grandparents because the person still has some right to live a self-determined life not overridden by the views of others, even those who know them best. Given the challenges women face having their healthcare decisions respected through the law (and the application of it), we must be careful in expanding any legal rights of (prospective) grandparents to override the autonomy of their daughters. It was right in this case that the CoP did not concede to the wishes of the prospective grandparents in analysing the best-interests test. Doing so would have reduced, or at least reframed, K's best interests according to the interests of others.

B. A Relational Approach?

Despite showing some respect for the liberal notion of individual autonomy of the incapacitated adult, the CoP has also implicitly incorporated the concept of relational autonomy in some instances, which leaves open the possibility for greater interference by grandmothers and wider familial networks under the application of the best-interests test. Relational autonomy is a theoretical approach developed predominantly by feminist scholars who argue for a more socially constitutive

---

[40] ibid [6].

analysis of autonomy.[41] It draws on the concept of relationality, which focuses on the interconnected or 'nested'[42] relations through which people live in the world. This means that being relationally autonomous is not an individualistic position in relation to the world but a relative position within a person's social context. On a relational approach we do not just analyse the individual decision and measure the extent to which it was rational and self-determining, but we can look to the conditions within which the person made that decision, their ways of thinking and self-reflection, and the influence of those around them.

Relational autonomy general subdivides further between procedural and substantive accounts, with both being evident in the operationalisation of the best-interests concept, as explained further below. Procedural approaches to relational autonomy look at the process by which decisions are made by the individual to determine whether or not they are autonomous, but they are neutral regarding the substance of the decision itself.[43] This means that the focus is on the decision maker, including their competencies and self-reflection abilities, rather than the course of action ultimately decided upon. Diane Meyers, for example, sets out a procedural account of autonomy as 'competency autonomy theory'.[44] In this approach she argues that people are autonomous to different degrees depending on the extent to which they have been able to develop the various competencies necessary for self-determination. Meyers' theory incorporates the relational element too, although writing before Mackenzie and Stoljar's seminal book on the topic, through recognising the importance of social context while requiring only that capacities are developed in an autonomous manner. This means that where a person has the competency to make decisions for themselves and has reflected, as an agent, on their own values, then even if what might externally be regarded as oppressive social conditions have become embedded within that person's belief system, on Meyers' account that person is likely to still be acting autonomously.[45] This highlights how a procedural account of autonomy, even considered relationally, is fundamentally distinct from liberal and substantive approaches.

In an intergenerational context, a procedural relational autonomy analysis could include considering the impact of the woman's mother on her opportunities to develop decision-making competencies and the extent to which she was facilitated to engage in self-reflection as an individual. For example, if a woman decides to refuse a blood transfusion because she feels under pressure to do so for religious reasons imposed by her own mother, this may be viewed as a

---

[41] Notwithstanding that there is a wide range of interpretations of the concept of relational autonomy with which different relational theorists may themselves disagree, see Mackenzie and Stoljar (eds) (n 8); Khader (n 8); MacKenzie et al (n 6); Oshana (ed), *Personal Autonomy and Social Oppression* (n 20); Oshana, *Personal Autonomy in Society* (n 20); Nedelsky (n 20).

[42] Nedelsky (n 20).

[43] For further analysis, see Mackenzie and Stoljar (eds) (n 8).

[44] D Meyers, *Self, Society and Personal Choice* (New York, Columbia University Press, 1989).

[45] Discussed further in J Lindsey, 'Maximising Women's Autonomy in the Regulation of Assisted Reproduction' (Master's thesis, King's College London, 2010).

non-autonomous decision under a procedurally relational account if the woman was unable to reflect on her own religious beliefs or given any opportunities to develop her own decision-making competency.[46] In contrast, substantive accounts of relational autonomy require us to look at the content of the decision as an indicator of whether or not it is autonomous.[47] In the example given, this would mean setting aside the influence of the mother on the woman's decision-making abilities throughout her childhood and adolescence, and instead analysing the mother's role in impacting the final decision to refuse a blood transfusion. For example, an outsider could determine whether the decision is substantively autonomous by weighing up whether or not a blood transfusion is in the self-determining interests of the woman and in accordance with her own values in wanting to, for example, protect the life of the foetus. Substantive relational accounts of autonomy in some ways have more in common with liberal accounts of autonomy than procedural accounts, because under liberal and substantive approaches, scholars have argued that certain decisions (or people) are not autonomous.[48] The result can mean that individuals who are seen as lacking autonomy can have their choices overruled. Thus, a lack of autonomy also impacts on liberty.[49]

Relational autonomy has been developed particularly as a response to overly individualistic conceptions of autonomy that have permeated legal philosophy, which value higher-order reasoning and rationality as necessary conditions for acting autonomously.[50] As Harding has explained, 'the subject that law seeks to regulate is often one that is artificially removed from her interpersonal context, especially when individual approaches to autonomy are elevated at the expense of relational understandings of decision-making'.[51] While I understand the feminist motivation for emphasising relations in rethinking autonomy, I am less

---

[46] There are many reported cases regarding refusal of blood transfusions by Jehovah's Witnesses, which is perhaps unsurprising given the difficult ethical issues raised by these cases: see *Re T (Adult: Refusal of Treatment)* [1992] Fam 95, *Re L (A Minor)* [1998] 6 WLUK 164; *HE v A Hospital NHS Trust* [2003] EWHC 1017; *E&F (Minors: Blood transfusion)* [2021] EWCA Civ 1888. While there are cases that indicate this approach, one difficulty with this area of law remains that reported judgments are relatively limited and often lack detail about the various parties involved; for a critique of reliance on reported judgments in this area see R Harding, 'The Rise of Statutory Wills and the Limits of Best Interests Decision-Making in Inheritance' (2015) 78 *MLR* 945; J Lindsey, 'Testimonial Injustice and Vulnerability: A Qualitative Analysis of Participation in the Court of Protection' (2019) 28 *Social & Legal Studies* 450; J Lindsey, 'Competing Professional Knowledge Claims About Mental Capacity in the Court of Protection' (2020) 28 *Medical Law Review* 1.

[47] Oshana (ed), *Personal Autonomy and Social Oppression* (n 20); Oshana, *Personal Autonomy in Society* (n 20).

[48] Coggon and Miola (n 20); Herring and Wall (n 5).

[49] For more detailed analysis on the different conceptions of autonomy in this context, see C Kong, *Mental Capacity in Relationship: Decision-making, Dialogue and Autonomy* (Cambridge, Cambridge University Press, 2017).

[50] For a useful overview in this context, see M Donnelly, *Healthcare Decision-Making and the Law: Autonomy, Capacity and the Limits of Liberalism* (Cambridge, Cambridge University Press, 2010).

[51] R Harding, *Duties to Care: Dementia, Relationality and Law* (Cambridge, Cambridge University Press, 2017) 17.

convinced that relationality is necessarily incompatible with liberal autonomy or feminist approaches to legal philosophy, despite the stark debates we see between relational and liberal theorists within healthcare law and beyond.[52] I have written elsewhere that, depending on your conception of rational self-interest,[53] it may be possible to incorporate relational thinking into the liberal conception, without abandoning the value that the liberal conception provides in terms of liberty and non-interference. For example, it can be rationally, morally and legally defensible to act in one's self-interest, where the definition of self-interest goes beyond individual bodily boundaries. This means that it is rationally in one's self-interest to care about the wishes and views of your family, friends and community, and that in weighing things up we analyses the variety of influences in our lives to come to a *contextually rational* decision.[54]

This can often be seen in responses to domestic and sexual abuse, something considered in chapter 7 of this volume. Where victims remain in relationships, or continue contact, with their abusers, their decisions can be criticised as highly irrational on the face of it. However, there are complex relational factors at work that, in many instances, mean the victim's decision to maintain a relationship at that point in time is an entirely rational one.[55] This argument is particularly acute in the context of intergenerational relationships, which are the subject of this book. Imagine a multi-generational household, consisting of grandparents, daughter and grandchild: a scenario whereby the parents are perhaps controlling of their adult daughter who, without her own parents' financial, material and social support, would not be able to care as effectively for her own child (their grandchild). In that scenario, remaining in the multi-generational household may be entirely rational and self-interested, if only in the short term while the daughter seeks to make alternative arrangements for herself and her child. Relationships are complicated, but taking those relationships outside of the bounds of self-interest and rational deliberation further exceptionalises, rather than normalises, them.

There are different conceptions of relational autonomy, but the core of each is that they reject the rational, atomistic, self-interested decision maker as the model for being autonomous. Despite the problems with the liberal conception of autonomy, my concern in replacing it with any form of relational approach, substantive

---

[52] Sherwin (n 20); J Christman, 'Relational Autonomy, Liberal Individualism, and the Social Constitution of Selves' (2004) 117 *Philosophical Studies: An International Journal for Philosophy in the Analytic Tradition* 143; AC Westlund, 'Rethinking Relational Autonomy' (2009) 24 *Hypatia* 26; C Mackenzie, 'The Importance of Relational Autonomy and Capabilities for an Ethics of Vulnerability' in C Mackenzie, W Rogers and S Dodds (eds), *Vulnerability: New essays in ethics and feminist philosophy* (Oxford, Oxford University Press, 2014) 33; B Clough, 'New Legal Landscapes: (Re)Constructing the Boundaries of Mental Capacity Law' (2018) 26 *Medical Law Review* 246; Khader (n 8).

[53] Lindsey (n 5).

[54] A similar argument has been made in different ways by, for example, Khader (n 8), who suggests that from the outside it may not be clear why a person is acting in a particular way, but from their standpoint they are making correct judgments based on their social situation.

[55] C Humphreys and RK Thiara, 'Neither Justice Nor Protection: Women's Experiences of Post-Separation Violence' (2003) 25 *Journal of Social Welfare and Family Law* 195.

or procedural, is that it can operate to justify paternalism by placing too much weight on context and the person's wider network, at the expense of avidly defending individual rights. In the specific context of grandparents it could, as I show in section IV, allow the wishes of a prospective grandmother to outweigh the wishes of her daughter. I make the argument here in respect of CoP proceedings, but if such a theoretical approach takes hold in jurisprudence, there is a risk of cross-fertilisation to other areas too, given the close link between the best-interests tests in family law and mental capacity law.[56]

C. Relational Autonomy in the Courts

We can see a relational approach taking hold in legal scholarship throughout social welfare and family law, predominantly a procedurally relational approach. Jonathan Herring, for example, has emphasised the value of relational autonomy across family, healthcare and mental capacity law.[57] Most specifically, we can see relationality through the application of the best-interests concept, which transcends these otherwise distinct areas of law with some clear overlap in the interpretation and application of the concept. Camillia Kong, for example, has more specifically argued that the MCA 2005 and associated law indicates that 'autonomy must assume a much more relational rather than individualistic temper'.[58] To some extent she is making a normative argument, but her statement captures a wider view that mental capacity law does, in fact, incorporate relational approaches to autonomy, and she makes this argument specifically in respect of the best-interests test.[59] If this is true, which it appears to be in certain interpretations of best interests at the very least, then it raises some concerns that come to the fore when seen in light of the possible expansion of grandparents' rights, but also in relation to best-interests assessments more broadly.

The current approach under the MCA 2005, drawing on several prior family law cases, including *Re F (Mental Patient: Sterilisation)*[60] and *Re A (Male Sterilisation)*,[61] has clearly embedded a relational approach. The 2005 Act provides

---

[56] This is particularly relevant here, because most CoP judges are family court judges too, or at least have experience in family law. Also see S Choudhry, 'Best interests in the MCA 2005: What can Healthcare Law learn from Family Law?' (2008) 16 *Health Care Analysis* 240; A Daly, 'No Weight for "Due Weight"? A Children's Autonomy Principle in Best Interest Proceedings' (2018) 26 *The International Journal of Children's Rights* 61.

[57] J Herring, 'Forging a Relational Approach: Best Interests or Human Rights?' (2013) 13 *Medical Law International* 32; J Herring, *Law and the Relational Self* (Cambridge, Cambridge University Press, 2019).

[58] See Kong (n 49) 67.

[59] Ibid.

[60] *Re F (Mental Patient: Sterilisation)* [1990] AC 1.

[61] *Re A (Male Sterilisation)* [2000] 1 FLR 549 560 F–H.

that regard must be given to the relevant circumstances of the decision[62] and to the views of:

(a) anyone named by the person as someone to be consulted on the matter in question or on matters of that kind,
(b) anyone engaged in caring for the person or interested in his welfare,
(c) any donee of a lasting power of attorney granted by the person, and
(d) any deputy appointed for the person by the court,

as to what would be in the person's best interests and, in particular, as to the matters mentioned in subsection (6).[63]

This means, in practice, that it is a legal requirement to consult those around the person to enable the decision maker (or the CoP) to make a judgement about what is in the person's best interests. This is a deeply relational approach; it requires, by law, consultation of the views of the people around the decision maker, and recognises the importance of relationships to understanding the person themselves. This is not simply a case of information gathering. It is an explicit recognition that the views of those close to us matter. It reinforces our socially constituted existence as humans. Of course, these views are primarily meant to be ascertained for epistemological reasons; to facilitate a better understanding of the person's best interests, rather than to supplant that with the wishes of the family member. However, this is a fine line and one that is not always clearly drawn by the courts. This highlights the potential risks of taking a relational approach to best interests.

In medical decision making for example, best interests is not simply about what is in the person's narrow medical interests, with the law approving the non-therapeutic donation of bone marrow for example, something that had no medical benefits for the person involved at all.[64] Such an approach might be welcomed for recognising that people do not always, or even primarily, act in their own self-interest but care deeply about the position of those close to them, even in relationships that may be less than positive. While this is clearly an accurate description of decision making for most of us, it is an approach that has also raised some concerns. For example, such a case highlights the potential conflict not only between children and their parents, but also between differing parental obligations towards different children, which might conflict,[65] an issue explored further in the example below. In *AN NHS Foundation Trust v MC*, the judge was highly critical of the evidence before him, which referred to the patient's best interests only in cursory terms:

> Nowhere is there at the centre of what is being considered either by the treating Trust or the Human Tissue Authority, the best interests of the donor. Ms Gollop for the Trust helpfully referred me to the passage within the accredited assessor's report and it is

---

[62] MCA 2005, s 4(2).
[63] ibid s 4(7).
[64] See *Re Y (Mental Patient: Bone Marrow Donation)* [1996] 2 FLR 787; *AN NHS Foundation Trust v MC* [2020] EWCOP 33.
[65] For a full discussion of the useful example of so-called 'saviour siblings', see S Sheldon and S Wilkinson, 'Should Selecting Saviour Siblings be Banned?' (2004) 30 *Journal of Medical Ethics* 533.

right that there is a passage headed 'Best Interests' but Ms Dolan is also right to say that it is cursory.[66]

This is precisely the difficulty where best interests move away from the individual to be seen in more substantively, rather than procedurally, relational terms. We can clearly see relationality in individual judgments of the CoP too. The judges do not expressly say they are using 'liberal' or 'relational' autonomy though. Instead, we can infer from the reasoning used how the concept of autonomy is being deployed. There are a number of high-profile CoP cases that engage autonomy, including *Wye Valley NHS Trust v B*[67] and *Westminster City Council v Sykes*,[68] but an earlier judgment of the CoP is particularly instructive here. *Re GC*[69] concerned an 82-year-old man who had been living with his nephew for a number of years in squalid conditions. An application was made to the CoP to consider whether or not it was in GC's best interests to live at his home, given the poor conditions and level of care he was receiving from his nephew. The CoP held that it was in his best interests to return to live at home, despite psychiatric evidence to the contrary. The reason for GC's return home, despite difficulties with the living conditions to which he was returning, was entirely relational – that he valued his familial relationship with his nephew and the 'emotional warmth, emotional security and the commitment of human relationship'.[70] GC did express a desire to return home to the care of his nephew, but this alone appeared not to be determinative of the court's judgment. In *GC* the court actively weighed up what was in his best interests, and explicitly referred to the balance-sheet approach to best interests in doing so,[71] which is unusual in reported judgments of the CoP. The use of the balance sheet and the factors considered under the balance-sheet approach show that the court did not simply defer to GC's own wishes, which would have reflected a liberal conception of autonomy. Instead, the court used the balance sheet to analyse a number of different factors, including the relational benefits of returning home in terms of the emotional and caring dimensions, and, as a result, found in favour of such a decision, despite the risks to GC.[72] This suggests that the court valued the relational factors in the case and they counterbalanced the other factors present, such as GC's own wishes and the risks of harm to GC. That is not to argue that the court took a paternalistic approach; quite the opposite – a paternalistic analysis would have resulted in the risks of harm *outweighing* the relational benefits and prohibiting a move home.

Even if the outcome would remain unchanged under a liberal autonomy analysis (ie GC would still have returned home), the judicial reasoning for the judgment matters. First, it shows greater respect to the agency of a disabled person

---

[66] *AN NHS Foundation Trust v MC* (n 64) [21].
[67] *Wye Valley NHS Trust v B* [2015] EWCOP 60.
[68] *Westminster City Council v Sykes* [2014] EWHC B9.
[69] *Re GC* [2008] EWHC 3402 (Fam).
[70] ibid [21].
[71] ibid [18].
[72] ibid [17]–[21].

if the reasoning for the decision is based upon that individual's own wishes. Furthermore, respecting GC's own wishes under a liberal approach is more closely aligned with the requirements under the United Nations Convention on the Rights of Persons with Disabilities, specifically Article 12, which prohibits a substituted decision-making approach for disabled people.[73] Second, if judges in the CoP move towards a relationally informed approach to best interests, this poses risks both to the individual and, more widely, for the understanding and development of the best-interests concept in other cases. I set out these difficulties in section IV, with analysis of possible consequences and concerns of this approach.

In addition to the clear relational dimension for mental capacity law, the case also importantly highlights the similarity in the analysis of best interests under the MCA 2005 and the Children Act 1989, despite obvious differences in application, with Hedley J stating:

> [T]he State does not intervene in the private family life of an individual, unless the continuance of that private family life is clearly inconsistent with the welfare of the person, whose best interests the court is required to determine. That is the same principle that governs State intervention under the Children Act 1989, and whilst the Children Act and the Mental Capacity Act deal with quite different problems and must be treated quite separately, in my judgment it is right that the fundamental principle governing the welfare agencies of the State's interventions in private life should be the same.[74]

This clear overlap between these otherwise distinct areas of family and mental capacity law shows that there is at least some degree of cross-fertilisation between these areas, which share the concept of best interests. This risks embedding relationality in best-interests decision making beyond the confines of mental capacity law given the close conceptual overlap with family law.[75] For example, as Davey discusses in chapter 6, application of the welfare checklist requires the court to consider before ordering adoption 'the relationship which the child has with relatives'.[76] Davey emphasises the value of grandparents and the benefits of recognising such rights through the law, and it is of course important to consider the child's relationship with relatives before something as final as adoption is ordered. However, within family law, analysis of the impact of relationships is too often viewed through the lens of the adults involved, whether that be the family members or professionals. For example, in chapter 5 Fisher-Frank outlines that the child,

---

[73] B Clough, '"People Like That": Realising the Social Model in Mental Capacity Jurisprudence' (2015) 23 *Medical Law Review* 53; A Arstein-Kerslake and E Flynn, 'Legislating Consent: Creating an Empowering Definition of Consent to Sex That Is Inclusive of People With Cognitive Disabilities' (2016) 25 *Social & Legal Studies* 225; A Arstein-Kerslake, *Restoring Voice to People with Cognitive Disabilities: Realizing the Right to Equal Recognition before the Law* (Cambridge, Cambridge University Press, 2017); A Keeling, '"Organising Objects": Adult Safeguarding Practice and Article 16 of the United Nations Convention on the Rights of Persons with Disabilities' (2017) 53 *International Journal of Law and Psychiatry* 77.

[74] *Re GC* (n 69) [14].

[75] See also Choudhry (n 56); Daly (n 56).

[76] Adoption and Children Act 2002, s 1(4)(f).

particularly in private family law proceedings, rarely has their own voice that is directly heard. This means that the child's best interests are analysed through the framing of those adults with the power to do so in proceedings, which in turn can shape the value placed on those relationships by the court. Of course, this is balanced by the expectation that professionals, and ultimately the family court judge, will be able to consider best interests with the child at the centre, but this relies on good evidence gathering and effective representation at court, which are not always present.[77]

A relational autonomy approach to best interests in family law cases could also result in difficulties, particularly where there are allegations of domestic abuse. I agree with Harwood's analysis in chapter 7 of this volume, that expanding the role of grandparents in this regard poses significant risks to children. Yet even doing so through the best-interests test itself poses risks. By way of example, if the courts are faced with an older child expressing a desire not to have contact with their grandmother, then the court could view this as a substantively non-relationally autonomous decision where there is an inherent assumption that kinship care is valuable and beneficial to children. Instead of deferring to the child's wishes, or analysing, procedurally, whether the child has sufficient competence to make an autonomous decision, the courts could look at the substance of the decision by the child to conclude that it indicates a non-autonomous decision that is not in their best interests.

Examples of this can most starkly be seen in so-called 'parental alienation' cases, a broad term that is difficult to define with precision, but which typically involves the concern that one parent (often the mother) is trying to alienate their child from another parent (or grandparent) without foundation.[78] This is despite the widespread debunking of parental alienation as a concept since it was first noted by the American child psychiatrist Richard Gardner.[79] A typical example of this arose in *Re H*,[80] which concerned a 12-year-old boy's contact with his father and paternal family, with Keehan J stating:

> The father had enjoyed a very good relationship with H up until March of 2018. H also enjoyed a close relationship with his paternal grandparents and paternal relatives. I am satisfied these were mutually loving, fulfilling and beneficial relationships.[81]

---

[77] For critiques of the evidence-gathering process in the family court, see AL James, A James and S McNamee, 'Turn down the Volume Not Hearing Children in Family Proceedings' (2004) 16 *Child and Family Law Quarterly* 189; AL James, 'Children, the UNCRC, and family law in England and Wales' (2008) 46 *Family Court Review* 53; A Brammer and P Cooper, 'Still Waiting for a Meeting of Minds: Child Witnesses in the Criminal and Family Justice Systems' (2011) *Criminal Law Review* 925; M Hill, V Welch and A Gadda, 'Contested Views of Expertise in Children's Care and Permanence Proceedings' (2017) 39 *Journal of Social Welfare and Family Law* 42.

[78] See C Bruch, 'Parental Alienation Syndrome and Parental Alienation: Getting It Wrong in Child Custody Cases' (2001) 35 *Family Law Quarterly* 527; JB Kelly and JR Johnston, 'The Alienated Child: A Reformulation of Parental Alienation Syndrome' (2001) 39 *Family Court Review* 249; J Birchall and S Choudhry, *'What About My Right Not to be Abused?' Domestic Abuse, Human Rights and the Family Courts* (Bristol, Women's Aid, 2018).

[79] Bruch (n 78).

[80] *Re H* [2019] EWHC 2723 (Fam).

[81] ibid [18].

Despite H's own wishes to remain living with his mother, Keehan J ordered that H should live with his father due to the mother's parental alienation, meaning a complete and radical upheaval to H's circumstances, including moving to a completely different geographic area, changing school and constructing new friendship groups. This decision is characterised by a substantive relational analysis; that the substance of H's decision to prefer the care of his mother indicates that he is not making an autonomous decision because, from a judicial perspective, he is acting under the oppressive influence of his mother and her unfounded views about the father.[82] Instead, respecting the child's own express wishes to remain with his mother, particularly at the age of 12, which is likely to be at the cusp of competence, would provide greater respect to the child's autonomy on a liberal account, rather than viewing his best interests in substantively relational terms.

IV. The Risks of Expanding Rights of Grandparents through Relational Approaches

In considering what all of this means more specifically for grandmothers in mental capacity law, I now turn to an example of the type of best-interests scenario that has the potential for a harmful relational approach to be incorporated that favours the grandmother's interests over that of the decision maker themselves.

(1) The NHS Acute Trust and (2) The NHS Mental Health Trust v C[83] concerned a pregnant woman, C, who had bipolar disorder and who was also detained under section 2 of the Mental Health Act 1983. The court heard oral evidence from Ms X, who was C's mother and the prospective grandmother of her unborn child.[84] The CoP proceedings related to C's forthcoming labour, as there were concerns that she would be unable to have a natural delivery and her labour would be difficult to manage. It was held that C lacked the capacity to make decisions about medical interventions relating to the birth as she was 'not able to weigh the pros and cons of such interventions, in what was likely to be a dynamic situation with the need to understand and weigh up options at relatively short notice'.[85] C's mother, the prospective grandmother, gave evidence:

> She understood why the application had been made, she would like C to experience some of the birth process but recognised the position needed to be kept constantly under review and, depending on C's state of mind, could see that a caesarean section may be the only option.[86]

---

[82] This is, perhaps, exacerbated by the statutory presumption of parental involvement under Children Act 1989, s 1(2A), albeit such a presumption does not exist in English law in relation to grandparents.

[83] *(1) The NHS Acute Trust and (2) The NHS Mental Health Trust v C* [2016] EWCOP 17.

[84] Legally, the status of the child at this point in time is a foetus. However, I use the term 'unborn child' here to indicate that in this scenario the child was born.

[85] *(1) The NHS Acute Trust and (2) The NHS Mental Health Trust v C* (n 83) [8].

[86] ibid [6].

It is unfortunate that the grandmother's oral evidence was summarised in only a few lines in this way; I have no doubt that her evidence was much richer than this passage reflects, a problematic phenomenon more generally when considered from a critical perspective.[87] However, the grandmother's wishes (or the judicial framing of them) can be interpreted in two ways. First, it could be seen that the grandmother's wishes are entirely about what is in the best interests of her daughter; that she is concerned for C because, on the one hand, she knows that C would want to experience the birth process, but, on the other hand, she knows that it could be harmful to C to have a vaginal delivery. The alternative interpretation is that the grandmother was balancing the interests of C against the interests of the unborn child and, indirectly therefore, her wish to have a healthy granddaughter. These two interpretations are, of course, not mutually exclusive, and on a relational analysis are difficult to separate. However, I suggest that it is essential that we do so, otherwise there is a risk of blurring the boundary between what is in C's exclusive best interests and what is in the interests of others, whether that be her unborn child or her own mother.

C's interests and the interests of her unborn child are, to many people, at least very closely related. In English law, the foetus has no rights until birth,[88] and so C's bodily interests, and bodily integrity, must take precedence. Similarly, even from C's subjective perspective, her interests may align with the objective interests of her unborn child, that is, C really wants her baby to have the best chance of survival. Conversely, though, if C's wish was to, in no circumstances, have any surgical intervention in her delivery, even if that risks the life of her unborn child, then the imputed wishes of C and the child are in direct conflict. Furthermore, it is not simply C's wishes and her child's interests that are in conflict, but potentially her interests and those of her existing children, something that particularly strengthens the grandmother's claim if she has existing bonds with her other grandchildren that she wishes to preserve. The potential for sibling conflict is perhaps more akin to the bone-marrow donation example previously noted, where we can see that such issues are not always resolved in the strict interests of the individual affected but by reference to their wider network. Drawing such an analogy here might suggest that C's best interests are best served by considering the wider interests of her network, including her own mother's wishes, which may be more closely aligned with the court's approach to weighing up the interests of the already living

---

[87] The Open Justice Court of Protection Project has provided much greater insights into the realities of CoP evidence, showing that what is summarised in the judgment is rarely a full picture – see at https://openjusticecourtofprotection.org/; see also Lindsey (n 46); J Lindsey, 'Protecting Vulnerable Adults From Abuse: Under-Protection and Over-Protection in Adult Safeguarding and Mental Capacity Law' (2020) 32 *Child and Family Law Quarterly* 157.

[88] For comparison between English law and US and German law on this point, see Halliday (n 3). There has been some discussion in a number of English cases regarding overriding the woman's decision-making rights to protect the foetus; see, eg, *Re T (An Adult) (Consent to Medical Treatment)* [1993] Fam 95. However, so far, English law has permitted this only in the case where the woman lacks the mental capacity to make a decision herself.

siblings. If the grandmother can provide evidence that is of use to the court in this regard then it may make it easier for a judgment that is not clearly in the mother's own interests to be reached.

Where these different interests come into potential conflict, the courts need to be much clearer about how they are weighing the evidence. The courts have, as already outlined, incorporated a wide range of evidence, but with an emphasis on how this illuminates the person's best interests. Yet it is not clear from this judgment, for example, whose interests the prospective grandmother's views support, and the opacity of the judgment in this regard is arguably intentional, to blur the boundaries of the best-interests analysis in favour of a particular outcome. If C's mother is giving evidence about what, based on her relationship with C, she thinks C would want then that is legitimate. But if C's mother is giving evidence based on her own wishes for her prospective granddaughter then it is not a legitimate approach. Perhaps it is not so easy to delineate, and that is why the courts have not done so, instead obscuring the issues and evidence within the reported judgment. However, it is my contention that they must do so clearly, to avoid a risk of restricting, or overriding, the daughter's autonomy. In less mutually supportive mother–daughter relationships, the distinction would be vital to avoid such a risk.

Given the lack of clarity in the reported case law from the CoP, let us imagine a similar scenario to the above, but with some key differences. Imagine that C has a difficult relationship with her mother. They see each other regularly and C values her mother, but C is emotionally dependent on her mother, perhaps due to a history of childhood neglect and periods of her teenage years where C was in care. C also has two other children, who are much-loved grandchildren. This scenario is reflective of the more difficult cases that reach the family courts, and highlights the complexities of intergenerational relationships for many families. Imagine, then, that during the hearing C's mother gives evidence to the court that she knows her daughter would want a natural birth and would not want any intervention whatsoever. The grandmother goes on to say, though, that on balance, she thinks C should have forced obstetric intervention because, without it, her current grandchildren could suffer and C and the foetus may die. It is the sort of evidence that one might expect to hear in a case such as this, evidence that it would not be particularly unreasonable for a grandmother to give. Yet how should the court treat this evidence? On a relational analysis of best interests, the grandmother's views do not go to the issue of what her daughter would want; rather, they highlight the impact of C's refusal of medical intervention on the grandmother and the existing grandchildren.

A relational autonomy-influenced approach has the potential to result in forcibly overriding the wishes of an individual in the name of their best interests as conceptualised by the wishes of another. Even though this is done under the pretext of best interests, in fact it could be the interests of others that are really being prioritised. Such an approach risks undermining individual freedom and bodily integrity under the guise of a seemingly benevolent concept of 'relational autonomy' that ought to be treated with caution here. I have highlighted ways in which this might be a particular problem in respect of discourse that expands grandparents' rights, but it also raises wider issues for the application of the best-interests test in mental capacity law and beyond, including in family law cases concerning children or where there are allegations of abuse.

V. Concluding Remarks

I am not rejecting the concept of relationality in this chapter. Nor do I repudiate relationally feminist approaches to autonomy, with which I broadly agree as a descriptor of our social world. Relationality is a more accurate understanding of human existence and reflects the value and significance of intergenerational (and other) relationships to most people. Feminist approaches to autonomy also importantly seek to reject the paternalistic subordination of a woman's will to others. Yet a relational approach to autonomy, substantive or relational, risks doing precisely that. It risks replacing a person's expressed wishes and feelings with the preferences of someone else. I have argued for caution when advocating a relational autonomy approach through the best-interests test of the law, given the potential for it to displace the person's own interests with the interests of others, and have explained how this represents a real risk in the context of expansion of grandparents' rights in particular.

In analysing the role of grandparents and the law, I am concerned that a relational understanding of autonomy can be, and perhaps is being, used to facilitate giving grandparents greater influence than is epistemologically justified to get to the person's wishes and feelings. In this chapter, I have shown how this has the potential to happen through the best-interests test under the MCA 2005. However, it may also impact upon decision making elsewhere across the Family Division, if courts are persuaded that grandparents, for relational reasons, ought to influence the interpretation of best interests.

4

On the Sidelines? Grandparents in Care Proceedings

JOAN HUNT

I. Introduction

Care proceedings constitute the most draconian intervention in family life, enabling the state to remove children from their parents and, in some cases, to sever all family ties. Protection against unwarranted state intervention is afforded to *parents* in three main ways. First, before a court can even *consider* making a care order (enabling a local authority (LA) to acquire parental responsibility and place a child away from home without parental permission), it must be satisfied that certain 'threshold' conditions[1] are met. Second, parents are automatically parties to proceedings. Third, parents have a right to public funding for their legal costs.

If a court decides a child requires substitute care, the ability of grandparents to keep them within the family is limited. There is no equivalent to the threshold conditions and no presumption that a child should be brought up by a relative (an arrangement commonly known as 'kinship care'). There are, however, some protections, intended to ensure that the possibility of such care is properly *considered* by local authorities and the courts. The Children Act 1989 specifies that where a child is looked after by an LA, he or she should be cared for by a 'relative, friend, or other person connected with him, unless that would not be reasonably practicable or consistent with his welfare'.[2] The Children and Young Persons Act 2008 strengthened this, directing that kinship care should be the *first* option considered,[3] a requirement reiterated in statutory guidance for England.[4] Relatives must also be taken into account when adoption is contemplated by a court or an

---

[1] Children Act 1989, s 31.
[2] ibid s 23(6).
[3] Children and Young Persons Act 2008, s 22C(7)(a).
[4] Department for Education, *Family and Friends Care: Statutory Guidance for Local Authorities* (London, Department for Education, 2011); Department for Education, *Statutory Children Act Guidance*, vol 1: *Court Orders and Pre-Proceedings* (London, Department for Education, 2014).

LA. Under the Adoption and Children Act 2002, 'the likely effect on the child (throughout his life) of having ceased to be a member of the original family'[5] must be considered, and 'the ability and willingness of any of the child's relatives … to provide the child with a secure environment in which the child can develop, and otherwise to meet the child's needs'.[6] This Act also introduced special guardianship orders (SGOs), which allow grandparents (and other long-term carers) to make the arrangement more legally secure.[7] Decisions in case law[8] have raised the profile of kinship care by emphasising the need for a thorough evaluation of all realistic placement options.

Although LAs and courts are therefore required to consider a kinship placement, the potential for grandparents to become kinship carers is affected in the first instance by whether they are aware that substitute care is being contemplated. They then have to get through an initial (viability) assessment, followed, if favourable, by a full assessment, both usually carried out by an LA social worker. There will be a separate report by the children's (CAFCASS) guardian[9] appointed to represent the child's interests and advise the court on the most appropriate outcome. If the court is satisfied with the arrangement, it may make a care order.[10] In that case, grandparents will have to meet the standards[11] designed for unrelated foster carers. These make only limited allowance for the very different circumstances of a kinship placement. The alternative to a care order is typically an SGO, where grandparents will be judged against the criteria specified in the Special Guardianship Regulations,[12] strengthened following concerns that the original criteria were insufficiently robust.[13]

Grandparents, moreover, commonly have to undergo these challenging assessments and make life-changing decisions when they are in an emotional turmoil resulting from the events prompting proceedings, often involving their own child's being deemed to be an inadequate parent. They may also have little experience of dealing with the complexities of the child welfare system, the law or the courts.

---

[5] Adoption and Children Act 2002, s 1(4)(c).

[6] ibid s 1(4)(f)(ii).

[7] Section 115(1) of the Adoption and Children Act 2002 was intended to provide legal permanency for children for whom adoption is not appropriate. It does not sever the link with parents, who retain their parental responsibility, but this is shared with the special guardian, who can exercise it to the exclusion of anyone else. Parents also require leave of the court to apply for revocation and must demonstrate a substantial change in circumstances.

[8] Notably *Re B (A Child) (Care Proceedings: Threshold Criteria)* [2013] UKSC 33, [2014] 2 FLR 1075; and *Re B-S (Children)* [2013] EWCA Civ 1146, [2014] 1 FLR 1035.

[9] A social worker from the Children and Family Court Advisory and Support Service (CAFCASS).

[10] Children Act 1989, s 31.

[11] Department for Education, *Fostering Services: National Minimum Standards* (London, Department for Education, 2011); Welsh Government, *The Care Planning, Placement and Case Review (Wales) Regulations 2015* (Cardiff, Welsh Government, 2015).

[12] Special Guardianship (Amendment) Regulations 2016 (SI 2016 /111); Special Guardianship (Wales) (Amendment) Regulations (SI 2018/573 (W.102)).

[13] Department for Education, *Special Guardianship Review: Report on Findings* (London, Department for Education, 2015).

Unlike parents, grandparents lack the protection afforded by automatically being parties to proceedings. Nor are they automatically entitled to legal aid, so that unless they can afford to meet what could be considerable costs, or the LA assists, their ability to participate effectively in proceedings, even when made parties, is limited and may result in their being marginalised when such momentous decisions are being made.

Grandparents, then, face a number of significant obstacles in seeking to provide a home for a grandchild subject to care proceedings.

II. Notification and Involvement Prior to Proceedings

The case summarised below[14] illustrates the issue of children losing the opportunity to be brought up in their birth family, simply because their grandparents had not been aware of the care proceedings:

> This was the rehearing of the case of child A, placed for adoption at seven months. The paternal grandparents (PGPs) only became aware of A's existence during care proceedings on a second child (J) by which point A's carers had applied for an adoption order, A having lived with them for 17 months. In A's care proceedings the *maternal* grandparents had been approached but were unwilling to care and neither they, nor the parents, would divulge any details enabling the LA to contact the *paternal* grandparents. Although the PGPs' application for an SGO for child A was successful in the court of first instance, the prospective adopters appealed,[15] the SGO was stayed, and at the rehearing, an adoption order was made. The PGPS, now special guardians for J, were adamant that had they known about A at the time they would have offered to care and throughout it was acknowledged that had they done so, it was very likely that A would have been placed with them.

A more common problem is where the LA does have grandparents' contact details but the parents refuse to allow them to be approached. In *Re H*,[16] Mr Justice Cobb reviewed statute law, applicable regulations and rules, concluding that none imposed any absolute duty on the LA, the CAFCASS guardian or the court to inform the extended family about adoption plans. More recently, the President of the Family Division emphasised the need for a consistent approach, whether the issue arose in adoption or care proceedings, setting out the process to follow when a parent refuses to allow the wider family to be approached.[17]

Grandparents, therefore, have no legal right to be informed, and the LA has no absolute duty to inform them. However, as *Re H* emphasised, the ethos of the

---

[14] *Re W (Adoption: Contact)* [2016] EWHC 3118.
[15] *Re W (A Child)* [2016] EWCA Civ 793, [2017] 2 FLR 31.
[16] *Re H (care and adoption: assessment of wider family)* [2019] EWFC 10, [2019] 2 FLR 33.
[17] *Re A, B and C (Adoption: Notification of Fathers and Relatives)* [2020] EWCA Civ 41, [2020] 1 FLR 747.

Children Act is 'plainly supportive of wider family involvement'.[18] It also endorsed a previous judgment, that 'cogent and compelling grounds'[19] should exist before the court could conclude public law proceedings while the wider family remained ignorant of the child's existence. Statutory guidance emphasises the need not only to identify, but also to involve the extended family as early as possible.[20] There is also now a formal pre-proceedings process,[21] offering opportunities for this to take place. Identifying and evaluating possible family carers *prior* to proceedings was highlighted by the then President of the Family Division[22] as a key element affecting the smooth running of care proceedings. However, the Care Crisis Review reported that 'it was clear … that all too often the wider family … are not involved before proceedings are issued'.[23]

Can more be done to ensure that family members are involved prior to proceedings? The Care Crisis Review urged that a working group be set up to agree amendments to pre-proceedings guidance. The Public Law Working Group[24] recommended further analysis of whether further statutory duties should be imposed on local authorities. A study of special guardianship[25] argued for protocols and practice to ensure that wider family engagement is explicitly addressed, and the Parliamentary Taskforce on Kinship Care recommended a duty on LAs to ensure that potential kinship placements are explored early on, reflecting its 'vision' of kinship care as the 'first port of call'.[26]

All these reports argue for the routine use of family group conferences (FGCs), or some form of family meeting, as a means of involving the extended family in early decision making. Although FGCs are not legally required, they are suggested in statutory guidance.[27] However, although 78 per cent of English LAs have an FGC service,[28] only a minority offer this routinely before a child is taken into care.[29] Research in six LAs found that the highest proportion of cases in which an FGC

---

[18] *Re H* (n 16) [45].

[19] *Birmingham City Council v S, R and A* [2006] EWHC 3065 (Fam), [2007] 1 FLR 1223 [73].

[20] Department for Education, *Family and Friends Care* (n 4).

[21] Department for Education, *Statutory Children Act Guidance* (n 4).

[22] J Munby, 'View from the President's Chambers: The Process of Reform: The revised PLO and the Local authority' (2013) 43 *Family Law* 680, 683.

[23] Care Crisis Review, *Care Crisis Review: Options for Change* (London, Family Rights Group, 2017) para 4.6.

[24] Public Law Working Group, *Recommendations to Achieve Best Practice in the Child Protection and Family Justice Systems: Special Guardianship Orders* at www.judiciary.uk/wp-content/uploads/2020/06/PLWG-SGO-Final-Report-1.pdf.

[25] J Harwin et al, *The Contribution of Supervision Orders and Special Guardianship to Children's Lives and Family Justice* (Lancaster, Lancaster University, 2019).

[26] Parliamentary Taskforce on Kinship Care, *First Thought Not Afterthought: Report of the Parliamentary Taskforce on Kinship Care* at https://frg.org.uk/involving-families/family-and-friends-carers/cross-party-parliamentary-taskforce-on-kinship-care (2021) 77.

[27] Department for Education, *Family and Friends Care* (n 4); Department for Education, *Statutory Children Act Guidance* (n 4).

[28] Parliamentary Taskforce on Kinship Care (n 26).

[29] See at https://frg.org.uk/involving-families/family-group-conferences.

was held before care proceedings was 30 per cent.[30] Stronger provisions therefore seem to be needed. The Parliamentary Taskforce[31] recommended that a legal duty should be placed on LAs to offer an FGC before a child enters the care system, initially through strengthening statutory guidance and subsequently through legislation, while the Independent Review of Children's Social Care[32] concluded that such meetings should be made mandatory before the pre-proceedings process is engaged.

III. Grandparents' Participation in Care Proceedings

In 1988, grandparents gained the automatic right to become parties in care proceedings.[33] That privileged status was removed by the Children Act 1989, which substituted the provision that anyone with an interest in, or affected by, the proceedings could acquire party status, but only with the leave of the court.[34] This filter, it was said, would 'scarcely be a hurdle at all to close relatives',[35] the courts would operate an 'open door'.[36] Indeed, government assurances were given that 'where the grandparent has maintained a close relationship with the child permission is unlikely to be much more than a formality'.[37]

Although this seems to have been the case in the early years of the Children Act, a more restrictive approach then developed.[38] More than two decades later the issue of party status has again come to the fore. *Re P-S*[39] concerned the placement of two half siblings with their respective PGPs and whether this should have been done under a care order with a view to a subsequent SGO, as the court of first instance had decided. The grandparents had not been made parties in the care proceedings, a point Ryder LJ declared himself 'at a loss to understand', since

> [i]t was clear … that the key issues in the case included whether each of the children should 'reside in a family placement under an SGO'. It may be that the apparent consensus between the local authority, the children's guardian and the grandparents on the

---

[30] J Masson et al, *Child Protection in Court: Outcomes for Children. Establishing outcomes of care proceedings for children before and after care proceedings reform* (School of Law, University of Bristol and the Centre for Research on Children and Families, University of East Anglia, 2019).

[31] Parliamentary Taskforce (n 26).

[32] J MacAlister, *The Independent Review of Children's Social Care: Final Report* at https://childrenssocialcare.independent-review.uk/wp-content/uploads/2022/05/The-independent-review-of-childrens-socialcare-Final-report.pdf.

[33] Children and Young Persons (Amendment) Act 1986, came into force 1988.

[34] Family Proceedings Court (Children Act 1989) Rules 1991 (SI 1991/1395 (L.17)), sch 2(iii).

[35] Law Commission, quoted Department of Health, *Introduction to the Children Act* (London, HMSO, 1989) 23.

[36] ibid.

[37] HL Deb, 6 February 1989, vol 503, col 1342.

[38] H Crook, 'Grandparents and the Children Act 1989' (1994) 16 *Family Law* 135, 138; G Posner, 'The Extended Family in Care Cases – Fallback or Centre Stage?' (2001) 23 *Family Law* 385, 387.

[39] *Re P-S (Children) (Special Guardianship)* [2018] EWCA Civ 1407, [2019] 1 FLR 251.

ultimate order they all sought obscured the immediate procedural issue before the court. Given the procedural unfairness that undoubtedly was the consequence, I have no hesitation in coming to the conclusion that it was wrong not to have made appropriate provision for the grandparents to obtain effective access to justice at the final hearing. To leave them on the side-lines without party status, without documents and without advice ... was unfair.[40]

In 2019 the Court of Appeal[41] again criticised a lower court for failing to address the issue of party status, but in very different circumstances, the care proceedings having concluded with care and placement orders, following several negative assessments of a great-aunt. After the first assessment, the great-aunt applied for party status but her application was adjourned, leave being granted only 11 months later, just prior to the final hearing. The Court of Appeal noted that the trial judge had encouraged the LA to consider funding legal advice for the great-aunt, 'in the event that there was a positive recommendation that the child be placed with her'. But as King LJ commented:

[I]t might be thought that the real need for legal representation ... would be if the assessment was ... negative ... It was recorded that [great-aunt] was to give evidence 'if advised' although it is unclear who it was anticipated would be giving her advice as she was still neither a party nor legally represented.[42]

At the final care hearing, the great-aunt acted as a litigant in person. The judge, it was noted, said that she had 'represented herself creditably' given the 'considerable complexities' of the case; that she had been in an 'entirely alien environment'; and that the mother's counsel gave her 'some assistance'. But 'crucially', she 'had the task of cross-examining the independent social worker and the Guardian entirely unaided'.[43]

Parties are entitled to see the papers, attend hearings and be legally represented. They thus have a right to argue their case not only in relation to having the child placed with them, but also with regard to the type of order proposed and the LA support package. Practice is reported to be very variable,[44] however, with one study[45] reporting that while all the special guardians 'wanted to have meaningful party status from the start of the proceedings so that they could effectively participate', 'most' had not had that advantage. Feeling excluded and ill-informed, they also felt they had lost the opportunity to argue for support. Those who had been parties stressed this latter advantage, plus the ability to defend themselves in court from misinformation, or information that was wrongly interpreted.

---

[40] ibid [55].
[41] *Re W (A Child)* [2019] EWCA Civ 196, [2020] 1 FLR 1966.
[42] ibid [28] and [29].
[43] ibid [45].
[44] J Harwin and J Simmonds, *Special Guardianship: Practitioner Perspectives* (London, Nuffield Family Justice Observatory, 2019); Harwin et al (n 25).
[45] Harwin et al (n 25) 132.

The Public Law Working Group[46] recommended that consideration should be given at an early stage to the issue of joining a proposed special guardian as a party. Hunt and Waterhouse concluded that where the issue is whether a child should live with kinship carers, under what order that should be, future contact arrangements, or the support package under an SGO 'then surely carers should have the right to be made parties and have a lawyer to represent their interests'.[47]

An application for party status is made under Family Procedure Rules 2010.[48] However, since they do not contain a specific test or guidance, the court has broad discretion, applying the overriding objective[49] of enabling the court to deal with cases justly. *Re B*,[50] in which the Court of Appeal upheld refusal of party status to a grandmother seeking a residence order, confirmed this discretion. The court of first instance had been correct in referring to section 10(9) of the Children Act 1989, which listed factors to which the court should have 'particular regard'. This, however, did not amount to a test; there might be other factors to consider, one of which was the prospects of the application's being successful; leave would not be given for an application that was not arguable. However, even having an 'arguable case' might not be sufficient in itself; 'it is only one consideration to be weighed against all the other factors in section 10(9)'.[51]

Where a grandparent is considered a 'realistic option', the impact of *Re P-S*[52] may be that party status is more frequently awarded than hitherto. Legal practitioners interviewed by Harwin and Simmonds[53] indicated that one of the most frequent reasons for a prospective special guardian's not being made a party was when there was an agreed positive assessment. The other scenario practitioners cited, however, was a negative assessment. Here one might have thought that the argument for party status was even stronger. Unfortunately, there appears to be no research examining the views on party status of grandparents who failed to secure the child's placement with them.

Where party status is not granted, the court may allow some involvement, such as sitting in court or having sight of court papers.[54] In *Re P-S*, for instance, the grandparents were brought into court for part of the final hearing in the care proceedings. However, given that the LA, the child and the parents all have full party status, this clearly leaves grandparents at a significant disadvantage.

---

[46] Public Law Working Group (n 24).
[47] J Hunt and S Waterhouse, *It's Just Not Fair! Support, need and legal status in family and friends care* (London, Family Rights Group, 2013) 154.
[48] Family Procedure Rules 2010 (SI 2010/2955 (L.17)), r 12(3).
[49] ibid r 1.1.
[50] *Re B (a child)* [2012] EWCA Civ 737, 2 FLR 1358.
[51] ibid [48].
[52] *Re P-S* (n 39).
[53] Harwin and Simmonds (n 44).
[54] Hunt and Waterhouse (n 47).

IV. Access to Legal Advice and Representation

The need for prospective kinship carers to have access to independent advice to make informed decisions has been consistently identified in research over a long period.[55] There is a surprising dearth of data, however, documenting the proportions of such carers who have accessed *legal* advice and those who were unable to do so; and, typically, what is reported does not specifically relate to care proceedings. Nonetheless, it is clear that improvements are needed.

Once the LA has initiated the pre-proceedings process, parents are entitled to publicly funded legal advice. Grandparents have no such rights. Similarly, if proceedings are brought, even if grandparents are parties, unlike parents they will only be publicly funded if their case is considered likely to succeed (the 'merits' test) and if their income and capital are below the Legal Aid Agency's specified threshold (the 'means' test).

In 2019, the Ministry of Justice proposed to extend the scope of legal aid to applications for SGOs made in *private* proceedings.[56] A briefing paper prepared by Family Rights Group, Association of Lawyers for Children, the Law Society and Resolution,[57] argues that changes are also needed for *public law* cases. Thus, once the prospective carer has had a positive viability assessment, they should be able to access legal advice, non-means- or merit-tested, to assist them during the full assessment; and if this is positive, they should be entitled to legal representation on the same basis. If either assessment is unfavourable, non-means- but merits-tested legal aid should be available, to enable the would-be carer to challenge the decision. The report of the All Party Parliamentary Group on Kinship Care, appropriately entitled *Lost in the Legal Labyrinth*, having identified 'significant challenges in accessing publicly funded legal advice and representation',[58] made recommendations for extending non-means-tested legal aid to potential kinship carers in certain circumstances, as did The Independent Review of Children's Social Care.[59]

Where grandparents cannot access legal aid, they may be fortunate enough to secure LA assistance with their costs. However, this is discretionary, and research indicates variation in the prevalence and level of such assistance and the

---

[55] J Hunt, *An Overview of the Last Two Decades of UK Research on Kinship Care* (London, Family Rights Group, 2020).

[56] Ministry of Justice, *Legal Support: The Way Ahead. An action plan to deliver better support to people experiencing legal problems* (London, Ministry of Justice, 2019).

[57] Family Rights Group et al, *Briefing Note to the Ministry of Justice – proposed changes to Family Legal Aid* at https://frg.org.uk/wp-content/uploads/2022/04/2204005-Briefing-from-FRG-Law-Society-Resolution-ALC.pdf.

[58] APPG, *Lost in the Legal Labyrinth: How a lack of legal aid and advice is undermining kinship care* (London, Family Rights Group, 2022) 7.

[59] MacAlister (n 32).

criteria used.[60] The Parliamentary Taskforce[61] made two recommendations. First, to amend statutory guidance to include explicit expectations that LAs will support, and where necessary fund, potential carers to access legal advice or representation. Second, that kinship care policies should clearly set out the criteria used to determine funding.

The issue of kinship carers' having to fund some, or all, of their legal costs is a common theme in the research.[62] Lack of funding can mean having to act as litigants in person. Some may feel confident doing so, and they should be assisted by the court. The child's solicitor or the CAFCASS guardian may also help. But should prospective carers have to depend on the support of professionals who are not there primarily to protect their interests, and who may even be opposing their position? Even those who have had the benefit of legal advice may be disadvantaged, particularly when so much, such as contact arrangements, may be resolved via negotiation outside the courtroom.

V. Assessing Grandparents as Potential Carers

Where grandparents take on care with parental agreement, the arrangement can be entirely informal. It does not even have to be notified to the LA. Where there are care proceedings, however, the grandparents must undergo rigorous assessment, typically by an LA social worker. Those assessments will then be scrutinised by the CAFCASS guardian, who also has to provide a report and a recommendation to the court. In some cases, where the LA's assessment is disputed by a prospective kinship carer, the court may order further assessment by an independent social worker. It might be questioned, of course, why grandparents offering to take care of their grandchildren should have to go through this process, even if the child's parents are in agreement. But once the court process is engaged the issue is no longer an intra-family matter; the state has a responsibility to ensure that children whose parents have proved unable to care for them adequately will receive safe and effective care in their new home for the duration of their childhood. The question is then what criteria should be used to evaluate a grandparent's application to care? Should they be the same as the threshold conditions that have to be satisfied to remove children from their parents, or should the standard be more demanding, in view of the adversities the children have already suffered and the potential

---

[60] S Bowyer, J Wilkinson and J Gadsby-Waters, *Impact of the Family Justice Reforms on Front-line Practice. Phase Two: Special Guardianship Orders* (London, Department for Education, 2015); Hunt and Waterhouse (n 47); J Wade et al, *Investigating Special Guardianship: Experiences, Challenges and Outcomes* (London, Department for Education, 2014).

[61] Parliamentary Taskforce (n 26).

[62] Hunt (n 55).

impact this may have on their life chances? The amended special guardianship regulations[63] indicate the latter.

A. Viability Assessments

Typically, the first step in the process is a viability assessment. There is no statutory basis or official guidance for these but, following concerns about their quality and variability, a Good Practice Guide[64] was developed and subsequently widely endorsed, including by the (then) President of the Family Division. Case law, it notes, clarifies that not 'every stone has to be uncovered and the ground exhaustively examined before coming to a conclusion that a particular option is not realistic'.[65] However, assessments that rule out a potential carer 'must evidence that this option is clearly and plainly unrealistic, and one that the court can and should confidently dismiss'.[66] There are no data on what proportion of viability assessments are negative. One study,[67] however, reports that prior to the assessment that resulted in 113 SGOs, a further 152 potential carers had been ruled out at viability stage. Concerns reported were that those ruled out did not fully understand that the SGO was intended to last until the child reached 18; would not be able to keep the child safe; failed to understand the child's needs; lived in overcrowded housing; or their capacity to care was affected by health problems or employment obligations.

A negative viability assessment does not *inevitably* mean that the person so assessed is ruled out as a kinship carer.[68] However, obtaining a repeat assessment is not easy, as was emphasised in *Re R*:

> The simple fact is that no second assessment can be ordered, nor should it be, unless the court is satisfied that it is ... necessary to assist the court to resolve the proceedings justly ... In determining whether an assessment is 'necessary', the court must adopt a robust and realistic approach, guarding itself against being driven by what in *Re S* I described as 'sentiment or a hope that "something may turn up"'.[69]

Again, data are lacking on how frequently repeat or full assessments are ordered after an unfavourable viability. However, social work practitioners have reported these being more frequently rejected than hitherto.[70] Some LAs are also reported

---

[63] Special Guardianship (Amendment) Regulations 2016 (n 12); Special Guardianship (Wales) Regulations 2005 (as amended 2018) (n 12).

[64] Family Rights Group, *Initial Family and Friends Care Assessment: A good practice guide* (London, Family Rights Group, 2017).

[65] ibid 6, citing *Re R (A Child)* [2014] EWCA Civ 1625, [2015] 1 FLR 715.

[66] Ibid 11, citing *Re S (A Child)* [2015] EWCA 25, [2017] 1 FLR 417.

[67] Harwin et al (n 25).

[68] S Bowyer and J Wilkinson, *Impact of the Family Justice Reforms: Phase 3 – exploring variation across 21 local authorities* (London, Department for Education, 2016); Harwin et al (n 25); J Hunt, *Practising in Kinship Care: The perspectives of specialist social workers* (London, Kinship, 2021).

[69] *Re R* (n 65) [66].

[70] Hunt (n 68).

to doubt the usefulness of viabilities because they can be challenged and result in an independent assessment's being ordered.[71] Although viability assessments seem to have been addressed in only two Court of Appeal judgments,[72] both were highly critical of the quality of the LA's work. In the first, the Court ruled that since the trial judge had been critical of the viability, they should have ordered an independent report, not relied on the CAFCASS guardian's report to correct its flaws. All this suggests that courts do not commonly simply accept LA recommendations to exclude potential kinship carers from further consideration.

If the Good Practice Guide[73] becomes embedded in practice, the chances of suitable carers' being wrongly excluded at this point should be reduced. Throughout there are reminders that the assessment should not simply evaluate current suitability but consider how to address any weaknesses. It reminds social workers of the 'emotional turmoil' of relatives who may be 'struggling to come to terms with what has happened';[74] that 'excessive weight'[75] should not be given to past parenting; that 'except in the most extreme circumstances',[76] a potential carer should not be ruled out because they will not meet fostering standards. Good practice also involves affording those being assessed an opportunity to comment on the draft report, and giving those negatively assessed written information on what steps they can take to challenge it. According to the Parliamentary Taskforce, however, application of the guidance has been 'patchy'.[77] It therefore recommended that it should be incorporated into statutory guidance.

In addition to challenges by those subject to viability assessments, the LA's conclusions may also be called into question by the CAFCASS guardian,[78] although there appear to be no data on how frequently this occurs.

B. Full Assessments

i. *Carer Experiences of Assessment*

This author's overview of research[79] indicates that most carers accept the need for assessment, and for some the process generates little criticism. A proportion, however (amounting to most or even all in two studies), are negative. The

---

[71] Bowyer and Wilkinson (n 68).

[72] *Re M-H (Assessment: Father of Half-Brother)* [2006] EWCA Civ 1864, [2007] 2 FLR 1715; *Re V-Z (Children)* [2016] EWCA Civ 475, All ER (D) 15 (Jun).

[73] Family Rights Group (n 64).

[74] ibid 8.

[75] ibid 21.

[76] ibid 24.

[77] Parliamentary Taskforce (n 26).

[78] See *Re W (Children)* [2014] EWCA Civ 1492, [2014] All ER (D) 228 (Nov); and *JV (final care and placement order)* [2014] EWFC B112.

[79] Hunt (n 55).

intrusiveness of the process, the overview reports, is a consistent theme, with carers reported to be 'bewildered, upset or angry' at the questions asked, feeling 'overwhelmed', 'demeaned', 'inadequate' and 'under scrutiny' or 'surveillance'. Many of the special guardians in one study considered that things they had said had been misinterpreted; another highlighted carers' distrust and sense of disempowerment in a process that could result in their losing the chance to care for the child; a third that fear of failing the assessment meant that special guardians felt unable to complain when they considered they had been treated badly. It should be noted, moreover, that all the interviewees in these studies succeeded in gaining care of the child; unsuccessful applicants might be even more critical.

While it is unrealistic to expect that being assessed can ever be less than a daunting experience, there are ways in which the process might be improved for prospective carers. Several research studies[80] have concluded, variously, that there is a need to train social workers in kinship care, to have input from specialist kinship workers into assessment and, where feasible, to establish specialist teams. Access to written, as well as oral, information about the process and the legal options is vital from the start, while signposting those being assessed to independent sources of advice, as recommended by the Parliamentary Taskforce,[81] could help to reduce their sense of disempowerment. According to one study,[82] only 49 per cent of LA staff said that potential carers would be advised to consult a lawyer, and just over a third that they would be routinely referred to organisations providing specialist advice.

ii. Negative Local Authority Assessments

The only information available on negative assessments is from cases where the LA's position differed either from that of the CAFCASS guardian or from the court decision. Wade and colleagues[83] found that this was a rare occurrence (3 per cent). However, since their sample cases were concluded before *Re B-S*[84] (discussed in section VI), this may now be an underestimate. Practitioners report it is happening more frequently, with LAs required to produce stronger evidence to support their conclusions; courts ordering repeat or independent assessments; and social work expertise being devalued,[85] with that of CAFCASS guardians being preferred, noted as a 'consistent message' by Harwin and colleagues.[86] As with

---

[80] See Hunt (n 68).

[81] Parliamentary Taskforce (n 26).

[82] Hunt and Waterhouse (n 47).

[83] J Wade, J Dixon and A Richards, *Special Guardianship in Practice* (London, BAAF, 2010); Wade et al (n 60).

[84] *Re B-S* (n 8).

[85] S Bowyer, J Wilkinson and J Gadsby-Waters, *Impact of the Family Justice Reforms on Front-line Practice. Phase One: The Public Law Outline* (London, Department for Education, 2015); Bowyer and Wilkinson (n 68); Hunt (n 68); Masson et al (n 30).

[86] Harwin et al (n 25) 107.

viability assessments, these findings indicate that a negative LA assessment is not necessarily the end of the road for relatives seeking to take on the care of a child. Quantitative data, however, are very much needed to establish how often and why relatives offering care are ruled out and how the courts are responding.

VI. Court Decision Making

A. Case Law

In *Re B-S*, Sir James Munby expressed

> real concerns, shared by other judges, about the recurrent inadequacy of the analysis and reasoning put forward in support of the case for adoption, both in the materials put before the court by local authorities and guardians and also in too many judgments.[87]

While noting that 'this is nothing new', he continued 'it is time to call a halt' to this 'sloppy practice'.[88] Judgment in this case was given after the Supreme Court decision in *Re B*,[89] which, as noted in *Re G*, gave a 'very clear wakeup call', bringing existing concerns into 'sharper focus'.[90]

Of these cases, only *Re G* involved a potential kinship placement. Nonetheless, the issues raised, and the decision-making framework articulated in *Re B-S*, have clear implications for cases that do involve such placements, potentially considerably strengthening the position of grandparents seeking to take on care. *Re B-S* pinpointed two essential requirements when the court is asked to approve an adoption plan.[91] First, there must be evidence addressing *all* the realistic options and an analysis of the arguments for and against each. Second, there must be an adequately reasoned judgment: the judicial task is to evaluate all the options, undertaking a global, holistic and multifaceted evaluation of the child's welfare that takes into account *all* the negatives and the positives, *all* the pros and cons, of each option. In outlining the spectrum of options it might be necessary to consider in a particular case, the judgment specifically mentions placement with relatives,[92] thus making it absolutely clear that these are encompassed in the statement in *Re B* that 'although the child's interests in an adoption case are "paramount" ... a court must never lose sight of the fact that those interests include being brought up by her natural family'.[93]

---

[87] *Re B-S* (n 8) [30].
[88] ibid [40].
[89] *Re B* (n 8).
[90] *Re G (A Child)* [2013] EWCA Civ 965, [2014] 1 FLR 670 [43].
[91] *Re B-S* (n 8) [34] and [44].
[92] ibid [27].
[93] *Re B* (n 8) [77].

Re B-S also highlighted the 'clear message' from *Re B* that orders contemplating non-consensual adoption are only to be made where 'no other course [is] possible in [the child's] interests', they are 'the most extreme option', a 'last resort – when all else fails', to be made 'only in exceptional circumstances and where motivated by *overriding requirements* pertaining to the child's welfare, in short, where nothing else will do'.[94]

B. The Impact on Practice

The impact of *Re B* and *Re B-S* was dramatic. Concerns about the diminishing use of adoption prompted the National Adoption Leadership Board to issue what became known as the Myth-Buster Guide.[95] Research reported social worker perceptions of a 'family at all costs' mentality operating in the courts; courts asking LAs to reconsider their recommendations for placement orders and LAs not applying for them in some cases where they previously would have done so.[96] There was a marked shift in the balance between placement orders and SGOs.[97] Masson and colleagues[98] reported that the impact of these case decisions

> pervaded the local authorities, not only because they were on the receiving end of decisions made by the courts but because of the advice given by local authority lawyers; the increased emphasis on identifying and assessing relative carers; the need to ensure care plans considered all realistic options and weighed their pros and cons; and the decisions taken by the local authority ADM (Agency Decision-Maker).

Responding to concerns about the post-*Re B-S* landscape, several Court of Appeal judgments sought to clarify the position, emphasising it had not changed the law; the primary aim was to bring practice into alignment with what was already required.[99]

Some of these judgments could impact adversely on the ability of grandparents to secure care of the child. In *Re R*,[100] for instance, the President gave guidance to 'urgently address' the impression that 'adoption is a thing of the past' resulting in a 'bending over backwards to keep the child in the family if at all possible'.[101]

---

[94] *Re B-S* (n 8) [22] (original emphasis).

[95] National Adoption Leadership Board, *Impact of Court Judgments on Adoption. What the judgments do and do not say* (London, NALB, 2014).

[96] Bowyer, Wilkinson and Gadsby-Waters (n 85); Bowyer, Wilkinson and Gadsby-Waters (n 60); Hunt (n 68); Masson et al (n 30).

[97] Harwin et al (n 25); Masson et al (n 30); Bowyer, Wilkinson and Gadsby-Waters (n 60).

[98] Masson et al (n 30) 140.

[99] eg *Re H (A Child)* [2015] EWCA Civ 1284, [2015] 2 FLR 1173; *Re R* (n 65); *Re S* (n 66); *Re W* (n 15).

[100] *Re R* (n 65).

[101] ibid [41].

Not only did he highlight that *Re B-S* does not require that every stone has to be uncovered, he also emphasised that '[n]or is there any basis for assuming that more than one negative assessment is required before a potential carer can be eliminated'.[102]

Re W[103] robustly took issue with the notion that children have a right to be brought up by their natural family or that there is a presumption to that effect. The Court of Appeal criticised both the CAFCASS guardian and the independent social worker for approaching their evaluation on this basis, and the judge for accepting their evidence without drawing attention to the erroneous approach: 'The existence of a viable home with the grandparents should make that option "a runner" but should not automatically make it "a winner"'.[104]

In this case (as noted earlier), at the point the grandparents offered to care, the child was already settled in an adoptive placement. In this situation, McFarlane LJ considered, the welfare balance to be struck 'must inevitably reflect these changed circumstances',[105] with the relationship that the child had established with new carers being at the core of the balancing exercise that must be carried out and the harm the child may suffer if that relationship is broken given consideration. He also offered a 'tentative formulation' that in terms of human rights, while 'it must be beyond question' that the relationship between the child and the prospective adopters was sufficient to establish family life rights under Article 8 of the European Convention on Human Rights, it did not follow 'as night follows day' that the paternal grandparents had any such rights.[106]

It is notable that two years earlier, where an aunt had succeeded in opposing an adoption order for a child who had been placed with prospective adopters for the past 13 months, permission to appeal was refused.[107] In *Re M'P-P*,[108] however, where one of the children had lived with the prospective adopters from being a day old, the Court of Appeal not only granted permission to appeal an order made in favour of an aunt, but also overturned the judgment and ordered a rehearing.[109] In *Re W*,[110] McFarlane LJ cited his own words in *Re M'P-P* concerning the importance of the status quo argument, going on to say that

> a balance has to have a fulcrum and if the fulcrum is incorrectly placed towards one or other end of that which is to be weighed, one side of the analysis or another will be afforded undue, automatic weight. ... [I]n proceedings at the stage prior to making a placement for an adoption order the balance will rightly and necessarily reflect weight being afforded to any viable natural family placement because there is no other existing

---

[102] ibid [65].
[103] *Re W* (n 15).
[104] ibid [70].
[105] ibid [65].
[106] ibid [79].
[107] *A & B v Rotherham* [2014] EWFC 47, [2015] 2 FLR 381.
[108] *Re M'P-P (Children)* [2015] EWCA 584, [2015] 2 FCR 451.
[109] *Re B and E (Children)* [2015] EWFC B203.
[110] *Re W* (n 15).

placement of the child which must be afforded weight on the other side of the scales. Where, as here, time has moved on and such a placement exists, and is indeed the total reality of the child's existence, it cannot be enough to decide the overall welfare issue simply by looking at the existence of the viable family placement and nothing else.[111]

Once a child is settled in a placement for adoption, therefore, grandparents are likely to have an uphill battle to secure care. Prior to this, however, as McFarlane notes in *Re W*, 'the balance naturally tilts towards a family placement where the relatives have been assessed … as being able to provide good, long term care'.[112]

Apart from this recognition of a 'natural tilt', there are two other ways in which *Re B* and *Re B-S* potentially strengthen the ability of grandparents to challenge a local authority plan for adoption. First, because decisions in the courts of first instance can be challenged on the grounds that their judgments do not meet the requirements of the decision-making framework established in these cases. Second, because it is no longer necessary for the Court of Appeal to find that the judgment was *plainly* wrong; now it only has to satisfy the lesser test of being 'wrong'.[113] In an early post-*Re B* judgment,[114] a grandmother was granted leave to appeal care and placement orders on both grounds; and in 2019 the Court of Appeal overturned such orders, ruling that the judgment had not been adequately reasoned[115] and that the specific grounds for appeal cited by the appellant (as set out below)[116] were made out:

(i) a failure sufficiently to analyse the factors set out in the welfare checklists contained in both s 1(3) Children Act 1989 and s 1(4) Children and Adoption Act 2002;

(ii) a failure to conduct an adequate holistic balancing exercise and to take into account such matters as the appellant's positive attributes; and

(iii) a failure to carry out an adequate evaluation of the risk factors and the proportionality of adoption.

Such claims may, of course, also be made and upheld in appeals against decisions to place with relatives.[117] It is also the case that even when a judgment is found to lack adequate reasoning, the decision may still be upheld.[118]

At the moment, insufficient data are available to establish whether the line of jurisprudence beginning with *Re B* has resulted in a higher proportion of successful challenges by grandparents, a changed approach in the lower courts and more children remaining in their extended families. This would require a systematic analysis of a representative sample of cases across all tiers of court. A brief

---

[111] ibid [75].
[112] ibid [65].
[113] *Re B* (n 8) [203].
[114] *Re J (A Child)* [2013] EWCA Civ 1100.
[115] *Re W (A Child)* [2019] EWCA Civ 1966, [2020] 1 FLR 1966.
[116] ibid [3].
[117] eg *A & B (Children: Care and placement orders)* [2014] EWFC B213.
[118] *Re FL (A Child)* [2020] EWCA Civ 20.

examination of publicly available judgments undertaken for this chapter reveals examples both of outcomes that did result in placement with the extended family and of those that did not. The evidence, however, does seem to support an on-going shift in practice towards an explicit consideration of potential kinship placements, with transcripts of judgments in the lower courts commonly referencing the decision-making framework specified in case law.

C. Court Timescales for Kinship Assessments

Court timescales present another potential hurdle for grandparents seeking to care. The Children and Families Act 2014 introduced a 26-week statutory time limit for the completion of care proceedings.[119] Extensions are permitted only where 'necessary to enable the court to resolve the proceedings justly', are 'not to be granted routinely' and require 'specific justification'.[120] Although in *Re S*[121] the then President of the Family Division identified 'cases where a realistic alternative family carer emerges late in the day'[122] as one of the forensic contexts in which an extension would be necessary, research indicates that in some courts the 26-week time frame has been rigidly adhered to, with extensions rarely granted.[123] However, the effect has not been that prospective carers are typically ruled out prematurely; rather, courts have insisted that assessments are expedited. This can mean that those being assessed have insufficient time to work through the trauma of what has happened in their family, to appreciate the need to protect the child from a parent and to arrive at a realistic evaluation of what lies ahead. As a result, some could be denied the opportunity to provide care while others are unprepared for the challenges caring for these children will bring, increasing the risk of placement breakdown.[124] Unresolved uncertainties about the viability of the placement could also result in the court's making a care order or attaching a supervision order to an SGO, both of which would subject the new carers to local authority surveillance, even if only for a limited time.

The question of restrictive court timescales in special guardianship cases was addressed in interim guidance issued by the Family Justice Council and subsequently incorporated into Best Practice Guidance published by the Public Law

---

[119] Children and Families Act 2014, s 14(2)(ii).
[120] ibid s 32(1)(a)(ii), (5) and (7).
[121] *Re S* (n 66).
[122] ibid [33].
[123] C Beckett, J Dickens and S Bailey, *Outcomes for Children of Shorter Court Decision-making processes: A follow-up study of the Tri-borough care proceedings pilot* (Centre for Research on Children and Families, School of Social Work, University of East Anglia, 2016); Bowyer and Wilkinson (n 68); Harwin and Simmonds (n 44); Harwin et al (n 25); Hunt (n 68).
[124] Wade et al (n 60).

Working Group.[125] This reinforces use of judicial power to extend proceedings, stating:

> The focus will always be on welfare and the fundamental requirement for a robust, evidence-based assessment. That will be the guiding factor as opposed to the statutory timescale of 26 weeks.[126]

Such cases 'will need to be removed from the CMS 26-week track'.[127] This latter stipulation is important in addressing any judicial reluctance to extend proceedings because they will adversely affect court performance statistics.

VII. Conclusions

This chapter has revealed a number of ways in which the position of grandparents seeking to take on care of their grandchildren needs to be strengthened if they are not to be on the sidelines in care proceedings and children's opportunities to remain in their extended families are to be maximised.

Once care proceedings have been instigated and it is likely that the children will need substitute care, if grandparents are seeking to provide that care then the default position should be that they are made parties to the proceedings. That is not to say that grandparents should have the privileged status they enjoyed, briefly, before the Children Act 1989: while they do constitute the largest single group of kinship carers in the United Kingdom, many children are placed with other relatives or connected persons. But the original 'open door' intention of the Act needs to be restored. When children, parents and LAs are all automatically parties, but potential kinship carers are not, they should not have to rely on the judge's allowing them a degree of participation.

As parties, potential carers should be entitled to have their legal costs publicly funded. It is fundamentally unjust that they should have to act as litigants in person, when all the other parties are legally represented. It is also unreasonable that those who are offering to care until a child reaches adulthood, with the enormous financial costs that will involve, should have to deplete their financial resources to meet the costs incurred in seeking to secure this. Responsibility for funding the legal costs of prospective carers should be clearly placed on the Legal Aid Agency; while some may be assisted by the LA, this is discretionary and, inevitably, variable.

Change is also needed to ensure that grandparents are consulted about LA concerns about the child before care proceedings are seriously considered. As a way of involving the extended family in decision making, FGCs are widely encouraged but their use is patchy. It now seems necessary to impose a legal duty on

---

[125] Public Law Working Group (n 24).
[126] ibid para 24.
[127] ibid paras 24 and 25.

LAs to offer an FGC, certainly before a child enters the care system and prefer-ably earlier, when the need for substitute care is becoming likely. Incorporating FGCs into routine social work practice with families could not only help to ensure that prospective carers are known, and familiar with the issues, but also harness the resources of the extended family to support the parents, which might enable the child to remain at home. It may also now be necessary, as the Parliamentary Taskforce[128] recommended, that a duty should be imposed on LAs to ensure early exploration of potential kinship carers. Local authorities should also be required to signpost potential carers to sources of legal information and advice, and, where necessary, assist with the costs of this.

Each of these process changes would help to ensure that grandparents are in a much better position to keep the child within their family than is currently the case.

The focus of care proceedings, however, is, and needs to remain, the interests of the individual child whose future is being determined. Giving grandparents a rebuttable right to care, or introducing such a presumption, risks blurring that focus. Nor is there evidence that the current law is inadequate, provided that the decision-making framework set out in *Re B* and *Re B-S*, which should ensure that the potential for a kinship placement is given proper consideration, is observed. Indeed, some have argued that the effect of these and subsequent significant cases has been an over-emphasis on such placements, to the potential detriment of the child's long-term welfare. Research is needed, however, to establish what is now happening in the generality of cases in the family courts, to ascertain whether there is a need for changes in the practice of courts, LAs and family justice practi-tioners, what the direction of any such changes should be and how they might be accomplished.

---

[128] Parliamentary Taskforce (n 26).

5

Special Guardianship Orders and Grandparents: 'Love Is Not Enough'

LIZ FISHER-FRANK

I. Introduction

A grandparent who is or wants to act as main carer for a grandchild may be advised to seek a Special Guardianship Order (SGO). These orders were introduced[1] to provide 'an alternative legal status for children that offered greater security than long-term fostering but without the absolute legal severance from the birth family that stems from an adoption order'.[2]

Grandparents can often be a first port of call as carer when parents are unable to look after a child.[3] This inability to care for a child may be due to, for example, issues around parental physical health, mental health, neglect, abuse and/or other social circumstances such as bereavement. The starting point for the child therefore will be that they will be from a disadvantaged background. Where there are concerns about parental care, or lack of it, a grandparent may take the private law route for an SGO per se, or may do so as an active step to prevent a local authority from taking child protection measures. Alternatively, public law care proceedings may be underway concerning a child and a grandparent may make an application for an SGO within the context of those proceedings. Therefore, SGOs can be made in both private and public law proceedings. Although SGOs may be made in favour of a wide range of individuals, including foster carers, friends and other relatives of the child, the emphasis in this chapter is on grandparents.

The numbers of SGOs are increasing. In 2011, 4,286 children were the subject of SGO proceedings. By 2021, this had risen to 7,112 children.[4] At the same time,

---

[1] Adoption and Children Act 2002, s 115.
[2] Special Guardianship Guidance DFES 2005 (amended 2017)) 6.
[3] An estimated 3.2% of households with grandparent as 'household reference person' in 2017; see at www.ons.gov.uk/peoplepopulationandcommunity/birthsdeathsandmarriages/families/adhocs/009645numberandpercentageofhouseholdswithagrandparentasheadofhouseholdlivingwiththeirgrandchildrenuk2006to2017.
[4] Family Court Statistics Quarterly: October to December 2021, Family Court Tables, Table 4.

adoption orders have been decreasing.[5] Also, an increasing number of SGOs are being made by the court of its own motion in care proceedings.[6] Although general data about the numbers of grandparent special guardians remain limited, the findings of a research study in 2008[7] confirmed that from 70 court files, 68 per cent of SGO orders made were to the 'grandparent generation', including grandparents, great-aunts and uncles. Research in 2019 found that SGOs were made to grandparents in 62 per cent of cases in a sample study.[8] Grandparents are therefore significant actors in special guardianship proceedings and orders.

Through real and fictional case studies, this chapter explores four key issues that shape the extent to which SGOs fulfil the promise of providing long-term stability whilst assisting another key aim of the order, ensuring opportunities to maintain relationships with the birth family. These four key issues are: the operation of parental responsibility;[9] the voice of the child; the interplay between SGOs and Child Arrangements Orders (CAOs);[10] and the court process in private and public law proceedings, placement breakdown and finances.

Having set out the evolution of the SGO in section II, section III of this chapter explores the concept of parental responsibility, which is bestowed by the making of an SGO.[11] What parental responsibility is in this context, who has it and what it means will all be discussed, concerning both the rights of birth parents and those of the grandparent carer. The bestowing of parental responsibility is significant since its absence can be a major impediment for both the grandparent with care of a child and, indeed, the child. The enhanced exercise of parental responsibility via an SGO in comparison with other legal options for a child's placement, such as a CAO, will also be explored.[12]

Section IV will consider the voice of the child in the making of SGOs in both private and public law proceedings. It will be seen that children's voices are heard differently in both sets of proceedings, which ultimately can result in the same order. It is argued that, at the very least, this lack of parity in hearing the voice of the child should be the subject of consideration and review. In proceedings resulting in an order that provides the grandparent special guardian with decision-making rights concerning the child, to achieve greater stability in the placement, the child should be fully engaged in the process.

---

[5] In 2015, there were 5,360 adoptions of looked-after children. By 2021, this had decreased to 2,870; see at www.explore-education-statistics.service.gov.uk/find-statistics/children-looked-after-in-england-including-adoptions/2021.

[6] Children Act 1989, s 14A(6)(b).

[7] A Hall 'Special Guardianship and Permanency Planning: Unforeseen Consequences and Missed Opportunities' [2008] *Child and Family Law Quarterly* 359, 371.

[8] J Harwin et al, *The Contribution of Supervision Orders and Special Guardianship to Children's Lives and Family Justice* (Centre for Child and Family Justice Research, Lancaster University, 2019) 88 at www.cfj-lancaster.org.uk/app/nuffield/files-module/local/documents/HARWIN%20main%20report%20SO%20and%20SGOs%20_%204Mar2019.pdf.

[9] Children Act 1989, s 3.

[10] ibid s 8.

[11] ibid s 3(1).

[12] ibid s 8.

The chapter then turns to consider other legal options available to grandparents, namely, a 'lives with' CAO.[13] Section V will compare the two orders and, in particular, will consider the application routes when applicants are unrepresented and have no option but to take proceedings as litigants in person.

Section VI will consider court processes in private and public law, placement breakdown and the funding of legal advice and representation in SGO proceedings. It will also consider the availability of legal aid, the potential for local authority provision of financial support with legal fees, and the resulting 'postcode lottery'. It will additionally examine the special guardian's financial and support needs. With reference to a case study, the potential difficulties in pursuing the route to an SGO alongside the impacts of the order once made to the grandparent special guardian, it will consider why 'love is not enough' and emphasise the importance of a legal order and the protection it provides.

This chapter is written from the perspective of a legal practitioner and draws from knowledge of legal frameworks and experience in advising and working with grandparents.

II. The Evolution of the Special Guardianship Order

The Adoption and Children Act 2002[14] introduced the SGO and the concept of the 'special guardian'. As well as reducing the numbers of children in care, it aimed to provide an alternative route to legal permanence for a child living with a carer who was not a birth parent, whilst providing stability for both the child and the carer. The order sits somewhere in between a 'lives with' CAO[15] (formerly a 'Residence Order')[16] and an Adoption Order.[17] The former was seen as 'too fragile, impermanent, vulnerable to repeated challenge and insufficiently supported'[18] and the latter as too harsh due to its almost absolute permanency.[19]

It has long been suggested that children in kinship care, that is children living with a family member, generally fare better than children in foster care. A 2018 study found that children in kinship care

> experience better outcomes in regard to behaviour problems, adaptive behaviours, psychiatric disorders, well-being, placement stability (placement settings, number of placements, and placement disruption), guardianship, and institutional abuse than do children in foster care.[20]

---

[13] ibid s 8(1)(a).
[14] Adoption and Children Act 2002, s 115.
[15] Children Act 1989, s 8.
[16] Children and Families Act 2014, s 12(2) and (3).
[17] Adoption and Children Act 2002, s 46.
[18] Hall (n 7) 362.
[19] Adoption and Children Act 2002, s 46(2)(a).
[20] M Winokur, A Holtan and K Batchelder, 'Systematic Review of Kinship Care Effects on Safety, Permanency, and Well-Being Outcomes' (2018) 28 *Research on Social Work Practice* 19, 26.

In a 2020 review of research into kinship care, it was found that 'children growing up in kinship care seem to be doing at least as well as (and in some studies better than) those in unrelated foster care'.[21]

The need for a different, more flexible route to permanence for a child was recognised in *The Review of Adoption Law* by the Department of Health and Welsh Office in 1992.[22] It noted that, particularly for older children living with a family member who was not their birth parent, the adoption route was not always suitable due to its harsh consequences, such as the termination of a birth parent's parental responsibility,[23] resulting in the child's legally becoming the adopters' child as if they were biological parents.[24] Likewise, 'open adoption', that is adoption with adoptive parents allowing post-adoption contact, remained unpopular.[25] This may arguably have been because 'the Government's reluctance to embrace open adoption reflects a deficit approach to birth families, who become the sum of their parental failures'.[26] It was felt that adoption as an option 'will continue to focus the search for permanency for children on stranger rather than kinship care',[27] the former arguably meaning contact was less likely. In 1992, the *Review of Adoption Law* by the Department of Health and Welsh Office proposed

> a new mid-way order, inter vivos guardianship, which would give the carers a status similar to a guardian despite the fact that the birth parents were still alive and correspondingly restrict the birth parents' exercise of parental responsibility without removing it.[28]

However, it was not until *Adoption: A New Approach*, a White Paper published in 2000, that the 'new option', named as 'special guardianship',[29] was introduced. This was to 'provide permanence short of the legal separation involved in adoption'.[30] Special guardianship would

> give the carer clear responsibility for all aspects of caring for the child or young person and for taking decisions to do with their upbringing ... [and] provide a firm foundation on which to build a lifelong permanent relationship between the carer and the child or young person, be legally secure, preserve the basic legal link between the child or young

---

[21] J Hunt, *Two Decades of UK Research on Kinship Care: An Overview* (Family Rights Group, 2020) at https://frg.org.uk/wp-content/uploads/2020/12/Overview-research-kinship-care.pdf, 10.

[22] Department of Health and Welsh Office, *Review of Adoption Law – Report to Ministers of an Interdepartmental Working Group, A Consultation Document* (London, HMSO, 1992).

[23] Adoption and Children Act 2002, s 46(2)(a).

[24] ibid s 67(1).

[25] E Neil, 'Rethinking Adoption and Birth Family Contact: Is There a Role for the Law?' [2019] *Family Law* 1178.

[26] M Ryburn, 'Ideology and Conflict: The Place of Adoption in English Child Welfare Services' (1995) 17 *Children and Youth Services Review* 721.

[27] ibid 722.

[28] C Ball, 'The Adoption and Children Act 2002 A Critical Examination' (2005) 29(2) *Adoption and Fostering* 6, 15.

[29] Department of Health, *Adoption: A New Approach* (Cm 5017, 2000) 24, paras 5.8–5.11.

[30] ibid para 5.9.

person with birth family, be accompanied by proper access to a full range of support services including, where appropriate, financial support.[31]

Special Guardianship Orders were then introduced by the Adoption and Children Act 2002[32] which inserted provisions concerning the order into the Children Act.[33]

III. Parental Responsibility and its Importance

The overarching aim of an SGO is to provide 'greater security' when a child is unable to live with a birth parent. A key element in the provision of this 'greater security' arises from the important way the order allows a special guardian to exercise their parental responsibility for the child in comparison to that of the birth parent(s). Parental responsibility is defined in the Children Act 1989 as 'all the rights, duties, powers, responsibilities and authority which by law a parent of a child has in relation to the child and his property'.[34] Prior to this definition, 'statutes referred to "parental rights and duties" or "parental powers and duties" or the "rights and authority" of a parent'.[35] The introduction of this concept and 'change of terminology was of enormous symbolic significance, characterising the parental role as one of responsibility to children rather than as rights exercised over them'.[36] In practical terms, a person with parental responsibility has the legal ability to make important decisions about a child's upbringing, including contact, protection and maintenance, discipline, education, religion, consent to medical treatment, marriage and adoption, naming and appointing a guardian for a child.[37]

A mother automatically has parental responsibility for her child.[38] Where a heterosexual couple are married, the father shares parental responsibility with the mother for their child.[39] An unmarried father can acquire parental responsibility by being named as father on the child's birth certificate,[40] by way of entering a Parental Responsibility Agreement[41] with the mother, obtaining a Parental Responsibility Order from the court[42] or by being named in a CAO[43] as a parent with whom a child is to live.[44] Similar provisions apply in relation to the acquisition

---

[31] ibid para 5.10.
[32] Adoption and Children Act 2002, s 115.
[33] Children Act 1989, ss 14A–14G.
[34] Children Act 1989, s 3(1).
[35] N Lowe et al, *Bromley's Family Law*, 12th edn (Oxford, Oxford University Press, 2021) 436.
[36] ibid.
[37] ibid 443–44.
[38] Children Act 1989, s 2(2)(a).
[39] ibid s 2(1).
[40] ibid s 2(2)(b), as introduced by the Adoption and Children Act 2002, s 111.
[41] ibid s 4(1)(b).
[42] ibid s 4(1).
[43] ibid s 8.
[44] For more information see section V.

of parental responsibility by a second female parent,[45] and further provisions relate to parental responsibility and step-parents.[46] In light of the importance of parental responsibility as a concept, it is crucial that when a grandparent is carer for a grandchild, that grandparent is bestowed with parental responsibility for the child to enable the grandparent to make important decisions regarding the child. The making of both an SGO[47] and a 'lives with' CAO[48] grants parental responsibility to the grandparent. This does not remove a parent's[49] parental responsibility, as more than one person can have parental responsibility for a child at the same time.[50] Where this is the case, each individual with parental responsibility can act alone and without the other.[51] However, starting from a position of equality and sharing of parental responsibility, as is the case where there is a CAO, this can inevitably lead to tension and conflict, as views on how parental responsibility should be exercised are often very likely to differ.

The stark difference for a grandparent with a SGO is that the grandparent can exercise parental responsibility to the exclusion of any other person with parental responsibility.[52] By dint of this, 'the special guardian appears to be in the driving seat'.[53] The enhanced ability to exercise parental responsibility above others who have parental responsibility could arguably lead to the 'greater security'[54] that was an intended aim of the order, which is not afforded in the same way via a CAO.

In exercising parental responsibility, a key issue facing special guardians in their decision-making role is in relation to parental contact. This is because an aim of the order was to preserve family ties.[55] However, inevitably, issues around contact, when and how it takes place, are likely to arise as the special guardian navigates complex family dynamics, practical arrangements and potentially conflicting views of the best interests of the child. For the special guardian in the 'driving seat', the knowledge of the enhanced ability to make decisions could provide the confidence to make difficult decisions that, where parental responsibility is shared under a CAO, could only be resolved via mediation and/or the courts. For example, a special guardian grandparent may feel it to be in the child's interests to reduce physical contact to indirect contact only for a period. This could be if a parent's commitment to contact is chaotic or sporadic and the resulting impact on the child's emotional well-being is significant. The enhanced parental

---

[45] Children Act 1989, s 4ZA.
[46] ibid s 4A.
[47] ibid s 14C(1)(a).
[48] ibid s 12(2).
[49] This also applies to any other carer with parental responsibility, other than a birth parent.
[50] Children Act 1989, s 2(5).
[51] ibid s 2(6).
[52] ibid s 14C(1)(b).
[53] L Jordan and B Lindley, *Special Guardianship What Does It Offer Children Who Cannot Live With Their Parents?* (London, Family Rights Group, 2006) 6.
[54] Special Guardianship Guidance (n 2) 6.
[55] S Davey, *Family Law* (London, Macmillan HE, 2020) 508.

responsibility of the special guardian arguably provides the tools to make this decision. This autotomy to make such a decision, however, conflicts with best practice recommendations.

In the Public Law Working Group's *Recommendations to achieve best practice in the child protection and family justice systems: Special guardianship orders* (June 2020),[56] a recommendation was made for 'renewed emphasis on parental contact'.[57] This was with a focus on the purpose of contact, the type and amount of contact, the professional support the potential special guardian may need, and the planning and support needed for the placement to remain secure in light of any contact problems.[58] The 'emphasis on parental contact' therefore could be seen as at odds with the 'greater security' intended to be afforded by the SGO.

Where issues do arise concerning parental contact, if agreement cannot be reached between a special guardian grandparent carer and a parent, it is for the parent to apply to the court for a CAO to confirm whether and how contact should take place. The special guardian would be respondent to the application. The court would then decide, based on the principle that the child's welfare is the court's paramount consideration,[59] with reference to the factors contained in the welfare checklist.[60] The ability of parental challenge through court proceedings, although of course essential, could in family situations be highly de-stabilising for the child and the placement. Also, the best practice recommendation for contact, along with the presumption of parental involvement with a child,[61] could mean the courts lean towards making CAOs for contact, which may be in the parent's interests but not in the interests of the child or those of the special guardian.

Despite the issues considered above, there remain some restrictions on how special guardians can exercise certain aspects of their parental responsibility. For example, a special guardian cannot take the child out of the United Kingdom (UK) for more than three months without the consent of the birth parents with parental responsibility or an order of the court.[62] Likewise, a special guardian cannot change a child's surname on the same basis.[63] This could be because the aim of the order is to preserve identity and family relationships via parental contact in a way that adoption, for example, does not.

The exercise of parental responsibility by the special guardian and the practical impacts that can have on the parents, special guardian and the child form a complex element in an SGO. In time, as the SGO matures, it would be interesting to assess what actual difference it makes. In the context for grandparents with

---

[56] Public Law Working Group at www.judiciary.uk/wp-content/uploads/2020/06/PLWG-SGO-Final-Report-1.pdf.

[57] ibid 30.

[58] ibid.

[59] Children Act 1989, s 1(1).

[60] ibid s 1(3).

[61] ibid s 1(2A).

[62] ibid s 14C(3)(b).

[63] ibid s 14C(3)(a).

special guardian status, for instance, this could create or increase tensions between grandparents and parents.

IV. The Voice of the Child

As was stated in the Nuffield evidence review,[64] there is little research or information about the child's voice on his or her experiences under a SGO once an order has been made. However, during court proceedings, depending on the age, development and understanding of the child involved, there is a focus on the child's voice on matters such as whether an SGO ought to be made at all or whether any subsequent orders ought to be made. As an SGO bestows enhanced parental responsibility on the special guardian, which can be exercised often to the exclusion of the parents, hearing the child's voice in the process is crucial.

The voice of the child as the subject of proceedings is heard very differently in private and public law proceedings. Given that the effect of the SGO is essentially the same whether it is made in public or private law proceedings, significant questions are raised by this differential treatment (which will be outlined and discussed in detail below).

In public law proceedings, the child is automatically a party to the proceedings, regardless of her/his age and understanding. A guardian is appointed from CAFCASS,[65] an independent public body formed in 2001.[66] CAFCASS is involved with children the subject of both public and private law proceedings, but its actual role in each set of proceedings is different.

In public law proceedings, the CAFCASS officer, known as a 'guardian',[67] appoints a solicitor who is paid by way of non-means-, non-merits-tested legal aid. The solicitor will also be an accredited member of The Law Society's Children Panel of specialist solicitors.[68] If the child has 'sufficient understanding' and maturity[69] (ie is '*Gillick* competent'), as assessed by the solicitor,[70] the solicitor will take instructions direct from the child and the guardian's role is to report to the court on what is perceived to be in the child's best interests. Therefore, where an application is made for an SGO within care proceedings, the child's voice about the proposed order should be thoroughly tested and promoted through the guardian

---

[64] J Harwin and J Simmonds, *Special Guardianship: A Review of the Evidence* (Nuffield Family Justice Observatory, 2020) at www.nuffieldfjo.org.uk/resource/special-guardianship-a-review-of-the-evidence, 11.

[65] The Child and Families Court Advisory and Support Service; see at www.cafcass.gov.uk.

[66] Criminal Justice and Courts Services Act 2000, ch II.

[67] Formerly known as a 'guardian ad litem'.

[68] See at www.lawsociety.org.uk/career-advice/individual-accreditations/children-law-accreditation.

[69] *Gillick v West Norfolk and Wisbech Area Health Authority* [1986] AC 112. Note the case of *CS (A Child) (Appeal FPR 16.5. Sufficiency of Child's Understanding)* [2019] EWHC 634 (Fam), where Williams J noted seven factors to be considered in terms of considering a child's understanding.

[70] Practice Direction 16A – Representation of Children, r 6.3.

and the child's appointed solicitor. As the guardian and solicitor are involved throughout the life of the care proceedings, they have the time to develop a meaningful relationship with the child. This potential to develop a real relationship with the child will enable the court to have a clear view of the child's wishes and feelings and best interests.

In contrast, in private law proceedings, where a grandparent may apply for an SGO, the circumstances are typically quite different. Often, there will be a very difficult family situation that requires a grandparent to become involved in a child's life. Thus, the potential to hear the child's voice is very different. As a starting point, and in contrast to public law proceedings, the child is not automatically a party to the proceedings. Making a child a party to private law proceedings is possible but rare, and requires unusual grounds.[71] That is, 'cases which involve an issue of significant difficulty and consequently will occur in only a minority of cases'.[72]

If such circumstances do exist, the child may be granted legal aid, but this is subject to a means and merits test.[73] Unlike care proceedings, therefore, there is no automatic right to legal aid, regardless of the merits of the case or the applicant's finances. Instead, the child (or his or her solicitor) will have to establish that there are merits to the child's being a party to the case and that the child meets the financial eligibility for legal aid, which generally is likely to be so, although it is not impossible for a child to have financial means such as a trust fund. In most private law cases where the child is typically not a party to the proceedings, the voice of the child is heard through the court's ordering a welfare report from CAFCASS,[74] dealing with such matters as required by the court. Generally, a CAFCASS officer will meet with the child 'alone on a sufficient number of occasions, proportionate to the issues in each case, to ensure they have heard and understood the voice of the child'.[75] The meeting should be in a neutral venue.[76]

Whether in public or private law proceedings, the court must consider the child's ascertainable wishes and feelings when making an SGO.[77] It is likely that the child's voice in public law proceedings, where he or she has the potential for a working relationship with the guardian and solicitor for the duration of the case, is going to have far more resonance than that of the child in private law proceedings. This is because the child in private proceedings may have only a few meetings with the CAFCASS Family Court Advisor, making, through no one's fault, a meaningful working relationship difficult.

---

[71] Practice Direction 16A – Representation of Children, Part 4, s 1.

[72] ibid Part 7.1.

[73] Legal Aid, Sentencing and Punishment of Offenders Act (LASPO) 2012, sch 1, pt 1, para 15(1).

[74] Children Act 1989, s 7.

[75] CAFCASS Operating Framework (2017) 12.

[76] See at www.cafcass.gov.uk/grown-ups/parents-and-carers/divorce-and-separation/what-to-expect-from-cafcass/section-7-report/.

[77] Children Act 1989, s 1(3)(a).

The impact and effects of an SGO are the same whether made in private or public law proceedings – it is the same order. This being so, there should be absolute equality in both sets of proceedings as to the voice of the child. The order, when made, gives the special guardian, as stated, heightened parental responsibility and the ability to exclude all others from decision making. It is crucial, therefore, that children, particularly where they are of an age to understand and fully participate in the court process, have the greatest opportunity to be heard in relation to the making of an order, particularly because of the huge impacts of the order on the child once it is made.

V. Special Guardianship Order or Child Arrangements Order?

Other routes exist for grandparents to secure the placement of a child with them on a legal basis. There are advantages and disadvantages, meaning that the potentially arduous process to obtain the 'greater security' of the SGO can be outweighed by the more manageable process of applying for another order.

The key alternative legal option for a grandparent is via an application for a 'lives with' CAO, which was formerly known as 'residence order', under section 8 of the Children Act 1989.[78] This is generally a quicker option than applying for an SGO and is more simple. This is partly because before an application for an SGO can be made, the applicant must provide the local authority with three months' notice of the proposed application.[79] This period is required to enable the local authority to undertake an assessment of the special guardian (as detailed in section VI of this chapter). Applicants may be deterred from the start, by the need to involve the local authority and for an in-depth assessment to be undertaken of them as a family. In contrast, the CAO process may not involve the local authority, as the court is able to obtain an independent report on the advisability of an order by way of asking CAFCASS[80] to undertake a welfare report.[81]

The ability to access advice and representation can have an impact on the route to an SGO or a CAO. The funding cuts introduced by LASPO 2012[82] in most circumstances removed applications for CAOs from the scope of legal aid. Since then, many people have been unable to afford legal advice and representation in such proceedings. In a 2014 study, the majority of court users were 'ineligible for

---

[78] Children Act 1989, s 8(1)(a).

[79] ibid, s 14A(7).

[80] CAFCASS is a public body created to safeguard and promote children's welfare, give advice to the court, make provision for a child to be represented in court, and to give support, advice and information to children and their families; see also the text associated with nn 65–67.

[81] Children Act 1989, s 7.

[82] Legal Aid Sentencing and Punishment of Offenders Act 2012.

or had been unable to obtain legal aid, but could not afford legal representation.[83] The cuts have resulted in a huge number of people resorting to initiating and representing themselves in proceedings as litigants in person. In 2013, 14 per cent of cases at disposal involved parties who were both unrepresented. For the same period in 2021, this rose to 37 per cent.[84] For the same periods, the cases in which both parties had representation decreased from 41 per cent in 2013 to 19 per cent in 2021.[85] The decrease in the availability of legal aid and the considerable increase in numbers of litigants in person have created difficulties for the individuals involved and the courts.[86] It has, however, meant that more resources are available to help people steer themselves through the process. For example, court forms have been adapted to be more user-friendly, and processes, such as making an application for a CAO, have gone online.[87] These necessary but slight process advancements for litigants in person arguably could mean that potential special guardians are put off the SGO process. For instance, see Case Study 5.1 (with names changed), drawn from a case supervised by the writer at Essex Law Clinic.[88] This is just one example of the reluctance of a grandparent to engage as a litigant in person via the SGO route.

Jan, grandmother of 3-year-old Ben, has been looking after him since he was born. Ben's mother Freya has a drug problem. Freya is sometimes home but often not. She does little for Ben and does not take him out of the house. Periodically Freya says she is going to take Ben to live with her and her new partner. Jan doesn't think this will happen. Jan, unable to afford a lawyer, visited Essex Law Clinic at Essex University, where students provide free legal advice under supervision. Jan was advised about both the SGO and CAO route, with an emphasis on the need to have parental responsibility for Ben. Despite being advised about the difference in the way of exercising parental responsibility, Jan opted to apply online for a CAO on the basis the process was far more manageable for her as a litigant in person.

Case Study 5.1

It appears, therefore, that the complexity of the SGO route, including the need for an assessment by the local authority, is a deterrent. In a Family Rights Group

---

[83] L Trinder et al, 'Litigants in Person in Private Family Law Cases' (27 November 2014) *Ministry of Justice Analytical Series* 7 at https://assets.publishing.service.gov.uk/government/uploads/system/uploads/attachment_data/file/380479/litigants-in-person-in-private-family-law-cases.pdf.

[84] See at www.gov.uk/government/statistics/family-court-statistics-quarterly-july-to-september-2021/family-court-statistics-quarterly-july-to-september-2021.

[85] ibid.

[86] Ministry of Justice, *Litigants in Person in Private Family Law Cases* (London, Ministry of Justice, 2014).

[87] See at www.gov.uk/government/publications/form-c100-application-under-the-children-act-1989-for-a-child-arrangements-prohibited-steps-specific-issue-section-8-order-or-to-vary-or-discharge.

[88] Essex Law Clinic, University of Essex, see at www.essex.ac.uk.

publication, when asked about the two orders, a grandparent stated 'I was acutely aware that by not going for the security that an SGO offers, the child ultimately suffers. However, the stress of going through the assessment process would be bound to impact on the child as well and that cannot be good.'[89]

In deciding on a CAO route, however, a grandparent's short-term gain may cause longer-term pain, particularly when the grandparent is exercising parental responsibility. The 'sharing' of parental responsibility under a CAO could lead to conflict in decision making, which could destabilise the child and the grandparent's role.

Despite the potential perceived advantages of the CAO process, the disruption rate of the order is considerably higher than that of SGOs. That is, over a five-year period, the SGO disruption rate was 5.6 per cent yet the CAO rate was 25 per cent (over a six-year period).[90] The stability of the SGO appears to support the contention of its 'greater security'. However, if the problem in private law proceedings is that the more manageable CAO process is more attractive, especially to litigants in person, perhaps steps, such as an online application form, could be taken to simplify the SGO process. This writer would argue that this would be of particular benefit to litigants in person, who would prefer a simpler process. In addition to simplifying the process and making it more 'user-friendly', there could be more public information about the order to create better awareness of it and its impact.

Whether an SGO or a CAO is made, the door remains open for further proceedings. A birth parent may potentially make numerous CAO applications for contact, specific issue or prohibited steps orders[91] if the grandparent carer is making decisions with which the birth parent disagrees. For example, a special guardian may decide that it is in a child's best interests to change to a school nearer to the special guardian's house or with a better OFSTED rating, which happens to be further away from the parents. While the grandparent may make a decision perceiving it to be in the child's best interests, this could create a barrier to the parents' continued involvement, due to the geographical distance or lack of day-to-day engagement with the school.

A decision of this nature could create a high level of tension for all parties involved, which could easily impact adversely on the child and even the stability of the placement itself. The special guardian grandparent in this example would be empowered to make this decision about the school without the knowledge of

---

[89] R Derriman, 'Special Guardianship: Reflections on a New Order' in L Jordan and B Lindley (eds), *Special Guardianship: What Does It Offer Children Who Cannot Live With Their Parents* (London, Family Rights Group, 2006) 58, 62.

[90] J Selwyn and J Masson, 'Adoption, Special Guardianship and Residence Orders: A Comparison of Disruption Rates' (2014) 44 *Family Law* 1709.

[91] Children Act 1989, s 8.

parents not involved in the day-to-day affairs of the child. The only option for the parents then would be to apply to the court under the Children Act 1989 for a prohibited steps order[92] to prevent the move, or a specific issue order[93] asking the court to decide which school the child should attend.

As noted, whether the exercise of parental responsibility is via an SGO or a CAO, there remains the potential for the parents or others with parental responsibility to make numerous applications to court to challenge the proposed decisions of the grandparent. This is clearly far from ideal, particularly in relation to achieving stability in the placement. There is provision for the grandparent to make an application to the court for a barring order,[94] that is, an order that no further applications be made under the Children Act 1989 without leave of the court. Generally, for the court to consider making such an order, there would need to be a persistent and unreasonable number of prior court applications. Unfortunately, this means that, by that stage, damage to the family dynamic is likely to be considerable, and the need to utilise further court proceedings in such a scenario supports the contention that 'love is not enough'.

VI. Process: Private Law and Public Law, Placement Breakdown and Finances

Special Guardianships Orders can be made in both private and public law proceedings, but the processes can have differences. The private law route is through an application by an individual over 18 years who is not the parent of the child. Applications can also be made within public law care proceedings instigated by the state, and/or the court can make an SGO of its own motion[95] within those care proceedings. The different routes can create distinct issues for the potential special guardian, particularly for those in the public law process, where principles to prevent delay can have a significant impact on the proceedings, and this will be considered further in section VI.B.

A. Private Law

The process of applying to the court in private law proceedings will be explained with the help of fictitious Case Study 5.2.

---

[92] ibid.
[93] ibid.
[94] ibid s 91(14).
[95] ibid s 14A(6)(b).

Jake (65 years) is the paternal grandfather of Sam. Sam has lived with Jake for 5 years and is now 10 years old. Sam's mother (Alisha) is a drug addict who periodically turns up demanding she has Sam back. Jake can usually talk her around. Sam's father died in an accident. Alisha now has a new partner. She has called Jake saying Sam must return to her care as they are now going to be a family unit. Jake is wholly opposed to this. He is unable to afford to pay a solicitor and must act as a litigant in person. He has been told he should apply for an SGO.

Case Study 5.2

Jake must notify his local authority that he intends to apply for an SGO. There is no prescribed method of doing this, but clearly in writing via letter or e-mail is advisable. He must give his local authority three months' notice of his intention to make the application.[96]

Jake must arrange a Mediation Information and Assessment Meeting (MIAM).[97] This is an initial meeting with a mediator to assess the viability, in the circumstances of the case, of mediation between Jake and Alisha. Generally, in most private law proceedings concerning children, this will be a requirement.[98] There are various exemptions[99] as to when mediation is necessary, however, including where there has been domestic abuse between the parties, there are no contact details for the respondent or one of the parties is out of the jurisdiction. Once a MIAM takes place, the mediator signs form FM1 to confirm this and an application to the court can be made. Alternatively, the applicant self-declares an exemption on that form. The application forms[100] are then submitted to the court with the court fee. Help is available with court fees should this be necessary.[101] It is not essential, but the applicant may also provide a statement about why he or she is making the application. This can be done on form C13A.[102]

In some circumstances an applicant will need 'leave' or the court's permission to make an application for an SGO.[103] In Jake's case, leave is not required as he is a relative of Sam and Sam has been living with him for more than one year. Likewise, leave is not required if a CAO is in place confirming that the child lives with the

---

[96] ibid s 14A(7).

[97] Children and Families Act 2014, s 10(1).

[98] Practice Direction 3A – Family Mediation Information and Assessment Meetings (MIAMS), para 12.

[99] Family Proceedings Rules, r 3.8 (1).

[100] Form FM1 at www.gov.uk/government/publications/give-information-for-a-family-mediation-assessment-form-fm1; and form C1 at www.gov.uk/government/publications/form-c1-application-for-an-order.

[101] See at www.gov.uk/get-help-with-court-fees.

[102] See at www.gov.uk/government/publications/form-c13a-supplement-for-an-application-for-a-special-guardianship-order.

[103] For individuals who do not require permission, see Children Act 1989, s 14A(5)(a)–(e).

applicant, or where the child has lived with the applicant (non-relative) for more than three years or where those with parental responsibility have consented to the application. It is therefore important to check whether leave is required. If it is, in making its decision the court will consider the nature of the application, the applicant's connection with the child and any risk of disruption to the child if the application should go ahead.[104]

The local authority must then report on the suitability of the proposed special guardian. Hence the three-month notice period provided by the applicant to the local authority, allowing time for this to take place. An assessment by the local authority will lead to a report for the court, giving information about the child, the applicant, the health of both, the impacts of the making of a SGO and/or other orders, resulting in a recommendation concerning the making or not of the order and of contact. Following further regulations to strengthen the assessment of special guardians,[105] the report must also address any harm and potential future harm that the child may suffer, and the child's needs (including future needs) and the ability of the applicant to meet those needs. Also, it must assess the applicant's ability to protect the child and must consider the likelihood of the placement's being sustained until the child is 18 years of age.

If the local authority's assessment and report about the applicant are positive, the application can proceed, and the local authority will devise an Assessment Plan, which will address issues such as support and training of the applicant. If it is negative, the applicant can challenge this by way of making an application to the court for ongoing assessment. The local authority is then made a party to the proceedings.

When deciding about the making of an SGO, the court will consider the factors contained in section 1(3) of the Children Act 1989, known as the Welfare Checklist. These factors are also considered in proceedings under section 8 of the Children Act 1989 (Child Arrangement Orders, Prohibited Steps Orders and Specific Issue Orders). This reflects very clearly how the Order can be felt to sit somewhere in between private and public law due to its private law roots and decision making, and the heavy involvement of the local authority in the process.

The factors considered by the court in the welfare checklist are:

- the child's wishes and feelings in light of his or her age and understanding;
- the child's physical, emotional and educational needs;
- the likely effect of a change in circumstances;
- the child's age, sex and background, and any characteristics the court feels are relevant;
- any harm the child has suffered or risk of harm;

---

[104] ibid s 10(9).
[105] Special Guardianship (Amendment) Regulations 2016 (SI 2016/111) regs 4 and 5.

- how capable the relevant person is, ie the applicant, of meeting the child's needs; and

- the powers available to the court.

B. Public Law

The other route to the making of an SGO is through the public law care proceedings. An increasing number of care applications are concluding with the making of an SGO rather than a care order. From a sample study using CAFCASS data, it was found that from 2010/11 to 2016/17, the number of care proceedings resulting in an SGO increased from 11 per cent to 17 per cent.[106] Also, in the same study, only 1 per cent of children subject to an SGO had an application for this order in their care proceedings,[107] thus reflecting the courts' increasing tendency to make such orders of their own motion.

Public law care proceedings may be issued by a local authority when it has concerns for a child. An interim[108] (temporary) care order may be applied for while further in-depth investigations are underway. An interim order will be made if the local authority has 'reasonable grounds for believing a child is suffering or is likely to suffer significant harm'.[109] As is consistent with the duty of the local authority under the Children Act 1989 to promote the upbringing of a child by his or her family,[110] the local authority should look to and assess members of the child's extended family, including grandparents, as potential carers when it has such concerns. That is, 'where a child cannot remain living with his or her parents, the local authority should identify and prioritise suitable family and friends' placements, if appropriate'.[111]

Therefore, we might re-imagine Case Study 5.2, as shown in Case Study 5.3.

> Sam, 10 years, lives with his mother Alisha. She has had a long-term drug problem, which has been relatively well managed. Alisha now has a new partner who has moved in to the house. He is known to the Local Authority as his children were removed due to drug dealing, dependency and violence. Sam regularly sees his paternal grandfather, Jake. Due to risk of future harm, the Local Authority has applied for an Interim Care Order re Sam.

Case Study 5.3

---

[106] Harwin et al (n 8) 26.
[107] ibid.
[108] Children Act 1989, s 38(1).
[109] ibid s 38(2).
[110] ibid s 17(1)(b).
[111] Department for Education, *Court Orders and Pre-proceedings: For Local Authorities* (April 2014) at https://assets.publishing.service.gov.uk/government/uploads/system/uploads/attachment_data/file/306282/Statutory_guidance_on_court_orders_and_pre-proceedings.pdf, 11.

In Sam's case, the local authority may identify Jake early in the care proceedings as a possible carer for Sam. If so, assessments of him would be undertaken in relation to his potential as main carer. The local authority may speak to Jake about a possible SGO's being made. Alternatively, it may plan, on the basis that it obtains a care order, to place Sam with Jake under that order.

However, difficulties may arise when a family member is identified as a potential carer only late in the care proceedings, when assessment of such a carer could create significant delay to the proceedings. Due to the potential harm delay can cause to an already vulnerable child, a tight time frame of 26 weeks[112] from application to disposal in care proceedings was introduced by the Children and Families Act 2014. This followed findings about delay by the Family Justice Review in 2011.[113] Prior to this, disposal times were considerably longer. For example, in the third quarter of 2012, the average time for disposal was 47.7 weeks.[114] The impact of the 26-week disposal period balanced with the need for assessment time, however, was the subject of a seminal case concerning grandparents, care proceedings and an SGO.

In *P-S (Children)*,[115] two boys were made the subject of 'short-term' care orders rather than SGOs to their grandparents. The concept of 'short-term' care orders was later declared as 'flawed', with reference to there being 'no mechanism for a care order to be discharged on the happening of a fixed event or otherwise be limited in time'.[116] In this case, the making of the care orders was contrary to the views of the local authority, the children's guardian and the parents. At first instance, informal guidance, providing that a child should live with a potential special guardian before an order is made, was also relied upon. The grandparents, who were not parties to the proceedings nor represented, were invited to attend the final hearing. The case raised, amongst other things, the failure to join the grandparents to the proceedings, the fact that they had no access to court documents and legal advice, and the fact that they took no proper role in the proceedings. According to Sir Ernest Ryder,

> The grandparents did not know what was happening, did not have the evidence upon which the court was making a decision, were unable to take advice and in the event, in my judgment, did not have effective access to justice.[117]

The case also raised the issue of the 26-week deadline to disposal, recognising the 'inevitable tension between the adverse effects of delay and the time needed for more complex welfare determinations where, for example, a placement order or

---

[112] Children Act 1989, s 32(1)(a).

[113] Family Justice Review 2011 at https://assets.publishing.service.gov.uk/government/uploads/system/uploads/attachment_data/file/217343/family-justice-review-final-report.pdf.

[114] See assets.publishing.service.gov.uk/government/uploads/system/uploads/attachment_data/file/217617/court-stats-quarterly-q3-2012.pdf.

[115] *P-S (Children)* [2018] EWCA Civ 1407.

[116] ibid [33].

[117] ibid [56].

special guardianship assessment are needed'.[118] Reference was also made to the increasing numbers of SGOs made in public law care proceedings by the court of its own motion. This case led the President of the Family Division to request that the Family Justice Council prepare guidance to assist the court when SGOs are an issue, with a view to addressing the points made in *P-S (Children)*. To support this, an evidence review of SGOs in public law proceedings was undertaken by the Nuffield Family Observatory.[119]

The findings from focus groups formulated for the Nuffield evidence review[120] include that preparation of special guardians for the role is limited, as is training; that local authority assessments are rushed; and that special guardians feel stress and are confused by the court process. Also, it found that the 26-week time frame causes problems; that there is a lack of consistency in potential extensions of the time frame; and that special guardians need more support when caring for a child who is likely to have suffered neglect and/or abuse. The findings from the research evidence,[121] which recognise the limited general research on special guardianship, found that children generally do well under an SGO, although there are several risk factors in achieving stability. These include the additional pressures on the special guardian in terms of the practical elements of care, such as meeting accommodation needs, as well as the impact on finances. Also, the review reflects on the emotional elements of care, such as supervising and managing contact inside a potentially a complex family dynamic whilst handling significant change.

In June 2020, the Family Justice Council Public Law Working Group published its final report, *Recommendations to achieve best practice in the child protection and family justice systems: Special guardianship orders*.[122] Within this report there is interim guidance on special guardianship.[123] In short, the guidance provides that potential alternative carers should be identified at an early stage, that assessments should be commenced promptly and that a full assessment would usually require a three-month time frame, as is provided for in private law proceedings. The guidance also covers, where proceedings are underway, the need to identify a potential carer and so notify the court and parties; and when that is late in the proceedings, an extension of the 26-week time limit should be allowed. However, delay should be proportionate to welfare.[124]

The consequence of the making of an SGO through the public law process is that the child is no longer deemed a 'looked-after' child. A child becomes 'looked-after' on the making of a care order/interim care order,[125] or when the

---

[118] ibid [18].
[119] Harwin and Simmonds (n 64).
[120] ibid 11–13.
[121] ibid 11–14.
[122] Public Law Working Group (n 56).
[123] ibid 62.
[124] Children Act 1989, s 1(2).
[125] ibid s 31.

local authority provides accommodation to the child.[126] The effect of being looked after means the local authority owes a large number of duties to the child, such as to safeguard and promote the child's welfare,[127] to consider whether the placement meets the child's needs,[128] to assess the child's needs for services[129] and to appoint an Independent Reviewing Officer to review the child's care plan.[130]

There is, therefore, a very high level of state intervention at, of course, considerable cost[131] regarding a child who is looked after. Bearing in mind that local authority support (eg from a personal adviser employed to provide advice and support) to a looked-after child leaving care[132] can (as from 2017)[133] extend to the age of 25 years if that person is in full-time education, the impact of the increasing numbers of children leaving the care system through the granting of SGOs could arguably have monetary implications for a local authority. Children who leave care through the making of an SGO are deemed to be 'care leavers',[134] however, meaning they have various rights, such as the entitlement of the child's school to Pupil Premium Plus in terms of education and the child's being deemed a priority in terms of school admissions.

More importantly, leaving care via an SGO could mean the loss of the state safety net comprising the local authority statutory duties to the child, which could mean that, in some circumstances, the child will be disadvantaged. This is important, as questions have been raised about the quality of assessment of a potential special guardian, resulting in approval of some special guardians who perhaps should not have been approved.

An example of this was in the tragic case of Shi-Anne Downer, which led to a Serious Case Review.[135] Due to parental alcohol and drug abuse, Shi-Anne was made the subject of an interim care order at birth and later a SGO in favour of her grandmother. At 18 months of age, Shi-Anne died of 150 internal and external injuries and her grandmother was charged with and convicted of murder. Part of the Serious Case Review considered the 'robustness of assessments, reports to court, care planning and court decision making processes', plus the way in which the grandmother's application for an SGO was 'evaluated, assessed, challenged and analysed during the proceedings'.[136] The Review's findings showed, amongst other

---

[126] ibid s 22.
[127] ibid s 22(3).
[128] Care Planning, Placement and Case Review Regulations 2010 (SI 2010/959) reg 4(3).
[129] ibid, reg 4(1).
[130] Children Act 1989, s 25A.
[131] See at www.nao.org.uk/report/children-in-care/. Average spend on a foster place for a child is £29,000–£33,000 pa. Average spend on a residential place for a child is £131,000–£135,000 pa. £2.5 billion spent supporting children in foster and residential care 2012–13.
[132] Children Act 1989, s 23 and s 24.
[133] Children and Social Work Act 2017, pt 3.
[134] Children Act 1989, s 23.
[135] Birmingham Safeguarding Children Board Serious Case Review Shi-Anne Downer 2017 at https://fostercareresources.files.wordpress.com/2016/01/scr_bscb_2015-16-02.pdf.
[136] ibid 5.

things, considerable failings in relation to the assessment process, with omissions not acted upon, inadequate health and background information relating to the grandmother, and no support or social-work involvement with the family after the order, despite the Family Court's being informed this would continue for six weeks. The author of the Serious Case Review concluded that a Supervision Order[137] (a year-long order where a local authority 'supervisor' is allocated to 'advise, assist and befriend'[138] a child) should have been made alongside the SGO.

It will never be known whether the appointment of a supervisor as suggested would have saved Shi-Anne. She was only 18 months old when she died. However, it is easily imagined that a person closely connected to her may have developed an awareness of a major problem.

C. Placement Breakdown

As with the tragic case discussed in section VI.B, sadly, potentially long-term care options do not always result in the outcomes hoped for by all involved. This can be particularly relevant where grandparent special guardians are involved. For example, the grandparent's health may be a major factor in leading to a breakdown of the placement. Likewise, grandparent special guardians may face more challenges in relation to the physical side of childcare when suddenly having to take on a parental role. Problems can include

> age, poverty, illness/disability, parenting alone, lower educational level; the length of time since they have parented; the effect of prior adversities on the children, which demand more than ordinary parenting skills; elevated levels of carer stress and inadequate support.[139]

The stability of the placement likewise could be impacted by the emotional effects on the special guardian and the child of the special guardian's attempts to facilitate (or not) contact with parents within a testing family dynamic.

Where difficulties arise, the special guardian should initially approach the local authority with a request for support. If, however, the issue is ultimately not resolvable, the special guardian can apply to the court to vary or discharge the order.[140] The local authority is also able to make such an application. Likewise, the child and/or the child's parents may apply to vary or discharge the SGO, but they need leave of the court to do so. The court will grant leave to the child only if he or she has 'sufficient understanding' to make the application,[141] and will only grant leave

---

[137] Children Act 1989, s 31.
[138] ibid s 35.
[139] J Hunt, 'Grandparents as substitute parents in the UK' (2018) 13(2) *Contemporary Social Science: Journal of the Academy of Social Sciences* 175, 176.
[140] Children Act 1989, s 14 D.
[141] ibid s 14D(4).

to the parents if there is a real prospect of parental success and if it is satisfied that there has been a 'significant change in circumstances'[142] since the making of the SGO. Change should be 'considerable, noteworthy or important'.[143]

In *Re M*, an SGO was made to grandparents within care proceedings regarding a 9-year-old boy whose mother suffered serious mental-health problems. The mother applied three years later for leave to discharge the SGO on the basis that her health was much improved. Leave was refused and the mother appealed. The mother was successful on the basis that the initial judge set the bar too high in terms of the change of circumstances needed, and that there had been no assessment of the mother's chances of success if leave were granted. Where there is a hearing about discharge of an SGO, the child's welfare will be paramount. The court will consider all the circumstances of the case and can request welfare reports[144] from CAFCASS, as it can in other private law proceedings.[145] The court can also discharge an SGO of its own motion within other proceedings. Therefore, although the order has evolved as a means of providing a child with 'greater security' and a safe alternative option for his or her care, there are – and of course may be – circumstances in which orders need to be discharged or varied, again establishing that 'love is not enough'.

D. Finances

A further argument that 'love is not enough' relates to the financial implications of making an application for an SGO in private law proceedings and those following an order's being made. In terms of legal costs and the availability of legal aid, as mentioned earlier regarding litigants in person, LASPO 2012 removed private law proceedings, such as section 8 Children Act Orders, divorce and financial orders, from the scope of legal aid. The only exemption to this is where an applicant for legal aid has suffered domestic abuse and there is evidence of that. Initially, post-LASPO 2012, the acceptable evidence of domestic abuse was limited, meaning it was difficult to obtain legal aid. This led to a successful judicial review[146] by Rights of Women,[147] and following Ministry of Justice research,[148] in January 2018, the list of information that could be classed as evidence widened considerably. Legal

---

[142] ibid s 14D(5).

[143] *Re M (Special Guardianship Order: Leave to Apply to Discharge)* [2021] EWCA 442 [28].

[144] Children Act 1989, s 7.

[145] ibid s 8.

[146] *The Queen (on the application of Rights of Women) v The Lord Chancellor and Secretary of State for Justice* [2016] EWCA Civ 91.

[147] See at https://rightsofwomen.org.uk/.

[148] F Syposz, *Research Investigating the Domestic Violence Evidential Requirements for Legal Aid in Private Family Disputes* (Ministry of Justice, 2017) at https://assets.publishing.service.gov.uk/government/uploads/system/uploads/attachment_data/file/719408/domestic-violence-legal-aid-research-report.pdf.

aid funding may also be available through an application for Exceptional Case Funding. That is, although outside the scope of legal aid, funding may be available due to the complexity of the case, the importance of it to the applicant, and whether withholding legal aid would mean the applicant would be unable to present his or her case effectively and without unfairness.[149] Applicants must still meet the means criteria. In 2019, the Ministry of Justice announced its intention to expand the scope of legal aid to include SGOs.[150] The current position is that legal aid may be available in special guardianship proceedings, subject to the means and merits test.

Many potential special guardians may not qualify for legal aid due to the financial means test, yet they may still unable to afford legal advice and representation. For example, those with capital in a property but limited income. In the Family Rights Group 2019 report *The Highs and Lows of Kinship Care*,[151] 845 kinship carers were questioned about kinship care, with 64 per cent of respondents being grandparents.[152] When asked about funding of proceedings, 58 per cent of respondents confirmed they had incurred legal costs, which ranged from £100 to £50,000. The average costs amounted to £5,446.[153] The report provides a clear picture of the importance of legal advice to those involved in SGOs. When asked if they knew enough about the legal options and their implications, 74 per cent of participants said 'no', 9 per cent felt 'not sure' and only 17 per cent responded 'yes'.[154] In some geographical areas, as a private law application for an SGO could in some cases potentially avoid the need for care proceedings, local authorities may provide funding towards an applicant's legal advice.[155] In the report, 37 per cent of people were helped by the local authority with some legal advice (which could only equate to one hour's information) or advice throughout.[156] This does inevitably raise questions about consistency and postcode lotteries in potential special guardians' access to advice.

In terms of funding and support post-SGO, the local authority and the potential special guardian should discuss likely financial needs and support before an order is made, and this should form part of the local authority's Support Plan. Financial support can be payable to 'facilitate' a person to become a special guardian under

---

[149] Lord Chancellor's Exceptional Funding Guidance (Non-Inquests) at https://assets.publishing. service.gov.uk/government/uploads/system/uploads/attachment_data/file/956612/Lord_Chancellor_ s_Exceptional_Funding_Guidance__Non-Inquests__January_2021.pdf.

[150] Ministry Of Justice, *Legal Support: The Way Ahead: An action plan to deliver better support to people experiencing legal problems* (2019) at https://assets.publishing.service.gov.uk/government/uploads/ system/uploads/attachment_data/file/777036/legal-support-the-way-ahead.pdf, 16.

[151] C Ashley and D Braun, *The Highs and Lows of Kinship Care: Analysis of a Comprehensive Survey of Kinship Carers* (Family Rights Group, 2019).

[152] ibid 6.

[153] ibid 32.

[154] ibid 33.

[155] Special Guardianship Regulations 2005 (SI 2005/1109) reg 6(2)(c)(i).

[156] Ashley and Braun (n 151) 32.

regulation 6(1)(a) of the Special Guardianship Regulations 2005.[157] Once an order is made, financial support can only be continued[158] where it is necessary for the special guardian to look after the child, the child needs 'special care', or where it is appropriate to contribute towards accommodation and maintenance of the child, including adaptations to the home, equipment and clothing.[159] On the making of an SGO, a special guardian can apply for Special Guardianship Allowance for either one-off costs or regular support. This is means-tested and the amount paid is generally in line with foster payments. Once paid, payment is reviewed annually, and the onus is on the special guardian to confirm any changes to his or her financial circumstances.[160]

Special guardians are entitled to the same benefits, such as child benefit, as birth parents. For children with complex problems, local authorities can apply for financial support from the Adoption Support Fund. This is in line with existing statutory provision for the assessment of adoption support, and was extended in 2016 to those families with an SGO in recognition of the fact that a child placed under an SGO is likely to have suffered prior to the making of the Order in the same way that a child in an adoptive situation may have. However, this funding is only available where a child was in care before the SGO, or left care and was made the subject of a CAO for the purposes of assessment of the potential special guardian. Once eligibility has been established, the local authority will assess the special guardian's support needs. If therapeutic help is needed, the local authority will apply to the Fund. At the time of writing, the current funding limit is £5,000 with potential for a further £2,500 per annum if specialist assessments are needed. These assessments could, for example, be around the child's and family's needs in terms of service provision.

Again, re-imagining Case Study 5.2, the practical and financial impacts are as shown in Case Study 5.4.

Jake has applied for and been granted a Special Guardianship Order regarding Sam. Jake's two adult sons, aged 19 and 21 years, still live with him in their 3-bedroom house. To create a space for Sam, Jake is left with no option but to convert the garage into a fourth bedroom. He needs to purchase new school uniform for Sam. Alisha (Sam's mother) is now on a drug rehabilitation programme 50 miles away, which means Jake will need to drive Sam to the unit so that contact can take place. Jake retired 3 years ago and is worried about how he is going to afford to care for Sam, who also needs weekly counselling sessions that Jake is paying for. Jake loves Sam, but when it comes to the practical impact on his finances now and in the future, he reflects that 'love is not enough'.

Case Study 5.4

---

[157] Special Guardianship Regulations 2005 (n 155).
[158] ibid reg 6(1)(b).
[159] ibid reg 6(2)(a)–(d).
[160] ibid reg 10(1).

VII. Conclusion

The SGO was introduced to sit somewhere between a CAO and an adoption order. The SGO has managed to find its place in the room, and certainly, in some places, it has reflected the intentions of policymakers and the expectations of stakeholders such as grandparents and parents. Special Guardianship Orders have, for instance, enabled the children to continue existing relationships whilst living away from their birth parents. They have also provided the special guardian with an enhanced parental responsibility safety net in terms of decision making that so easily could destabilise environments. The clear intention, for the Order to help maintain relationships, is supported by provisions in the legislation aimed at maintaining identity, such as the inability to change a child's name without consent or the leave of the court. It can be easily argued that SGOs are a bridge between the private law and public law. Despite there being two routes towards making an Order, once made, the impacts and effects of the SGO are the same. However, the two processes have differences, particularly around the representation of the child and the amplification of the child's voice in proceedings resulting in an SGO (in terms of legal aid, allocation of a specialist solicitor for the child, the role of the guardian). Does this distinction matter? For the child at the centre of the case, it is strongly felt that there should be absolute parity. As stated initially, a child the subject of SGO proceedings is highly likely to have suffered trauma, whether bereavement, neglect or abuse. The child and the child's voice should be heard and considered in the same way in both sets of proceedings. Considering that a key element of an SGO is that the special guardian can exercise parental responsibility above and beyond anyone else, it is suggested that there should be every opportunity to hear the child's voice in private law proceedings in the thorough way it is heard in public law proceedings.

Moving forward, it is also argued that there should be better and more data about the Orders, with a particular focus on the make-up of special guardians. If a high proportion of special guardians are grandparents, age, health and other factors are particularly important, as these issues could feed into the requirement for additional or alternative support. It would also be useful to trace and compare data about grandparent applications and outcomes regarding SGOs, 'lives with' CAOs and adoption orders. There should be consideration as to how the process of applying for an SGO can potentially be simplified, as it has been with 'lives with' CAOs, due to the huge number of litigants in person generally taking proceedings. The arguably clunky application process for a SGO involving the local authority could easily put off potential carers, who then opt for the online, straightforward CAO process. If this latter route is followed, the carer then faces the problem of sharing decision making with others with parental responsibility, which is likely to lead to tensions and disputes. Also, there should be greater public awareness of the SGO route. Although the SGO is still relatively new, it would be interesting to assess, in time, the impact on the child who grows up under a SGO compared to under a CAO, and what difference the enhanced parental responsibility makes.

Finally, special guardians clearly need further support to fulfil their role. This could be particularly relevant for a grandparent special guardian, who may be juggling other adult children in the home, work, retirement and complex needs of the child whilst trying to facilitate contact and manage decision making.

6

Grandparents: Anchors in Uncertain Times, Alternatives to Adoption?

SAMANTHA DAVEY

I. Introduction

Unfortunately, some parents are unable to provide a safe environment for their children due to reasons such as drug and/or alcohol abuse;[1] profound learning disability; mental illness or domestic abuse.[2] Challenging circumstances might make long-term placements necessary for these children via fostering, kinship care (potentially with a special guardianship order in place[3]) or adoption.[4] The state's aim of providing the child with a safe and loving home, outside of parental care, is balanced against other considerations in the process of providing a child with long-term care. One potential consideration, in the context of determining a 'best fit' long-term placement, is the child's identity rights. The child's identity is protected via Article 8 of the European Convention on Human Rights (ECHR), the right to respect for 'private and family life'.[5] Identity is also protected via the United Nations Convention on the Rights of the Child (UNCRC) via Articles 7 and 8. Article 8 UNCRC identifies the need to protect 'family relations' as an aspect of identity, which is traditionally construed in terms of the parent/child relationship. It is argued that 'family relations' envisaged under Article 8 UNCRC can be interpreted to apply also between the child and others in his or her wider kinship or cultural network, such as grandparents. While this chapter largely focuses on legal frameworks within UK law, the observations within the chapter could be argued to be applicable within other European jurisdictions with similar systems in place for children in care and, thus, similar flaws in the decision-making processes. This

---

[1] B Featherstone, A Gupta and S Mills, *The role of the social worker in adoption – ethics and human rights: an enquiry* (London, The British Association of Social Workers, 2018) 33.

[2] ibid 13.

[3] Provided for under the Children Act 1989, s 14A. For more detail on special guardianship orders, see Chapter 5 of this volume.

[4] Adoption and Children Act 2002, s 46.

[5] *Gaskin v UK* App no 10454/83 (ECtHR, 7 July 1989).

chapter pays particular attention to children with pre-existing relationships with their grandparents, and to the potential relevance of the grandparent/grandchild relationship when children cannot be raised by their parents.

So far, scholarly attention on the child's identity rights under the UNCRC has been focused on the child's right to know his or her origins.[6] Research on the protection of 'family relations' envisaged under Article 8 UNCRC has tended to explore the protection of relationships between children and parents. This chapter provides a unique contribution to academic literature in this field because of its emphasis on the protection of extended 'family relations' in the development of the child's identity itself and the role of decision-making processes by child welfare professionals and legal practitioners in upholding or failing to protect a child's identity rights. This research has focused on largely ignored aspects of the UNCRC, such as the need for a more complex account of identity. It is argued that the child's identity, and more specifically the 'family relations' that may form part of that identity, is an important consideration that may need to be balanced against other competing interests, such as the child's best interests under Article 3 UNCRC and right to protection from 'physical … injury or abuse' under Article 9 UNCRC. The child's right to participate in decision making is protected under Article 12 UNCRC. It cannot be presumed either that children will want to reside with grandparents in all cases. Children, taking into account their evolving capacities, may express a desire not to be raised by or spend time with their grandparents. It is thus acknowledged that there are instances where the need to protect a child from significant harm under Articles 3, 9 and 12 UNCRC will outweigh the importance of protecting a child's 'family relations'. Not all grandparent relationships are beneficial to children, and there may be circumstances where these relationships could even be detrimental, where grandparents are unable to protect their grandchildren from physical or emotional harm, or to raise children in a manner conducive to the protection of children's rights under Articles 3, 9 and 12. Despite the need to balance these competing interests, it is argued that insufficient emphasis is placed on children's identity rights under the UNCRC, even where a measured 'weighing' process is employed when a child's welfare is at stake.

This chapter, exploring the UNCRC from a socio-legal stance, challenges the existing conception of 'identity' and considers potential barriers to the protection of the child's identity rights under Article 8 UNCRC, in the context of decisions about long-term, non-parental care. These factors include insufficient viability assessments that over-emphasise factors such as a carer's age, or the reluctance of social workers to recommend post-adoption contact. While, in practice, many relationships in a child's extended network may be of social, emotional and practical value to children, the focus of this chapter is on grandparents, because

---

[6] S Besson, 'Enforcing the Child's Right to Know Her Origins: Contrasting Approaches under the Convention on the Rights of the Child and the European Convention on Human Rights' (2007) 21 *International Journal of Law, Policy and the Family* 137.

they are often the first prospective carers considered by social workers when birth parents are unable to care for their children.

Research, including work undertaken within chapter 2 of this edited collection by Bendall and Davey, shows that many grandparent/grandchild relationships are beneficial, practically and emotionally, to both grandchildren and grandparents.[7] In fact, there is a growing body of literature that demonstrates that grandparent involvement is associated with improved mental health and positive social behaviour in children.[8] Specifically, it is suggested that, metaphorically and psychologically, those within a child's kinship and cultural networks, such as grandparents, may be powerful 'anchors', linking children to their memories and identities, and 'bridges' to future social and emotional development in adolescent years and adulthood.

This chapter will consider the concept of identity, Family Constellation Theory (FCT) and how a modern conceptualisation of FCT in conjunction with the UNCRC, which encompasses a diverse range of relationships, contributes to understanding both children's identity rights and the benefits of kinship care. While there are many theories that consider the relevance of both genetic and emotional connections, FCT is one of the few psychological theories to focus on the importance of relationships beyond that of the parent and child. Individuals who form part of a child's extended kinship network, such as grandparents, have an important role to play in the context of Article 8 UNCRC and Article 8 ECHR. The discussion will thus consider specific legal provisions of the ECHR and UNCRC. In doing so, the chapter will explore the circumstances in which grandparents become kinship carers and the challenges they may face in doing so, before concluding by exploring the ways in which protection of children's identity can be improved via the grandparent/grandparent relationship.

It is not the purpose of this chapter to argue that grandparent care is always in a child's best interests. Grandparents may, in certain circumstances, be unsuitable carers or be unable to provide care, and in those situations foster care or adoption may be in a child's best interests instead. In cases where grandparents are willing and able to provide care in circumstances where the protection of the child and

---

[7] P Coleman and A Hanlon, *Aging and Development* (Abingdon, Routledge, 2017) 115; V Bengtson, 'Beyond the Nuclear Family: The Increasing Importance of Multigenerational Bonds' (2001) 63 *Journal of Marriage and Family* 1.

[8] J Yorgason, L Padilla-Walker and J Jackson, 'Nonresidential Grandparents' Emotional and Financial Involvement in Relation to Early Adolescent Grandparent Outcomes' (2011) 21 *Journal of Research on Adolescence* 552; B Hayslip Jr and G Smith, *Resilient Grandparent Caregivers: A Strength-Based Perspective* (New York, Routledge, 2013); T Bol and M Kalmijn, 'Grandparents' resources and grandchildren's schooling: Does grandparental involvement moderate the grandparent effect?' (2016) 16 *Social Science Research* 155; A Buchanan and S Attar-Schwartz 'Grandparenting and adolescent well-being: evidence from UK and Israel' (2018) 13 *Contemporary Social Science* 219; B Hayslip and C Fruhauf, *Grandparenting: Influences on the Dynamics of Family Relationships* (London, Springer, 2019); A Buchanan and A Rotkirch (eds), *The Role of Grandparents in the 21st Century* (Abingdon, Routledge, 2020).

his or her identity have been carefully balanced against other fundamental rights, children may receive equally effective (or superior) care from grandparents when compared against other permanence options, such as long-term foster care or an adoption order.[9]

II. Identity and Family Constellations: Who is the Child?

A. How Do We Understand 'Identity'?

The term 'identity' is 'multidimensional'[10] and, as Blauwhoff notes, 'has so far not been given a legal definition.'[11] 'Identity' is a challenging concept to define, but the focus of this chapter is on 'personal identity' encompassing a 'narrative identity', that is the 'continuity of psychological connections between a person's past and present'.[12] Blauwhoff explains that 'In order to be able to create a narrative identity of one's own, it will … often be necessary to tap into the memory that other people may have of ourselves. A narrative identity therefore bridges the historical past to the present and future.'[13] Grandparents have significance in this context, since they can provide an account of children's parents and wider familial connections, as well as the child's historical and genealogical origins. Such knowledge is key in helping a child understand his or her identity and protecting and promoting the child's identity rights.

More specifically, in terms of a human right to *personal* identity, it is apparent that such a right exists under the ECHR[14] and the UNCRC.[15] Marshall observes, however, that 'it is not at all clear what this right actually means'[16] and it can be 'interpreted in different ways'.[17] Marshall observes that 'identity is largely created by social forces', 'moral and social identity … are intelligible only in terms of the social network in which they are an element'.[18] McLaughlin suggests that 'An identity therefore gives an individual's life meaning by framing it in a social and historical context. It provides a bridge between current consciousness and past experiences.'[19] This is especially true for the grandparent/grandchild relationship, as considered in the preceding paragraph.

---

[9] Adoption and Children Act 2002, s 46.

[10] RJ Blauwhoff, *Foundational Facts, Relative Truths: A Comparative Law Study on Children's Right to Know their Genetic Origins* (Mortsel, Intersentia, 2009) 20.

[11] ibid 20.

[12] ibid. See also EH Erikson, *Identity: Youth and Crisis* (New York, Norton, 1968).

[13] Blauwhoff (n 10) 20.

[14] J Marshall, *Personal Freedom through Human Rights Law?* (Leiden, Brill, 2009) 89.

[15] Also see J Marshall, *Human Rights Law and Personal Identity* (Abingdon, Routledge, 2014) 141.

[16] ibid 8.

[17] ibid 85.

[18] Marshall (n 14) 89. See also J Triseliotis, 'Identity and Genealogy in Adopted People' in E Hibbs (ed), *Adoption: International Perspectives* (Madison, CT, International Universities Press, 1991) 35, 35.

[19] K McLaughlin, *Surviving Identity: Vulnerability and the Psychology of Recognition* (East Sussex, Routledge, 2012) 29.

Many adoptive parents and foster carers may have access to information on a child's past, or may have engaged in 'life story'[20] work with the child, mapping out his or her personal history. However, many grandparents are likely to have more detailed knowledge of a child's life, including his or her social connections in the community as well as shared genealogy. As O'Donovan argues, 'Ancestry and identity ... are not a simple matter of linear biological relationships or normative definitions of family but necessarily involve contemplation of kinship – the dual role of blood ties and social structures.'[21] Personal identity, then, can be seen as 'a mixture of genetics and social conditioning',[22] with family relationships at the 'heart of understandings of identity'.[23] Ronen claims that identity is influenced by others around us: 'Identity should not be seen as developing in a vacuum, but rather always through dialogue and sometimes struggles with significant others – those persons who matter to the individual constructing their identity'.[24]

It is argued here, specifically, that in the absence of birth parents, the grandparent/grandchild relationship and thus grandparents are crucial to a child's sense of personal identity. Identity is most often linked to genetic identity, with considerable stress on 'biological origins'[25] in case law[26] and in literature. As Marshall suggests, '[i]nterpreting a right to personal identity in this way seems to connect to strong and emotive language in wider society and in the proliferation of genetic searching, family heritage and genealogy'.[27] Children who are placed into care often have a history based on notes from (sometimes multiple) social workers, rather than on direct first-hand accounts from family members. The stories from the past, which are a notable part of the grandparent role, help children to form a sense of themselves.

The emphasis on genealogy, however, can be seen, for instance, via the historical 'natural parent'[28] presumption, which pointed to a preference for genetic connections over social and emotional connections.[29] Some cases also seemed to indicate a 'hierarchy' in genetics, with birth parents at times favoured over grandparents in residence disputes, even when secure bonds had been developed

---

[20] This is where a document is produced outlining a child's family history.

[21] J Reid 'Lost Identities: denying Children their Family Identity' in R Sheehan, H Rhoades and N Stanley (eds), *Vulnerable Children and the Law: International Evidence for Improving Child Welfare, Child Protection and Children's Rights* (London, Jessica Kingsley, 2012) 235, 236.

[22] Marshall (n 14) 90. See also K O'Donovan, '*Enfants Trouvés*, Anonymous Mothers and Children's Identity Rights' in K O'Donovan and G Rubin (ed), *Human Rights and Legal History* (New York, Oxford University Press, 2000) 237.

[23] Marshall (n 15) 123.

[24] Ya'ir Ronen, 'Redefining the Child's Rights to Identity' (2004) 18 *International Journal of Law, Policy and the Family* 147, 149.

[25] Marshall (n 15) 119.

[26] *Re H (Paternity: Blood Tests)* [1996] 4 All ER 28.

[27] Marshall (n 15) 119.

[28] *Re KD (A Minor) (Ward: Termination of Access)* [1988] AC 806; *Re D (Care: Natural Presumption)* [1999] 1 FLR 134. For discussion, see J Fortin, 'Re D (Care: Natural Parent Presumption) Is blood really thicker than water?' (1999) 11 *Child and Family Law Quarterly* 435.

[29] Fortin (n 28); K Everett and L Yeatman, 'Are some parents more natural than others?' (2010) 22 *Child and Family Law Quarterly* 290.

between children and grandparents via long-term care.[30] Moreover, as Eekelaar observes, grandparents may argue a right to a relationship with a grandchild based on genetics alone.[31] Therefore, if genetics forms part of a child's identity, the arguments that apply in favour of protecting and respecting the parent/child biological link apply to many grandparents too. It is argued that while 'genetics' is an important factor to contemplate, it is not a sufficient reason, by itself, for valuing grandparental impact on identity and for being a preferred alternative to non-consensual adoption. Grandparents, and other kinship carers, may have established strong emotional bonds with children and/or may form an important part of a child's cultural networks. These key relationships may be important in and of themselves, but may also provide a 'doorway' to relationships that make the child feel more connected within himself or herself, strengthening the child's emotional well-being and sense of who he or she is in the world. Grandparents are a tangible connection to the child's immediate family and a 'living' account of the child's past and, where grandparents are related by blood, the child's genealogy.

In fact, during the last two decades, the superior courts have moved away from the 'natural parent' presumption[32] and have placed substantial weight on secure social and emotional connections.[33] As Marshall notes, '[t]he child's genetic parentage plays a large role in his or her identity and is one of the main factors in terms of determining who a person is, but it is not the only factor'.[34] Blauwhoff argues that narrative identity is 'able to accommodate the idea that blood ties could be crucial to a person's identity, but it does not dismiss the importance of having a social family either'.[35] Thus, while genetic identity is important, and relevant from a human rights perspective, the importance of grandparents may in cases where established relationships exist between child and grandparent, largely be seen via well-developed social and emotional bonds. The importance can also be seen where grandparents can help a child to make sense of his or her past and promote a child's sense of 'connectedness' based on detailed knowledge of the child's life, which might be more challenging for unrelated foster carers or adopters.

B. Family Constellation Theory

'Family Constellation Theory',[36] developed by Hellinger and colleagues as a sub-division of family systems theory, is based on the premise that historical and cultural

---

[30] *Re D (Care: Natural Presumption)* [1999] 1 FLR 134.

[31] J Eekelaar, *Family Law and Personal Life* (Oxford, Oxford University Press, 2006) 70.

[32] *Re B (A Child)* [2009] UKSC 5, *Re E-R (A Child)* [2015] EWCA Civ 405; *Re W (A Child)* [2017] 1 WLR 889. For discussion see Everett and Yeatman (n 29).

[33] *Re G (Children)* [2006] UKHL 43.

[34] Marshall (n 15) 127.

[35] Blauwhoff (n 10) 21.

[36] SR Liebermeister, *The Roots of Love, A Guide to Family Constellation: Understanding the ties that bind us and the path to freedom* (Cambridge, Perfect Publishers, 2006).

origins underpin our identity, relationships and interactions with wider civil society.[37] The foundation of the theory is that members of a family are interconnected and part of an 'organic system',[38] which may be viewed as 'a complex system of atomic particles [that] is affecting and being affected by every other part'.[39] The act of adoption[40] then can be seen as not just complex legally, but potentially complex emotionally, due to the fact of removing a child from one psychological family system and 'transplanting' him or her into another. As Deblasio observes, '[t]he legal ties may be terminated, but the human bonds may be less straightforward to eradicate'.[41] Although for the purposes of the law the child has been integrated into a new family, the child's bonds to birth family such as grandparents may persist. It is argued that, depending on the circumstances, these bonds may be linked to the child's identity.

Family Constellation Theory is based on the principles of 'order' and 'belonging', emphasising that every family member has his or her place in the system.[42] Although Hellinger's analysis focused on a more traditional conception of the family, often individuals outside of the birth family could nonetheless form part of the 'system'. 'Family members' can therefore include those genetically connected, but also those with a role in a child's life, such as parents and grandparents, and also others with a role in children's lives, such as step-parents. Sélénée observes that, according to FCT, the drive to belong 'is part of what binds us to our family system and to each other'.[43] The importance of 'belonging' is crucial in the context of a child's identity after parental separation and adoption, so FCT is a helpful theoretical basis and framework to consider in the context of identity. The Theory entails exploration of a much wider family network, therefore reflecting the diversity of connections and influences on a child, beyond his or her parents. Thus FCT involves exploring how wider familial networks, including grandparents and even now deceased and absent family members, may affect the dynamics of the family unit.[44] Liebermeister notes a surprising phenomenon whereby 'a later member of the family, a child, identifies with an earlier family member without having any idea that this is happening. He carries his relative's feelings as his own and acts out that person's life ...'.[45] These consequences are based on what is referred to by Hellinger et al as the 'systematic conscience',[46] which is intangible but felt by all

---

[37] B Hellinger, G Weber and H Beaumont, *Love's Hidden Symmetry: What Makes Love Work in Relationships* (Phoenix, AZ, Zeig, Tucker & Co, 1998).

[38] Liebermeister (n 36) 5.

[39] ibid 2.

[40] Provided for under the Adoption and Children Act 2002.

[41] L Deblasio, *Adoption and Law: The Unique Personal Experiences of Birth Mothers in Adoption Proceedings* (Abingdon, Routledge, 2021) 157.

[42] M Sélénée, *Connected Fates, Separate Destinies* (London, TJ Books, 2021) 4.

[43] ibid 5.

[44] Liebermeister (n 36) 7.

[45] ibid 33.

[46] Hellinger et al, 3–4 (n 18).

members in a family system. Adoption itself has an impact on the child, his or her parents, grandparents and others within the family system.[47] The absent child has an intangible, emotional effect on his or her birth family and vice versa.

A probable issue with an adoptive placement is that children may carry unconscious conflicts with them into new relationships. Research by Howe, for instance, has shown that birth mothers are often 'psychologically present'[48] in the minds of adopted children, regardless of their physical absence. While placement with grandparents may not be without challenges, it is argued that protecting relationships with extended kin may provide increased conscious understanding of deeper family conflicts that are felt by the child (and his or her carers). These conflicts could exist because of neglect and abuse the child has experienced, due to the absence of the birth parents, or due to other factors that impact on the child's psyche. Continuity within a safe, supportive, social, cultural network familiar to the child may be more beneficial in this context.

Although application of FCT may draw scepticism on the basis that it has 'esoteric'[49] origins, phenomenological research[50] demonstrates that it provides a useful way of understanding lived experiences and identity. It has also had useful application in therapeutic contexts.[51] Similarly to the application of relationality considered in chapter 2 of this volume, the theory considers the importance of wider familial networks to well-being and one's sense of connectedness. Family Constellation Theory can be conceptualised to assign roles to family members (which may include those without genetic links, who have shaped a child's life in some way) and bring order to a diverse range of relationships that may affect and shape a child's identity.

While FCT tends to centre around the parent/child relationship, many other types of relationships are considered to impact on personal identity, since the Theory places an emphasis on family 'systems'. Grandparents are part of this family system, with many grandparents forming close, loving bonds with their grandchildren. Grandparent relationships may affect a child's development and identity, consciously and unconsciously.[52] The importance of extended family as part of a child's identity is also reflected in aspects of the UNCRC. Despite the significance of grandparents historically, grandparents lack recognition of their rights in English law.[53] This author argues that the insufficient priority placed on the grandparent/grandchild relationship may, in some circumstances, serve to weaken

---

[47] M Grand, *The Adoption Constellation: New Ways of Thinking About and Practicing Adoption* (Scotts Valley, CA, Create Space, 2010).

[48] D Howe, *Adopters on Adoption: Reflections on parenthood and children* (London, BAAF, 1996) 4.

[49] C Watters, *Mental Health and Wellbeing: Intercultural Perspectives* (London, Bloomsbury, 2019) 97.

[50] ibid.

[51] ibid.

[52] A Green, 'Grandparents, communicative memory and narrative identity' (2019) 47 *Oral History* 81.

[53] F Kaganas and C Piper, 'Grandparent contact – another presumption?' (2020) 42 *Journal of Social Welfare and Family Law* 176.

protection of children's identity rights and fail to acknowledge the importance of grandparents within the 'family constellation'.

Liebermeister observes that the loss of a parent (or parental figure), through either death or an extended absence in the provision of care, is traumatic and affects the child's psyche.[54] Thus, removal of a child into care and, potentially, a subsequent adoption is not always associated with improvement in mental health.[55] Children may, for instance, suffer 'genealogical bewilderment'[56] through the distress of not knowing about their birth family or having uncertain knowledge of them (unless children have suffered severe neglect and/or abuse). In a minority of cases,[57] adoption placements may be disrupted or break down completely.[58] Lansdown suggests it is essential to consider whether adoption 'is consistent with the promotion of the child's rights to an identity'[59] and indicates there should be a presumption that 'as far as is possible, there should be continued and extensive contact with members of the birth family'.[60] Certainly, when the matter of adoption is viewed through the lens of FCT, the child may be affected negatively by absent birth parents. Most children with less biographical information tend to fare worse emotionally than children who have more knowledge of their roots and have had placements with kinship carers prior to adoption.[61] Thus, perhaps some of these difficult feelings could be mitigated with more information, but this does not address the loss of the relationships or of the opportunity to develop these relationships. It is believed, for instance, that even very young children may experience feelings of grief or loss when separated from a birth parent (or another primary carer). Thoburn argues that

> too little attention has been paid, in some of the cases that have gone badly wrong, to the child's likely behaviour when separated from carers to whom he or she is attached. This applies especially to pre-verbal children, toddlers and disabled children whose only way of articulating their confusion and grief … will be to behave in a way which may bring them into conflict with the parents they currently live with.[62]

Many children with adoptive parents are settled in their placements and may not prioritise discovery of genetic and cultural origins. Nonetheless, research shows

---

[54] Liebermeister 102–03 (n 36).

[55] A Paine et al, 'Early adversity predicts adoptees' enduring emotional and behavioral problems in childhood' (2020) 30 *European Child Adolescent Psychiatry* 721.

[56] R Barn and N Mansuri, '"I Always Wanted to Look at Another Human and Say I Can See That Human in Me": Understanding Genealogical Bewilderment in the Context of Racialised Intercountry Adoptees' (2019) 3 *Genealogy* 71.

[57] Often unreported.

[58] J Selwyn, D Wijedasa and S Meakings, *Beyond the Adoption Order: Challenges, Interventions and Adoption Disruptions* (London, BAAF, 2015).

[59] G Lansdown, 'The welfare of the child in contested proceedings' in M Ryburn (ed), *Contested Adoptions: Research, law, policy and practice* (Aldershot, Ashgate Publishing, 1994) 70.

[60] ibid.

[61] Paine et al (n 55).

[62] J Thoburn, 'Reunification from care: the "permanence" option that has most to offer, but the lowest success rate' (2009) 18 *Seen and Heard* 44, 48.

that often even children who are happy within their adopted families may still feel conflicted about where their 'loyalties'[63] lie, which may cause emotional difficulties. According to Blauwhoff, 'adopted children are more likely than other children to suffer identity problems'.[64] Children may experience negative emotions other than grief later in life. Liebermeister, for instance, suggests that 'an adopted person frequently remains angry with the original parents'.[65] They may also experience anger towards their adoptive parents.[66] These feelings of anger are often associated with a sense of rejection, which is a common occurrence with adoptive arrangements,[67] regardless of how loving the adoptive parents might be. Although kinship placements may still present emotional challenges for children and carers alike, living with grandparents may help to salve a child's anger. Being raised by grandparents may have an 'anchoring' effect, since it enables children to maintain some link with their previous life with their birth parents, helping to ground a sense of personal identity and protect a child's rights under Article 8 ECHR and Article 8 UNCRC.

This sense of 'identity' is reinforced not simply via 'genetics' but through the importance of culture. Grandparents may be able to provide details about a child's cultural background to 'fill in gaps' for the child. Grandparents may be central figures in outlining a child's historical origins and in facilitating relationships with other birth family members, including the parents. In some cases, where appropriate, safe and in accordance with their wishes, children may be able to have contact with birth parents (either indirect or direct). Grandparents may therefore be able to use their role within the 'family system' to foster the development of a future relationship during adulthood (in accordance with the child's wishes and evolving capacities under Article 12 UNCRC).

Indeed, it is important to recognise the value of existing connections beyond the parent/child relationship and the impact of these on children's sense of identity. The child cannot be seen in isolation from the family unit. Herring has considered the importance of 'relationality',[68] in that a child's rights (such as identity) may be 'interrelated' with the rights and interests of other family members rather than be opposed to them.[69] He suggests that '[i]n a radical sense our relationships

---

[63] C Thomas, *Adoption for Looked After Children: Messages from research* (London, BAAF, 2013) 25.

[64] Blauwhoff (n 10) 8. See also HD Grotevant et al, 'Adoptive Identity and Adjustment from Adolescence to Emerging Adulthood: A Person-Centred Approach' (2017) 53 *Developmental Psychology* 2195.

[65] Liebermeister 196 (n 36).

[66] Howe (n 48) 87.

[67] D Hindle and G Shulman, *The Emotional Experience of Adoption: A Psychoanalytic Perspective* (Abingdon, Routledge, 2008) 81; HJ Hamilton, *The Secrets in My Eyes* (Manitoba, Friesen Press, 2016); S Roszia and A Davis Maxon, *Seven Core Issues in Adoption and Permanency* (London, Jessica Kingsley, 2019) 62–80.

[68] J Herring, *Law and the Relational Self* (Cambridge, Cambridge University Press, 2020). See also Barn and Mansuri (n 56).

[69] See ch 2 of this volume for detailed discussion of the importance of 'relationality' and its role in adapting the law and legal practices to acknowledge the importance of extended kin, such as grandparents.

constitute ourselves.[70] This perspective also applies in relation to the child's identity, since it is not just the child's identity and emotions that may be affected adversely by adoption; the entire family constellation may be affected, and there may be a rippling effect on the emotional well-being of birth parents and the extended family. Deblasio notes that 'the adversarial family justice system creates a damaging interplay of blame and trauma, causing long-term harm to families.'[71] As Parr highlights, 'When their child is finally adopted birth relatives are often left powerless and with an immense of loss.'[72] Thus, placement outside of the birth family and the child's existing social and emotional connections can affect the welfare and rights of others connected to him or her, including grandparents. As noted in chapter 2 by Bendall and Davey, rights cannot always be treated in isolation, with a 'relational' approach being crucial towards understanding the relevance of grandparent/grandchild relationships.

While placement with grandparents will not necessarily eliminate all the emotional and practical challenges a child will face, grandparent care may make the transition from parental care easier. Where there are pre-existing relationships, placement with a grandparent may be a more 'incremental' step and be less of an upheaval for a child, especially where a child has lived with or spent a considerable amount of time with a grandparent. Cantwell, for instance, has observed:

> Among the identified advantages of kinship care are preservation of the child's family, community and cultural ties; avoidance of trauma resulting from moving in with strangers; and less likelihood of multiple placements. However, kinship or friendship is no guarantee of welfare, protection and ability to cope.[73]

Thus, it is suggested that the priority should be protecting pre-existing relationships between grandparents (along with other kinship carers) and grandchildren. In the case of children, including those placed into care at birth, retention of links with grandparents, birth family and other members of the child's extended network is important when viewed through the lens of Article 8 ECHR and Article 8 UNCRC. Kinship placements provide the benefit of continued connection to birth family, acknowledge the extended family's interests and facilitate direct connection to a family framework. The kinship network is crucial since it encompasses genetic, social and emotional connections within which children's identities are firmly embedded. While it is important to protect a child's right to identity, encompassing his or her ties to extended kin, of course this cannot be at the expense of a child's emotional and physical well-being. Such placements must, ultimately, be in the child's best interests (ie within the scope of Article 3 UNCRC).

---

[70] J Herring, *Vulnerable Adults and the Law* (Oxford, Oxford University Press, 2016) 12.

[71] Deblasio (n 41) 2.

[72] V Parr, 'The Forgotten Corner of the Adoption Triangle' (2005) 15 *Seen and Heard* 43.

[73] N Cantwell, 'The Human Rights of Children in the Context of Formal Alternative Care' in W Vandenhole et al (eds), *Routledge International Handbook of Children's Rights Studies* (Abingdon, Routledge, 2015) 257, 263.

As considered in detail later, weak viability assessments may mean that the child's best interests, and the benefits of a kinship placement (with a grandparent, for instance), may not be explored sufficiently. It is argued that every regard ought to be given to the possibility of grandparent care, where it is safe and possible to do so, due to the importance of the kinship link to the child's identity.

C. Identity, Race and Culture

As established previously, the importance of the grandparent/grandchild relationship to identity may extend beyond a rudimentary understanding of genetics and the value of social and emotional bonds. O'Donovan observes the intersectionality between individual and group identity: 'The focus on context demands we pay attention to all strands of identity such as ethnicity, culture, race, class and that we belong to multiple identity categories.'[74] These features of identity are also crucial in the formation of wider bonds within cultures and communities,[75] which may serve children throughout their lives. It is argued, therefore, that grandparents not only have a genetic connection that it is important to acknowledge (and, where appropriate, protect), but also, often, have an important role within the 'family system' in helping children make sense of highly specific features of their identity, such as culture, religion and ethnicity. Grandparent care also increases the likelihood of encouraging and protecting ethnic and cultural identity, which are important factors when professionals make decisions about long-term care and in the context of FCT. This is relevant as regards non-consensual adoption cases, where adoption might be the preferred option over grandparent care.

Until the Adoption and Children Act 2002 was amended, there was a requirement to give 'due consideration' to race (and thus racial matching) in the adoption process. This was repealed by section 3 of the Children and Families Act 2014 to speed up the adoption process, especially for children from ethnic minorities who tend to be over-represented in the care system.[76] This repeal mirrors the approach taken in US law, which amended equivalent legislation on adoption law, the MEPA,[77] in 1996.[78] This amendment received 'vociferous'[79] opposition and was seen as minimising the importance of black culture.[80] Similarly, there has been concern about the removal of the 'due consideration' requirement within English

---

[74] O'Donovan (n 22) 242–43.

[75] Marshall (n 15) 145.

[76] For discussion, see L Ferguson. 'Families in All Their Subversive Variety: Over-Representation, the Ethnic Child Protection Penalty, and Responding to Diversity Whilst Protecting Children' (2014) 63 *Studies in Law, Politics, and Society* 43.

[77] Multiethnic Placement Act 1994.

[78] E Bartholet, 'Contested Child Protection Policies' in JG Dwyer (ed), *The Oxford Handbook of Children and the Law* (Oxford, Oxford University Press, 2020) 415, 427.

[79] RR Banks, 'Race and the Adoption of Children' in Dwyer (ed) (n 78) 227, 229.

[80] ibid 230.

law.[81] Although this shift in approach affects all ethnic minority children, it has the most impact on black children because they comprise the highest proportion of ethnic minority children in care.[82] Hughes argues that the removal of 'due consideration' is the 'wrong solution'[83] to the problem of the high number of black children in care and that it is 'discriminatory'.[84] Arguably too, such an approach minimises the importance of 'race' as a component of identity, covered by Article 8 UNCRC. Hughes notes that

[a]dopted children have to deal with the fact of being adopted. The additional emotional burden to their identity development and sense of self as a result of being inappropriately placed is an unnecessary burden which we consider is not in their interests.[85]

Trying to racially match children protects the development of their identity in many ways, including by increasing the likelihood that children will be provided with 'tools'[86] on how to navigate racial hostilities. Transracial placements can undermine children's self-confidence and self-esteem.[87] Children may feel anger due to powerlessness, or a sense of being 'different',[88] especially in such placements.[89] Such adoptions may 'reinforce power imbalances by using white middle-class standards'.[90] Moreover, adoption may give 'children a legal status that may leave them feeling alienated in their own culture'[91] if they are not placed with adopters of the same race. According to O'Halloran, 'the emerging consensus is that where possible placement arrangements should reflect a child's ethnic background and cultural identity'.[92] Hughes and Wilson reflect that

a black child's race, culture and language are central to who they are and the person they become in later life. Black children have many issues to grapple with and their identity and sense of belonging are fundamental to their ability to think of themselves positively ...[93]

---

[81] J Hughes, 'Black children's lives matter: NAGALRO campaign to reinstate the repealed provisions of s1(5) Adoption and Children Act 2002' (2021) 31 *Seen and Heard* 62.

[82] Department for Education, *Children looked after in England including adoption 2019 to 2020* (ONS, Department for Education, 2020) at https://explore-education-statistics.service.gov.uk/find-statistics/children-looked-after-in-england-including-adoptions/2020.

[83] Hughes (n 81) 62.

[84] ibid.

[85] ibid.

[86] J Hughes, 'The Acculturation Process of Adella' (2020) 30 *Seen and Heard* 35, 35.

[87] ibid; Banks (n 79) 235–36.

[88] J Feast and T Philpot, *Searching Questions: Identity, Origins and Adoption* (London, British Association for Adoption and Fostering, 2003); T Patel, *Mixed-Up Kids? Race, identity and social order* (Lyme Regis, Russell House, 2009) 50–51.

[89] K O'Donovan, 'Interpretations of children's identity rights' in D Fottrell (ed), *Revisiting Children's Rights* (Dordrecht, Kluwer, 2000) 73 at 74.

[90] Patel (n 88).

[91] Lansdown (n 59) 71.

[92] K O'Halloran, *The Welfare of the Child* (Abingdon, Routledge, 1999) 253.

[93] J Hughes and Y Wilson, 'NAGALRO's Black Children's Lives Matter: Response to the "Adoption Strategy – Achieving Excellence Everywhere"' (2022) 32 *Seen and Heard* 63.

Most black children tend to enter the care system at an older age[94] and are thus more likely to have pre-existing relationships with their grandparents compared to white children. The removal of children from ethnic minorities (especially black children) into care and placement for subsequent adoption has given rise to concern about whether sufficient protection is provided to these children's identities.[95] Huh and Reid express concern that 'if children are uprooted from their own culture, their sense of ethnic identity may become confused or conflicted'.[96] Moreover, Banks argues that '[a] denial of carers of the need, early in a child's life, for accurate ethnic identification may lead to intense anxiety, confusion[97] and later anger when racial slurs are encountered'.[98] In these circumstances, where grandparents share the same racial characteristics, such placements may be of particular importance to help to protect children's identity rights under Article 8 ECHR and Article 8 UNCRC, through acknowledging their ethnicity and/or culture. Where children are trans-racial, matters may be more complicated, as a child may identify more closely with one race than another. In such circumstances, grandparent care may need to be more closely scrutinised to ensure that a grandparents' cultural and social networks will serve the child's need to develop his or her racial and cultural identity. It is also argued that it is of particular importance in such cases to make children central to these decision-making processes about their understanding of 'who' they are and 'where' they want to live, in accordance with a child's evolving capacities under Article 12 UNCRC.

In fact, the European Court of Human Rights (ECtHR) has regarded ethnic identity as an essential component of individual identity that is protected under Article 8 ECHR.[99] Marshall articulates the importance of protecting minority rights under Article 8: 'When your identity is different to that of the majority in any society ... there is the potential vulnerability to prejudice and discrimination.'[100] Grandparent care may be beneficial to children from ethnic minorities, since grandparents may be of the same race and be part of the same social and cultural networks as the grandchild. Thus, an awareness of identity and origins is important in developing a sense of personal identity.[101] It is argued that identity is formed via place within a family unit and through individual relationships, such as the grandparent/grandchild relationship. Although some children may experience a sense of grief and loss when separated from their parents, for black children especially, the likelihood is greater that adoption will involve loss of

---

[94] ibid.

[95] Hughes (n 81).

[96] NS Huh and WJ Reid, 'Intercountry, transracial adoption and ethnic identity: A Korean example' (2000) 43 *International Social Work* 75, 75.

[97] Patel (n 88) 106–07.

[98] N Banks, 'Issues of attachment, separation and identity in contested adoptions' in Ryburn (ed) (n 59) 105, 118.

[99] *Ciubotaru v Moldova* App no 27138/04 (ECtHR, 27 April 2010).

[100] Marshall (n 15) 157.

[101] Banks (n 98) 119.

cultural as well as familial connections due to the relative paucity of carers available from ethnic minorities in proportion to the number of children from ethnic minorities in care.[102] Therefore, the protection of 'identity' and potential benefits of grandparent care are even more important for children from ethnic minorities, where children themselves express a wish to maintain these relationships.

Recent research by the Family Rights Group into local authorities seeking to create or re-establish links between children in care and their wider familial and friendship networks, has shown that these relationships are valued by young people. Children in care seek to 'develop their sense of identity'[103] and find the maintenance of kinship networks or 'relational stability'[104] beneficial to their well-being. Arguably, where grandparent care is not appropriate, 'open adoption' (ie adoption with contact taking place between children and their birth family) should be explored more fully. The difficulty is that most adoptions are 'closed'[105] and take place without face-to-face contact between children and their parents or extended birth family, including grandparents. Ryburn has argued that adoption would benefit from 'flexibility and inclusiveness', for example by maintaining contact between children and natural grandparents post-adoption.[106] There is intrinsic value in protecting children's identity via the maintenance of grandparent relationships, where it is safe and in a child's wider best interests under Articles 3, 9 and 12 UNCRC to do so.

D. The Value of Kinship Care to Identity

While 'identity' is often drawn from conscious, established relationships, the power of the unconscious should not be underestimated. Most adoptions are of children between 1 and 4 years of age,[107] a time of significant growth of neural networks[108] and unconscious learning.[109] Children learn skills, such as acquiring language, from their experiences. but may have no conscious awareness of doing so.[110] Arguably, then, these important developmental processes also facilitate the

---

[102] J Selwyn, L Frazer and A Fitzgerald, *Finding Adoptive Families for Black, Asian and Black Mixed-Parentage Children: Agency policy and practice* (London, NCH, 2004).

[103] Family Rights Group, *Lifelong Links: Embedding practice* (Oxford, Family Rights Group, 2022) 5.

[104] ibid 16.

[105] E Neil, 'Rethinking adoption and birth family contact: is there a role for the law?' [2019] *Family Law* 1178.

[106] Ryburn (ed) (n 59) 17.

[107] Department for Education, *Children looked after in England including adoptions* (London, Department for Education, 2021).

[108] D Siegel, *The Developing Mind: How Relationships and the Brain Interact to Shape Who We Are*, 3rd edn (New York, Guildford Press, 2020).

[109] ibid.

[110] J Dunn, K Kirsner and S Lewandowsky, *Implicit Memory: Theoretical issues* (Abingdon, Taylor and Francis, 2014) 249.

unconscious development of identity vis-à-vis familial relationships. Benions suggests:

> It is common knowledge that even little children who are too young to understand the biological significance of their parents to them, can accept that several people may be important to them without confusion. For instance, two year olds already know that Granny and Grandpa are significant to them, as well as Mummy and Daddy.[111]

Children can be affected by parental separation in various ways, such as a sense of divided loyalties. Blauwhoff argues that unconscious loyalty towards birth parents may be innate:

> Since loyalty is represented ... as a function of nature rather than nurture, it would be understandable why so many adopted children seem to experience identity problems, because loyalty towards the socio-legal parents would almost irretrievably entail a form of disloyalty towards birthparents.[112]

This type of unconscious conflict could be minimised with the retention of familial links via a kinship placement or an 'open adoption', as considered earlier.[113] Research has demonstrated that many children removed from home sought out their birth families because they had 'become their main point of personal identity'.[114] Therefore, regardless of whether children have memories of birth family, they have an impact on children's psyche. As Ronen points out, 'the child's loss of earlier relationships along with all traces of their pre-adoption identity is widely recognised as potentially damaging to some children'.[115] For children who maintain a grandparent/grandchild relationship, the grandmother especially can be seen as a 'reservoir of memories and connections to their social network'.[116] Reid argues that extended family are important to identity:

> Ancestry and identity ... are not a simple matter of linear biological relationships or normative definitions of family but necessarily involve consideration of kinship – the dual role of blood ties and social structures.[117]

Grandmothers thus are often a 'bridge' to extended kinship and cultural networks, which can be beneficial for children's welfare. These connections help to improve children's sense of 'belonging' and 'identity', which can be more challenging in adoptive placements, since adopted children often feel they do not 'fit in'.[118]

---

[111] R Benions, 'Natural Contact for Children in Care' (1992) *Seen and Heard* 31, 32.

[112] Blauwhoff (n 10) 14.

[113] Thoburn (n 62). See also PA Costa, A Gubello and F Tasker, 'Intentional Kinship through Caring Relationships, Heritage and Identity: Adoptive Parents' Inclusion of Non-Biological and Non-Affinal Relationships on Family Maps' (2021) 5 *Genealogy* 85.

[114] C Hardy, 'Permanence in Practice' (1995) 6 *Seen and Heard* 28, 32.

[115] Ronen (n 24) 154.

[116] A Souralova, *New Perspectives on Mutual Dependency in Caregiving* (Abingdon, Taylor and Francis, 2016) 101.

[117] Reid (n 21) 237.

[118] Howe (n 48) 87.

Therefore grandparents are an important part of the 'family system' or 'family constellation', and may help to mitigate feelings of loss and anger as well as the trauma that can result from separation from and/or mistreatment by parents.[119] Kinship care can be valuable in 'reining in the damage to challenging children, especially given that the children's needs may be volatile, intermittent and flexible'.[120] This is particularly the case for older children, who are likely to have memories of and bonds with their birth family. As mentioned, statistically most adoptions take place between the ages of 1 and 4. Banks suggests that adoption placements for children aged between 1 and 4 are often perceived as unlikely to have problems, when in fact around 54 per cent of such children demonstrate difficult behaviours, including problems sleeping, eating, concentrating or managing emotions.[121] Therefore, decisions regarding permanent placements for children warrant the careful balancing of the potential benefits and dis-benefits of particular kinship arrangements, against the possible benefits and dis-benefits of adoption.

Despite the clear advantages that come with the stability of an adoption placement, research shows that adoption is far from perfect. Placement with a family or friend carer, followed by SGOs or residence orders, are far less likely to face placement disruption than when children are placed with unrelated carers[122] and children are 'overwhelmingly'[123] positive about their kinship care experiences, despite the lack of financial and practical report received by carers (such as grandparents) when compared against adoptive parents.[124] Therefore, where it is possible for grandparent care to take place (or, indeed, other kinship placements) there is a robust argument for doing so, based on the importance of protecting existing social and emotional connections and integration into cultural and social networks, which may be beneficial to the child.

Although adoption is sometimes treated as a 'holy grail' for each child, as Deblasio argues, 'the system cannot guarantee that children are safer in care or that adoption will be the happy ending'.[125] Therefore, it can be concluded that while adoption may offer many benefits, grandparent care may have the distinct benefit of enabling children to place themselves within their 'family constellation' and have a firmer sense of identity. Section III explores which rights frameworks may be applicable when children cannot be reunited with their parents and it becomes necessary for social workers to explore long-term placement options.

[119] J Alper and A Edwards, 'Assessing Potential Kinship Placements' in J Alper and D Howe (eds), *Assessing Adoptive Parents, Foster Carers and Kinship Carers* (London, Jessica Kingsley, 2017) 149, 155.
[120] Children and Young Persons Bill 2008 (HL) 17 March 2008, available online at https://publications.parliament.uk/pa/ld200708/ldhansrd/text/80317-0009.htm.
[121] Banks (n 98) 109.
[122] Selwyn et al (n 36).
[123] J Hunt, *Two decades of UK research on kinship care: an overview* (Family Rights Group, 2020) 9.
[124] Kinship, *Out of the Shadows: A vision for kinship care in England* (Kinship, March 2022).
[125] Deblasio (n 41) 61.

III. The ECHR, UNCRC and English Law

A. Law and Policy Frameworks in English Law

The relationships between grandchildren and grandparents must be seen on a spectrum that ranges from a non-existent relationship (ie grandparents who have never met their grandchildren) to grandparents who are heavily involved in the lives of their grandchildren and have developed powerful mutual bonds. These bonds may have been developed via regular contact or through grandparents and grandchildren living together. Some grandparents have served as 'substitute parents',[126] who have taken over care from parents on a temporary or ongoing basis. This caregiving may be an arrangement from birth, or a response to a parenting 'crisis' that has necessitated state intervention. This might include, for instance, Social Services involvement in family life. In these circumstances, children might be cared for or live with their grandparents in an unofficial capacity with the agreement of the mother (who has automatic parental responsibility[127]) or both parents, as appropriate. Such caregiving arrangements might even have been approved by Social Services without a care order in place. In other situations, children might be living with their grandparents with the seal of judicial approval obtained via a court order. This could be through a child arrangements order specifying the child's residence,[128] a special guardianship order,[129] a care order[130] or, in rare cases, an adoption order in favour of grandparents.[131] In other circumstances, grandparents may put themselves forward as carers and may be rejected as a form of alternative care. As considered below, there are cases where this may be due to the lack of an in-depth viability assessment.

Under section 22C(7)(a) of the Children Act 1989, when a child is looked-after, local authorities must give preference to relatives or friends as connected person foster carers. Moreover, under section 22(4)(d) of the Act, local authorities are duty-bound to consider 'any other person whose wishes and feelings the authority consider to be relevant' (eg, extended kin such as grandparents) before placing children with unrelated carers (either as long-term foster placements, or short-term foster placements preceding removal of the child into a different family unit and the subsequent making of placement and adoption orders or fostering for adoption placements). When an adoption order is made and the welfare checklist is applied under section 1(4)(f) of the Adoption and Children Act 2002, the

---

[126] J Hunt, 'Grandparents as substitute parents in the UK' in Buchanan and Rotkirch (eds) (n 8) 45; J Poehlmann, 'An attachment perspective on grandparents raising their very young grandchildren: Implications for intervention and research' (2003) 25 *Infant Mental Health* 149.
[127] Within the meaning of the Children Act 1989, ss 2–4.
[128] ibid, s 8.
[129] ibid s 14A (as amended by the Adoption and Children Act 2002).
[130] ibid s 31.
[131] *Re T (A Child: Refusal of Adoption Order)* [2020] EWCA Civ 797.

court must consider 'the relationship which the child has with relatives' before making an adoption order. This demonstrates that legislative frameworks make some provision for grandparents, albeit indirectly.

Grandparents' interests (and children's relationships with grandparents) tend to be minimised in adoption proceedings.[132] This is the case, as already considered, despite the fact that many grandparents (and other kinship carers) may have an important 'anchoring' role in their grandchildren's lives via the commitment to and mutual bonds they have formed with each other. Research demonstrates that children themselves see the advantages of living with kin, such as stability, avoidance of being in care, maintaining links with family and friends, maintaining racial and cultural heritage.[133] In kinship placements, some grandparents are not only a stable and continuous presence but also provide a tangible connection to children's genealogical roots.[134] Moreover, as Tingle has found via empirical research, 'They [grandparents] are fearful, too, of their adopted grandchild growing up not knowing its family of birth and of being rootless because of it.'[135] Thus, a child removed from his or her 'family constellation' may grow up with a sense of loss, which serves, at least in part, to define identity. In other words, who we become is formed not just by the significant people present in our lives, but also by the absence of those who are significant and who may provide tangible links to social and cultural networks. This challenge might be avoided via the increased utilisation of grandparent care. This would, in turn, lead to greater protection of children's identity under Article 8 ECHR and the UNCRC (see sections III.B and III.C).

Grandparents may encounter several hurdles to looking after grandchildren who have been subject to care proceedings[136] (see also discussion in chapter 4). They may be rejected as carers for their grandchildren due to unsuccessful initial viability assessments or court-ordered assessments conducted by social workers. In many cases, a thorough assessment will have been undertaken that protects and promotes children's best interests. Unfortunately, due to time constraints or lack of training, often these assessments may not always be of sufficient quality to deliver the best long-term care option for children. Grandparents face additional barriers to challenging unsuccessful assessments, such as the lack of automatic eligibility to legal aid[137] and the lack of automatic party status.[138] This problem has long been an issue in care and adoption proceedings, as shown by David Hinchcliffe's

---

[132] S Davey, *A Failure of Proportion: Non-Consensual Adoption in England and Wales* (Oxford, Hart Publishing, 2020) 167–69.

[133] B Broad, R Hayes and C Rushworth, *Kith and Kin: Kinship Care for Vulnerable Young People* (London, Jessica Kingsley, 2001) 29.

[134] Souralova (n 116) 101.

[135] N Tingle, 'A view of wider family perspectives in contested adoptions' in Ryburn (ed) (n 59) 175, 176.

[136] Care orders are made under the Children Act 1989, s 31.

[137] A Daly, 'Good Relations: Kinship Care in Liverpool, UK and the Views of Professionals on Human Rights' (2021) 13 *Journal of Human Rights Practice* 67.

[138] D Bloomfield, 'A Grandfather at Court: Rights and Reality' [2004] 14 *Seen and Heard* 36.

comments, found within the Hansard debates on the bill that became the Children Act 1989:

> I had fought for a woman who is the grandparent of a six-year-old child. She brought up the child, was the only figure in the child's life and loved and cared for him in the absence of a mother. Then he was adopted, and she had no rights. She could not get legal aid, because she had no right to be heard in court. I am angry about that. The law is wrong.[139]

Tingle is critical of the current legal framework, describing it as 'unjust law that gave scant recognition to the important part that many grandparents play in the lives of their young relatives'.[140] The removal of children for adoption is 'traumatic'[141] for grandparents and could be avoided in many cases by opting for grandparent care. Tingle's research provides a case study of a grandmother and grandchild that is illuminating. The grandmother had regular contact with a child, who was removed from the father due to the father's mental illness and child abuse. Once in care, contact between the child and grandmother was terminated and the child was placed for adoption. The placement was unsuccessful. The social workers involved in the case asked the grandmother for assistance, and once she resumed regular contact with the child, the child's behavioural issues improved considerably.[142] Although this example draws on research from the 1990s,[143] it is just as relevant today. This example shows that where adoption is in the child's best interests, retaining contact with kinship carers such as grandparents may be beneficial to the child's well-being and sense of self. This may thereby protect the child's identity rights under Article 8 ECHR and Article 8 UNCRC.

As already considered, there may be reasons why grandparents may be unsuitable carers. Factors such as age and ill-health, for instance, are relevant welfare factors under section 1(4) of the Adoption and Children Act 2002. There may be cases where grandparents may be neglectful and/or abusive or emotionally harmful to grandchildren due to racist or misogynistic outlooks on life, which may detrimentally affect children's welfare. It is argued, however, that there may be cases where disproportionate weight is attached to grandparental vulnerabilities based on health and age, thus failing to provide sufficient emphasis on the child's right to identity under Article 8 UNCRC and the need to protect diverse relationships extending beyond the textbook 'nuclear' family. In other circumstances, where kinship care is not in a child's best interests, open adoption might be beneficial. Open adoption may provide an opportunity for a child to develop and maintain his social and cultural networks and minimise the child's sense of grief and loss.

---

[139] D Hinchcliffe, HC Deb 27 October 1989, vol 158.
[140] Tingle (n 135) 175.
[141] Featherstone, Gupta and Mills (n 1) 28.
[142] Tingle (n 135) 180.
[143] See, eg, T Festinger, 'Adoption Disruption: Rates and Correlates' in D Brodinzky and M Schechter (eds), *The Psychology of Adoption* (Oxford, Oxford University Press, 1990) 201.

B. Relationships and Identity under the ECHR

The 'family constellation' is relevant to the work undertaken by social workers to find a permanent home for a child who requires substitute care. Social workers develop a 'genogram', mapping out relevant family members who can provide such care. While this document focuses on genetic relatives, it may include extended networks, including step-parents and step-grandparents. When family members are ruled out, other options are explored, such as long-term fostering and adoption. As Kelly and Das observe, '[a]doption can be a remarkably successful intervention in the lives of abandoned and neglected children'.[144] Moreover, for many children in care, it is the best measure to protect them from harm, protect their ECHR rights and promote their welfare within the meaning of the welfare checklist in section 1(4) of the Adoption and Children Act 2002.

Adoption does, however, have serious and irreversible consequences for the relationships between children and their birth families, and may constitute an interference with their mutual right to respect for private and family life under Article 8 ECHR. Non-consensual adoption has been described as 'life changing'[145] and even 'draconian',[146] since it terminates the birth parents' parental responsibility[147] and severs the legal link between children and their birth families. Adoption is typically irrevocable,[148] with few exceptions.[149] The courts are reluctant to set aside adoptions, unless procedural irregularities exist.[150] As Ronen argues, 'the legal system lacks the tools to fully safeguard the child's sense of belonging in each and every case'.[151] Therefore, out of all court orders that can be made in relation to children, adoption has the greatest impact on the child's identity throughout his or her life. While adoption is a long-term measure of care that may protect children's welfare and right to protection from harm under Article 3 ECHR, it may also clash with children's other rights. These include the protection under Article 8 ECHR, the right to respect for private and family life, which protects children's family relationships (including extended family such

---

[144] G Kelly and C Das, 'Should Adoption Be an Option' in D Fottrell (ed), *Revisiting Children's Rights* (Dordrecht, Kluwer, 2000) 254.

[145] Featherstone, Gupta and Mills (n 1) 3.

[146] Kelly and Das (n 144) 254; *P, C and S v UK* [2002] ECHR 604. Also P Parkinson, 'Child protection, permanency planning and children's right to family life' (2003) 17 *International Journal of Law, Policy and the Family* 147.

[147] Parents have automatic parental responsibility when registered as birth parents on the child's birth certificate. Adoption has the effect of terminating this parental responsibility and vesting it in the adoptive parents.

[148] *Webster v Norfolk County Council and others* [2009] EWCA Civ 59.

[149] For discussion of examples of cases where revocation has occurred, see P Morgan, 'ZH v HS & Ors (Application to Revoke Adoption Order): three groups of revocation cases' (2020) 42 *Journal of Social Welfare and Family Law* 246.

[150] *Webster* (n 148).

[151] Ronen (n 24) 156.

as grandparents) and 'identity'[152] rights. It is apparent from the jurisprudence of the ECtHR that the 'mutual enjoyment' between 'grandparent and child, of each other's company'[153] qualifies as family life.[154]

The existence of family life under Article 8 ECHR can, however, be construed as dependent on the reality of personal ties[155] and demonstrable benefit to the child's welfare.[156] Draghici suggests that '[f]amily-related guarantees under the ECHR are therefore a constellation of rights amenable to different organisational criteria'.[157] Thus, depending on the facts of the case, although grandparents will be able to engage rights to a relationship with their grandchildren under Article 8 ECHR, this may be on the basis either of a right to respect for private life or of a right to respect for family life.[158] According to the ECtHR, children have the right to know facts pertaining to their identity,[159] and 'identity' can be regarded as the 'inner core'[160] of one's right to respect for private life under Article 8 ECHR. The UNCRC, especially Article 8, has relevance under the umbrella of Article 8 ECHR. It is argued that the right to identity under the UNCRC, encompassing the right to 'family relations', may also be protected under Article 8 ECHR. The UNCRC has, since its conception, been influential on the ECHR and has importance for the ECtHR's interpretation of identity. Furthermore, 'identity' is encompassed within the child's best interests, which is not only a substantive right protected by Article 3 UNCRC but is also protected within the scope of Article 8 ECHR.[161]

C. Identity and the UNCRC

Although the UNCRC is non-binding, it is the most authoritative legal document on children's rights[162] and an 'important interpretative tool'.[163] This is because it provides more detail on the individual rights of children compared with the ECHR. Moreover, the UNCRC includes a cluster of 'familial' rights,[164] and provides for

---

[152] *Mikulić v Croatia* [2002] 1 FCR 720. See also Y Al Tamimi, 'Human Rights and the Excess of Identity: A Legal and Theoretical Inquiry into the Notion of Identity in Strasbourg Case Law' (2018) 27 *Social and Legal Studies* 283.

[153] *L v Finland* [2000] 2 FLR 118, para 101.

[154] *Monaco de Gallicchio v Argentina* Comm No 400/1990 HRC (3 April 1995).

[155] *Todorova v Italy* App no 33932/06 (ECtHR, 13 January 2009).

[156] S Choudhry and J Herring, *European Human Rights and Family Law* (Oxford, Hart Publishing, 2010) 271.

[157] C Draghici, *The Legitimacy of Family Rights in Strasbourg Case Law* (Oxford, Hart Publishing, 2017) 32.

[158] *Marckx v Belgium* App no 6833/74 (ECtHR, 13 June 1979).

[159] *Gaskin* (n 5).

[160] *Jäggi v Switzerland* App no 58757/00 (ECtHR, 13 July 2006).

[161] *Gaskin* (n 5). See also J Collinson, 'Making the best interests of the child a substantive human right at the centre of national level expulsion decisions' (2020) 38 *Netherlands Quarterly of Human Rights* 169.

[162] G Van Bueren, *The International Law on the Rights of the Child* (Leiden, Brill, 1995).

[163] U Kilkelly, 'The Impact of the Convention on the case-law of the European Court of Human Rights' in D Fottrell (ed), *Revisiting Children's Rights* (Dordrecht, Kluwer, 2000) 87.

[164] See Arts 7–9 UNCRC.

the collective rights of children and adults, via provisions including Articles 5, 7, 8, 20 and 30, and also the United Nations Guidelines for the Alternative Care of Children.[165] Articles 2, 7, 8, 16 and 30 UNCRC, in particular, all have the effect of protecting children from various forms of interference with identity.[166] It is suggested that the UNCRC acknowledges the importance of children's relationships with parents and extended kin. Additionally, it has been argued elsewhere that the UNCRC is so significant that it ought to be considered when determining the proportionality of non-consensual adoption.[167] Lansdown has noted the potential value of the UNCRC in this regard:

> The use ... of the key principles of the [UN] Convention as a yardstick to measure every decision in adoption would begin to offer an external consistency and rigour to the decisions taken in all adoption matters, and in particular to those in the very difficult circumstances where parents and professionals disagree.[168]

In other words, where there is scope for disagreement over which measure of long-term care might be best, including grandparent care, the UNCRC could have a helpful role. Here, it is suggested that the principles of the UNCRC ought to have greater significance when choosing options for long-term care, particularly Article 8 UNCRC. Article 8(1) UNCRC has defined identity as 'including nationality, name and family relations'. Hodgkin and Newell note that 'a child's identity means more than just knowing who one's parents are ... Siblings, grandparents and other relatives can be as, or more, important to the child's sense of identity as his or her parents are.'[169]

Similarly, FCT acknowledges that 'family relations' past and present form part of a child's identity. The cases brought before the ECtHR that have involved contemplation of identity rights recognised under the UNCRC have impliedly (eg *Gaskin v UK*[170]) or explicitly (eg *Odièvre v France*[171]) tended to focus on the children's right to know who they are, rather than on the role of family members in forming personal identity itself. It is argued that a child's 'identity' should be interpreted as broadly as possible, through acknowledging 'family relations' as part of a child's identity itself, as envisaged within the UNCRC. In fact, there are further steps that could be taken to recognise and acknowledge the importance of the 'family constellation' and the impact on a child's identity. Ronen, for example, proposes 'redefining the child's right to identity as a right to state protection of ties meaningful to the child'.[172] This would involve seeking the child's wishes and

[165] Davey (n 132) 176.
[166] R Hodgkin and P Newell, *Implementation Handbook for the Convention on the Rights of the Child*, 3rd edn (New York, UNICEF, 2007) 113.
[167] Davey (n 132) 46–48.
[168] Lansdown (n 59) 67.
[169] Hodgkin and Newell (n 166) 114.
[170] *Gaskin* (n 5).
[171] *Odièvre v France* App no 42326/98 (ECtHR, 13 February 2003).
[172] Ronen (n 24) 147.

feelings about his or her relationships, an exploration of the child's culture and reflection on how 'these ties delineate the child's identity'.[173] Ronen further adds that '[i]dentity should not be seen as developing in a vacuum, but rather always through dialogue and sometimes struggles with significant others – those persons who matter to the individual constructing their identity'.[174] Therefore, relationships that have helped to 'construct' the child's existing identity are deserving of protection if they are capable of protecting the child's welfare. As argued earlier, when considered through the lens of FCT, grandparents may be key to some children, and may help children maintain their existing identities and maintain and develop networks within their existing cultures.

Article 5 UNCRC has a contribution to make towards the concept of how the protection of family ties, in turn, protects identity. It provides that 'States Parties shall respect the responsibilities, rights and duties of parents or, where applicable, the members of the extended family ...' As Kamchedzera observes, Article 5 has a 'flexible conception'[175] of family since it refers to 'members of the extended family or community'.[176] Article 5 also does not hold the child in isolation, since 'Article 5 of the CRC is very much about parents and other key carers',[177] with the Committee on the Rights of the Child making specific reference to grandparents.[178] Hodgkin and Newell observe that there is an 'overall trend towards greater diversity in family size, parental roles and arrangements for bringing up children',[179] and note the increase in grandparent-headed families.[180] This acknowledgement of the importance of protecting diverse family forms can be seen in General Comment 18, where it is stated:

> Where diverse concepts of family, 'nuclear' and 'extended' exist within a State, this should be indicated with an explanation of the degree of protection afforded to each ... State Parties should also indicate whether and to what extent such types of family and their members are recognised and protected by domestic law and practice.[181]

This increased recognition of the impact on a child's well-being of family networks beyond the nuclear family can be seen via FCT. As shown from chapter 10, jurisdictions such as Nepal place emphasis on the importance of extended family networks. This is not necessarily the case, however, in western jurisdictions such as the UK. The UNCRC, interpreted expansively, therefore has an important role to

---

[173] ibid.
[174] ibid 149.
[175] G Kamchedzera, *A Commentary on the United Nations Convention on the Rights of the Child: Article 5 The Child's Right to Appropriate Direction and Guidance* (Leiden, Martinus Nijhoff, 2012) 14–15.
[176] Committee on the Rights of the Child, General Comment No 7, 2005, CRC/C/GC/7/Rev 1, para 15.
[177] Kamchedzera (n 175) 20.
[178] Committee on the Rights of the Child (n 176) para 19.
[179] Hodgkin and Newell (n 166) 76–77.
[180] ibid.
[181] UN Doc HRI/GEN/1/Rev.1, 28 (1994).

play in protecting diverse relationships. Recognition of extended family units, it is argued, is key because of the vital role various family members may play in raising, educating, mentoring and supporting children, but also because of the impact of their absence on a child's psyche. Ronen suggests that Article 5 UNCRC 'supports the psychological rationale for the definition of the right to identity'.[182] In other words, the development of family ties through social and emotional bonds may form part of the child's identity itself. Kamchedzera also considers the importance of Article 5 UNCRC for the grandparent/grandchild relationship, arguing that:

> The correlative duties to the child's rights are ... not on families or communities. Instead, the duties are on individuals who may belong to relevant social units. This interpretation would also justify court decisions that have upheld the rights of grandparents to bring up and to have contact with a child ...[183]

Hodgkin and Newell note that psychological parents (which could include grandparents where a pre-existing relationship exists) 'are intimately bound up in children's identity and thus their rights under article 8'.[184] Therefore, it is argued that Articles 5 and 8 UNCRC, in conjunction, provide comprehensive protection to children's identity through protecting relationships with extended kin, including grandparents. Identity can also be construed to include personal and ancestral history,[185] encompassing various influences since birth, such as carers and the child's race, culture, religion and language, physical appearance, abilities, gender identity and sexual orientation. Thus, the mutually reinforcing nature of Articles 5 and 8 UNCRC highlight the importance of acknowledging the impact of the family constellation on identity.

Preservation of these elements of identity (ie race, culture, religion, etc) can also be argued to be upheld via Article 20 UNCRC. Hodgkin and Newell observe that 'Article 20 ... provides that children deprived of their family environment should where possible have continuity of upbringing, particularly with regard to their ethnic, cultural and linguistic background.'[186]

Moreover, Article 20 UNCRC refers to family, not parents, an important distinction since the state should seek placement within wider family (in accordance with Article 5 UNCRC) before looking elsewhere.[187] Thus, according to Ronen, Article 20 'can be seen as seeking to protect the child's ties to a personal world' despite the lack of explicit reference to identity.[188] Article 20 can further be seen as fitting well within the scope of FCT. While FCT focuses on the effect of 'missing' family members, Article 20 can arguably be viewed as attaching weight to the effect

---

[182] Ronen (n 24) 161.
[183] Kamchedzera (n 175) 20.
[184] Hodgkin and Newell (n 166) 106.
[185] Barn and Mansuri (n 56).
[186] Hodgkin and Newell (n 166) 113.
[187] ibid 278.
[188] Ronen (n 24) 161.

of 'missing' a wider family environment and the ethnic, cultural and linguistic benefits that the birth family can provide. Although adoption can be a very beneficial arrangement for many children, placement with extended kin provides the best form of protection to the identity aspects considered under Article 20, including 'family relations' with extended kinship networks, including grandparents.

Protection of the child's identity can also be seen via Article 30 UNCRC. The provision contains a requirement that children from minority backgrounds have the right to enjoy their own culture and practise their own language and religion. Thus, viewed through the lens of FCT, an adopted child may suffer the loss of important social and emotional heritage drawn from culture, language and religion. Lansdown is critical that current adoption practice 'largely ignores'[189] this facet of Article 30 UNCRC. This failure to acknowledge the importance of culture can be seen from the lack of a requirement to match children with prospective adopters from the same racial group or cultural group. The UNCRC therefore, through the provisions considered above, affords protection to kinship networks and aspects of identity, including ethnicity and culture. The importance of familial networks and the 'absence' of individuals (such as grandparents), which could be interpreted expansively to include absence of recognition of culture, are key elements of FCT. It can be concluded that the UNCRC, directly and indirectly, protections and promotes considerations inherent within FCT.

IV. Law, Carer Assessments, Family Constellations and Identity

The legal frameworks and rights facilitate 'family constellations' and a recognition of the importance of wider families in the formation of 'identity'. Kelly and Das acknowledge that it is legitimate to regard adoption without parental consent as proportionate to the aim of 'protecting children from persistent abuse and neglect',[190] but that adoption will only be a proportionate measure if 'all available efforts have been made and opportunities given to remedy the problems in the child's family'.[191] Viability assessments, which are used to identify potential long-term carers for children in care, can serve as a stumbling block to this process.

Under the Children Act 1989, local authorities have a statutory duty to look for kinship carers. Once a possible carer, such as a grandparent, has been identified, the first stage is a viability assessment. This is an assessment that, according to Morgan,

> will involve looking at the carer's experience of child-raising, their financial and working position, their accommodation, age, health and motivation for being willing to raise

---

[189] Lansdown (n 59) 73.
[190] Kelly and Das (n 144) 260.
[191] ibid 261.

the child, as well as their understanding of why the local authority is concerned about the child.[192]

Social workers may, depending on the local authority, apply the *Good Practice Guide on Assessments* to assist in conducting initial and subsequent care assessments.[193] If the outcome of the viability assessment is positive, the court will order a full assessment to take place under section 14A(8) of the Children Act 1989. In terms of the substance of the assessment, social workers should consider a range of factors and, using their own judgement, determine whether a grandparent is a 'viable' carer. These factors are based on grandparents' personal characteristics, lifestyle choices and opinions. As Hunt identifies, there may be practical constraints that impact on grandparents' ability to 'parent' children, such as 'age, poverty, illness/disability, parenting alone, lower levels of education, the length of time since they have parented, the effect of prior adversities on the children'.[194] Moreover, grandparents may reject a finding of fact in a court of law that a child has sustained neglect or abuse at the hands of a parent.

Research has shown that viability assessments can be of variable quality[195] and they have been subject to judicial criticism.[196] Grandparents may have been subject to comprehensive assessment or to a modest 'viability assessment' (eg grandparents living abroad, contacted via telephone or video conference). These factors, alone or together, are relevant considerations that may militate against the use of grandparent care as an option for the short-term care and/or a long-term placement of a child.

The admirable work of the late Bridget Lindley brought attention to the gaps in the viability assessment process.[197] This work led to the development of a viability tool[198] that is used by some local authorities, but there is yet to be research that fully evaluates the use of the tool and whether it has led to improvement in viability assessments. It is clear, however, that there are still further challenges that may prevent a thorough assessment. Because of inexperience[199] or excessive paperwork, many social workers struggle 'to carry out the kind of complex family work demanded by kinship care',[200] which means that important factors in grandparents'

---

[192] P Morgan, *Family Law* (Oxford, Oxford University Press, 2021) 809.

[193] *Initial Family and Friends Care Assessment: A Good Practice Guide* at https://bettercarenetwork. org/sites/default/files/VIABILITY-MASTER-COPY-WHOLE-GUIDE.pdf 4; Reid (n 21) 236.

[194] Hunt (n 126) 46–47.

[195] Grandparents Plus, *Rethinking Family Life: Exploring the role of grandparents and the wider family* (London, Grandparents Plus, 2009) 24–25; J Harwin and J Simmonds, *Special Guardianship: A review of the evidence* (London, Coram BAAF, 2020).

[196] *Re B-S (Children)* [2013] EWCA Civ 1146; *K, T and U (Placement of Children with Kinship Carers Abroad)* [2019] EWFC 59.

[197] *Good Practice Guide* (n 193).

[198] ibid.

[199] J Hunt, *Two Decades of UK Research on Kinship Care: An Overview* (London, Family Rights Group, 2020) 35.

[200] Grandparents Plus (n 195) 25.

favour may be overlooked in the process of screening grandparents as potential carers. As Deblasio observes, evidence presented in court and administrative practice are 'explicably linked'.[201] It is argued that a viability assessment is a form of 'administrative practice'[202] that directly impacts on grandparents' likelihood of becoming kinship carers when other options, such as non-consensual adoption, might be on the table. Without a positive viability assessment, grandparents' chances of being considered as carers or of being granted a child arrangements order or special guardianship order will be low. Thus, the importance of grandparents within the 'family constellation' could be minimised. In such circumstances, children's identity rights under the ECHR and the UNCRC may not be fully protected if children lose significant, diverse relationships extending beyond the 'binary' model of parenthood and/or connections with wider social and cultural networks.

Another inherent problem, as identified in chapter 4 of this volume, is the timing of grandparent involvement. While many grandparents are informed in a timely manner that their grandchildren are to be adopted, this is not always the case. In some cases, court proceedings are underway before grandparents become aware that a grandchild is to be adopted. In such circumstances, they face an uphill struggle to put themselves forward as kinship carers. Sometimes grandparents are not informed at all, for instance because birth parents oppose grandparent care. The organisation Grandparents Plus has argued that grandparents ought to be notified about care and adoption proceedings, unless it can be shown that to do so would not be in the best interests of the child.[203] Grandparents Plus has stated that viability assessments treat relatives the same as non-relatives, suggesting that it is inappropriate to apply the same assessment to kinship carers, who may be ruled out because they do not 'fit' the ideal profile. Reasons for exclusion, they propose, may include being a smoker or living in a small house, and they suggest that such an approach 'is like fitting a square peg into a round hole'.[204] Family members are often aggrieved when after 10-minute interviews with professionals like psychiatrists, these professionals produce reports that include negative comments[205] that can impact on grandparents' likelihood of becoming kinship carers. Often, grandparents' relationships with social workers are 'very strained'.[206]

Although the report was published in 2009, subsequent work by Hunt (covered in chapter 4), demonstrates that grandparents and extended kin still face challenges in becoming carers. It is argued that a more flexible, nuanced viability assessment that is tailored to grandparents[207] would be the best approach. Although the Good Practice Guide encourages this type of approach, it is not known how

---

[201] Deblasio (n 41) 197.
[202] ibid.
[203] Grandparents Plus (n 195) 36.
[204] ibid 25.
[205] Tingle (n 135) 182–83.
[206] ibid 181.
[207] Grandparents Plus (n 195) 25.

many local authorities apply its principles in practice. There is a need for more transparency and consistency across local authorities, to ensure that sufficient weight is placed on children's identity rights, thereby providing more protection to children's rights under Article 8 ECHR and Article 8 UNCRC. This would also provide further acknowledgement of the importance of grandparents within the family constellation.

Ageism towards the elderly, Herring suggests, is a significant 'social problem'.[208] Age is clearly a factor that may impact on the likelihood of grandparents' being regarded as 'viable' kinship carers. Unfortunately, Coleman and Hanlon express concern that such 'negative and ageist attitudes towards ... older people can be widespread and problematic'.[209] Many grandparents, therefore, are regarded by social workers as being 'too old'[210] to be caregivers. Moreover, Buchanan and Rotkirch observe that ageism, in a range of contexts, has the potential to undermine 'the importance and status of grandparents'.[211] Decisions to rule out grandparents as carers based on age may be based on a 'stereotype'[212] that grandparents lack good health due to their age. Coleman and Hanlon opine that stereotypes can lead to 'assumptions that older people are senile, lonely, ill, demented or disabled'.[213] Although a disadvantage of an increased lifespan is potentially 'higher levels of disability and frailty',[214] it can be argued that parents themselves could suffer from disability and ill-health, or be older parents. As Clarke and Roberts observe, 'more older people are experiencing grandparenthood and even great grand parenthood than ever before'.[215] Thus, disproportionate weight should not be placed on such factors, when determining whether a child ought to be placed with grandparents or prospective adopters.[216]

While age is a factor that might impact on a kinship carer, including a grandparent, and his or her ability to provide long-term care, it should be balanced carefully alongside other factors, such as the strength of the child's relationship with his or her grandparent and the availability of developing and maintaining wider social and cultural networks. Research demonstrates that legislation on equality, including the Equality Act 2010, has not eradicated such age discrimination.[217]

---

[208] J Herring, *Life through the Life Course* (Bristol, Bristol University Press, 2021) 42.

[209] Coleman and Hanlon (n 7) 91.

[210] Grandparents Plus (n 195) 24.

[211] A Buchanan and A Rotkirch, 'Twenty-first century grandparents: global perspectives on changing roles and consequences' in Buchanan and Rotkirch (eds) (n 8) 1, 5.

[212] Grandparents Plus (n 195) 24.

[213] Coleman and Hanlon (n 7) 95.

[214] ibid 134.

[215] L Clarke and C Roberts, 'Policy and rhetoric: The growing interest in fathers and grandparents in Britain' in A Carling, S Duncan and R Edwards (eds), *Analysing Families: Morality and rationality in policy and practice* (London, Routledge, 2002) 166.

[216] S Mills, 'Perpetuating Ageism Via Adoption Standards and Practices' (2011) 26 *Wisconsin Journal of Law, Gender and Society* 69.

[217] V Heaslip and J Ryden, *Understanding Vulnerability: A Nursing and Healthcare Approach* (Hoboken, NJ, Wiley, 2013) 1994. Generally see M Sargeant, *Age Discrimination: Ageism in Employment and Service Provision* (Abingdon, Routledge, 2016).

Grandparents Plus suggest a campaign to promote forthcoming age discrimination legislation and 'to promote a culture of respect for older and younger people'.[218] While age is certainly a relevant factor to be considered during assessment, the weighing process may be 'out of balance' if significant attention to grandparental age takes place at the expense of attention to children's identity rights. Moreover, stressing age as a factor in the provision of care may even result in discriminatory practices[219] that are at odds with section 5 of the Equality Act 2010. A recent decision along such lines, *Mander v Windsor and Maidenhead RBC*,[220] demonstrates the importance of non-discrimination in the selection of prospective long-term carers. In this case, a couple were not added to the register of adopters based on racial characteristics. This approach was determined, by the court, to amount to race discrimination. It is argued, therefore, that ruling out kinship carers (or prospective adopters) because of age could also amount to discrimination.

That is not to say that grandparent care, despite its advantages, is without its challenges. Kinship carers are undoubtedly at risk of 'intra-familial conflict over the division of responsibilities and decision-making powers',[221] and are also less likely to access the services and support available to foster carers.[222] Research by Hunt has shown that children in grandparent care may require more help in developing social networks,[223] which can also affect the development of children's identity. Hunt notes that there can be an issue with the 'generation gap, with grandparents having old-fashioned views about rules and appropriate behaviour and sometimes being overly restrictive about social activities'.[224] Undoubtedly, though, there are ways to alleviate such issues if they arise in kinship placements. For example, proactive targeting of grandparents so that they attend children's centres, Sure Start and other local services[225] could provide grandparents with further support and socialisation for children outside of nursery care and school settings. It is therefore 'vital'[226] to ensure that grandparents receive a wide range of support, such as respite care, education, mental-health services, counselling, legal help, transport,[227] so that they can thrive in their role as kinship carers and help children thrive and develop their identities, in accordance with their evolving capacities under Article 12 UNCRC.

---

[218] Grandparents Plus (n 195) 19.
[219] Mills (n 216).
[220] *Mander v Windsor and Maidenhead RBC* (2019) 12 WLUK 79.
[221] Cantwell (n 73) 263.
[222] ibid.
[223] Hunt (n 126) 51.
[224] ibid 49.
[225] Grandparents Plus (n 195) 12.
[226] Hunt (n 126) 52.
[227] ibid.

V. Conclusion

If grandparents can provide alternative care to adoption, in a manner consistent with promoting a child's welfare, this promotes children's identity rights within the scope of Article 8 UNCRC and Article 8 ECHR. This chapter has identified potential barriers to the provision of alternative care by grandparents. These barriers include variability in carer assessment practice and age. Factors such as age may be relevant considerations. Regardless, over-emphasis on these factors may be to the detriment of the child's welfare and identity rights, provided for explicitly under Article 8 UNCRC and Article 8 ECHR, and implicitly via Articles 5, 20 and 30 UNCRC.

It is argued that the bundle of 'identity' rights within the UNCRC ought to be prioritised. The UNCRC, viewed through the lens of 'Family Constellation Theory', protects the rights of children, including their identity rights under Article 8 UNCRC. An incidental, beneficial effect would be improved protection of grandparents' relationships with their grandchildren. Grandparent care may be as effective (or better) than adoptive placements if grandparents are mentally, emotionally and physically capable of caring for their grandchildren. Grandparent care has many benefits. These include the development and maintenance of familial relationships, knowledge of origins and a prospective 'anchoring' role for grandparents who have strong existing mutual bonds with their grandchildren. In situations where grandparents may be unable to act as long-term carers there may, nonetheless, be benefits from open adoption.

It has been argued that 'identity' should be an explicit, rather than implicit, factor to be considered when weighing up non-consensual adoption versus grandparent care. While grandparent care might not be appropriate in every case, there are many situations where such care will afford effective protection of the child's identity. This chapter has therefore explored the extent to which issues identified during viability assessments constitute relevant factors to be balanced against the child's identity and relationships with his or her birth family, which are protected under the Article 8 UNCRC and Article 8 ECHR. It is proposed that viewing the UNCRC and family constellations in juxtaposition highlights the importance of emphasising grandparents' role in grandchildren's lives when children cannot be raised by their parents.

Adoption is a beneficial arrangement that may be the 'anchor' needed for many children. It is argued, however, that emphasis must be placed on the importance of placement with extended family members, including grandparents. Grandparents can help their grandchildren make sense of their past and provide meaningful connections and relationship continuity, which facilitate the child's development of personal identity. Thus, it is submitted that protection of the relationships between children and their wider kinship and cultural networks, such as the grandparent/grandchild relationship, may afford greater protection to children's identity rights, especially under Article 8 UNCRC and Article 8 ECHR.

7

Symbolic and Expedient 'Solutions', Grandparents and the Private Family Justice System: The Risk of Unintended Consequences

JOANNA HARWOOD

I. Introduction

The principal challenge at the heart of family law is having to make decisions about children's futures in the face of conflicting arguments from the parties to a dispute, without being able to know with any certainty how those decisions will play out in practice.[1] Private family law responds to this challenge of 'future uncertainty',[2] in part, through recognising some family members as more significant than others to the promotion of children's welfare within the statutory framework, including through differentiating between those who need to seek permission from the court before applying for orders to spend time with children and those who can apply directly, and by guiding the courts' decision making at the substantive hearing stage. Judges also have some flexibility to find solutions to the challenge of future uncertainty in individual cases when deciding how cases should progress once they leave court. This chapter explores the challenge of future uncertainty in relation to grandparents' relationships with the private family justice system by extending, for the first time, the use of autopoietic theory from other areas of family law to this specific context. By doing so, the chapter provides a framework that connects theory with practice, which can be used to evaluate the merits of the

---

[1] For discussion of this challenge of 'future uncertainty', see M King, 'Future Uncertainty as a Challenge to Law's Programmes: The Dilemma of Parental Disputes' (2000) 63(4) *Modern Law Review* 523.

[2] A term originally used by King (ibid). Michael King has been influential in applying autopoietic theory to understand family law's navigation of this future uncertainty. Until now, an autopoietic approach has not been applied in the context of grandparents and the private family justice system, potentially owing to the current nature of these debates.

calls for statutory reform to promote grandparents' involvement in grandchildren's lives and the role they may play once cases leave court. This framework reveals the significant risks that attach to reliance on symbolic and expedient solutions within the legal system to solve problems that emanate from outside the legal system itself.

The calls for statutory reform to promote grandparents' relationships with their grandchildren include the removal of the requirement that grandparents must seek leave from the court before applying for child arrangements orders to spend time with their grandchildren, when this time is being denied by one or both of the child(ren)'s parents.[3] There has also been a more recent call for the existing statutory presumption of parental involvement to be extended to include the promotion of grandparents' relationships with their grandchildren.[4] At the later stages of parties' progression through the private family court, there is evidence that, rather than being neglected by the legal framework, grandparents are being called upon by the courts, in some cases, to perform an unduly extensive role in the post-separation family once cases leave court. The evidence here is that grandparents are being tasked with monitoring the time spent between a parent who has perpetrated domestic abuse and their child(ren), in response to limited alternatives for progressing contact, with concerns raised that children's safety is threatened since grandparents are insufficiently qualified to be performing this protective function.[5] This concern has become more pronounced in the light of the shift away from the courts' involvement in cases post-order, with a reduction in the number of post-order reviews to monitor how the arrangements made for children are progressing once those cases leave court.[6]

The perception driving the calls for statutory reform is that grandparents are losing out on valuable relationships with their grandchildren,[7] and that the law can

---

[3] The Children and Families Act 2014 removed the terms 'contact' and 'residence', replacing these with 'child arrangements orders'. These orders determine where a child shall live and if/with whom they should spend time. Since 'child arrangements orders' do not differentiate between contact and residence, and this chapter focuses solely on contact, 'contact' is used throughout this chapter to refer to the time spent between children and their parents/grandparents. Grandparents who turn to the private family justice system to secure time with their grandchildren do so for different reasons. In some cases, contact might be being refused to grandparents when parents remain together; in other cases, grandparents might or might not have a pre-existing relationship with their grandchildren but contact is being refused following parental separation, by either one or both parents, with this latter category being among the most contentious. For discussion of the most common circumstances in which grandparents turn to the private law family courts, see, eg, L Dickson, 'Grandparents and Contact: What's the Solution?' (2019) 49(Oct) *Family Law* 1091, 1092. This chapter focuses on the cases in which both parents are alive.

[4] The statutory presumption of parental involvement directs the courts to 'presume, unless the contrary is shown, that involvement of that parent in the life of the child concerned will further the child's welfare': Children Act 1989, s 1(2A).

[5] As explored later in this chapter, see, eg, the concerns raised by the All-Party Parliamentary Group on Domestic Violence, *Parliamentary Briefing: Domestic Abuse, Child Contact and the Family Courts* (All-Party Parliamentary Group on Domestic Violence and Women's Aid 2016) 21.

[6] See, eg, Ministry of Justice, *Assessing Risk of Harm to Children and Parents in Private Law Children Cases: Final Report* (London, Ministry of Justice, 2020) 145–46.

[7] For the calls for reform to remove this leave requirement, see, eg, the arguments in Family Justice Review Panel, *Family Justice Review: Interim Report* (Ministry of Justice, Department for Education

provide the solution to that problem. These calls can be located within a broader trend within private family law of using statutory reform for symbolic ends, the intention being not to change the courts' practice but rather to attempt to change the behaviour of the parties to the dispute, inside and outside court, by sending 'messages' on how those parties should behave.[8] Underpinning the calls both to remove the leave requirement and to extend the statutory presumption of parental involvement to include grandparents is the perception that giving grandparents enhanced status within the statutory framework will stop parents from denying grandparents a relationship with their grandchildren, since parents will, the argument goes, change their behaviour in line with the expectations set out within that statutory framework.[9] The deployment of grandparents to perform a protective role in domestic abuse cases is driven not by these symbolic aims but rather by expediency, with grandparents tasked with stepping in to compensate for the lack of funding for professional supervision of contact. Whilst informed by different motivating factors, uniting the calls for both symbolic statutory reform and the expedient deployment of grandparents to perform a protective function are attempts to control the uncertainty of children's futures through generalisations on the importance of grandparents in children's lives.

Autopoietic theory provides a framework for understanding how significant problems arise when attempting to translate these generalisations into a legal system that must be based on the particular circumstances of each individual child. It offers a 'depiction of society as consisting of closed, self-referring systems of communications', with each system only able to 'reproduce another in that first system's own terms'.[10] Within family law to date, the theory has provided an

---

and Welsh Assembly Government, March 2011) paras 5.37–5.38; and Family Justice Review Panel, *Family Justice Review: Final Report* (Ministry of Justice, Department for Education and Welsh Government, November 2011) paras 4.41–4.48. Whilst not supported unanimously by grandparents' groups, Grandparents Apart has called for a presumption to promote grandparents' involvement in the lives of their grandchildren (for discussion, see F Kaganas and C Piper, 'Grandparent Contact: Another Presumption?' (2020) 42(2) *Journal of Social Welfare and Family Law* 176). See also J Deuchars and J Loudoun, *Grandparents Speak Out for Vulnerable Children: To Be in Our Grandchildren's Lives* (GAUK Scotland, 2006) at http://grandparentsapart.co.uk/wp-content/uploads/2018/08/Grandparents-Book. pdf. As discussed later in this chapter, the call for a statutory presumption for grandparents has gained some traction within Parliament since. See, eg, House of Commons, *Access Rights to Grandparents*, HC Deb 2 May 2018, vol 640. For discussion more generally of the campaigns by grandparents' organisations, see Kaganas and Piper (within this footnote).

[8] See, eg, the discussion outside the context of grandparents' relationships with the private family justice system in F Kaganas, 'A Presumption that "Involvement" of Both Parents is Best: Deciphering Law's Messages' (2013) 25(3) *Child and Family Law Quarterly* 270. See further A Newnham, 'Shared Parenting, Law and Policy: Considering Power Within the Framework of Autopoietic Theory' (2015) 11(4) *International Journal of Law in Context* 426.

[9] See, eg, J Stather, 'Enhancing the Rights of Grandchildren to See Their Grandparents' *Family Law Week* (May 2018); Nigel Huddleston MP, HC Deb 2 May 2018, vol 640, cols 173–74WH. See also Dickson (n 3) 1903.

[10] M King, '"Being Sensible": Images and Practices of the New Family Lawyers' (1999) 28(2) *Journal of Social Policy* 249, 252. See also G Teubner, 'How the Law Thinks: Toward a Constructivist Epistemology of Law' (1989) 23(5) *Law & Society Review* 727; M King, 'Child Welfare Within Law: The Emergence of a Hybrid Discourse' (1991) 18(3) *Journal of Law and Society* 303; M King and C Piper, *How the Law Thinks About Children*, 2nd edn (Aldershot, Ashgate, 1995); Newnham (n 8).

explanation of the law's navigation of future uncertainty, with the self-referential nature of the system allowing children's welfare to be defined within the legal system's own terms and norms.[11] When applied to the context involving grand-parents, the theory highlights the reinterpretations and retranslations of meaning that take place between policy intentions, the statutory framework, the courts' interpretation of that framework and the understanding of the law possessed by families themselves.[12] The theory shows how understandings within one broadly defined 'system' are not neatly transferred into another, instead going through a process of 're-entry' into a format compatible with each particular system, which can then give rise to misinterpretations and mistranslations.[13]

The framework provided by autopoietic theory demonstrates why symbolic statutory reform, in relation to both the leave requirement and the statutory presumption of parental involvement, will serve neither grandparents nor children, since parents and grandparents are not guaranteed to respond in any predictable way to either the policy intention behind reform or legal rules themselves.[14] As this chapter shows, the more likely outcome of statutory reform will be unintended consequences, including renewed grandparent dissatisfaction with the legal system and an increased risk that the courts will reach judgments that threaten the safety and welfare of children, in particular in cases involving allegations of harm. Autopoietic theory is also valuable in identifying how the expedient deployment of grandparents as 'protectors', in cases in which a child is to spend time with a domestically abusive parent, risks undermining the safety and welfare of children. This is due again to the misinterpretations and mistranslations that can take place between the courts' intentions in designating grandparents as 'protectors', and parents' and grandparents' interpretations of those intentions, particularly when there are significant limits to the information being fed back into the legal system on how contact is progressing. The application of autopoietic theory to these issues is timely, owing to the Ministry of Justice's current exploration of whether reform is needed to the statutory presumption of parental involvement and the calls for the reinstatement of post-order reviews in child arrangements disputes involving allegations of harm.[15]

---

[11] See, eg, King (n 1) 525; G Teubner, R Nobles and D Schiff, 'The Autonomy of Law: An Introduction to Legal Autopoiesis' in D Schiff and R Nobles (eds), *Jurisprudence* (London, Butterworth, 2003) 897, 917–19; Newnham (n 8) 427.

[12] For further discussion outside the context of grandparents and the private family justice system, see, eg, R Nobles and D Schiff, 'Why Do Judges Talk the Way They Do?' (2009) 5(1) *International Journal of Law in Context* 25, 30–31; Newnham (n 8) 427, 432–33 and 441.

[13] Newnham (n 8) 427–28. See further G Teubner, 'Legal Irritants: Good Faith in British Law or How Unifying Law Ends Up in New Divergences' (1998) 61(1) *Modern Law Review* 11; R van Krieken, 'The Socio-Legal Construction of the "Best Interests of the Child": Law's Autonomy, Sociology and Family Law' in M Freeman (ed), *Law and Sociology* (Oxford, Oxford University Press, 2006) 437.

[14] For discussion outside the context of grandparents' relationships with the private family justice system, see, eg, Newnham (n 8).

[15] Ministry of Justice (n 6); Ministry of Justice, *Assessing Risk of Harm to Children and Parents in Private Law Children Cases: Implementation Plan* (London, Ministry of Justice, June 2020). At the time of writing, an inquiry has also recently commenced by the Children and Families Act 2014

The chapter first outlines the general contribution autopoietic theory has already made to account for the way in which the family justice system navigates the challenge of future uncertainty. It then applies insights provided by the application of this theory to both the calls for statutory reform and the deployment of grandparents to play a protective role in domestic abuse cases. By doing so, the chapter foregrounds the value of autopoietic theory in identifying the necessarily imperfect interactions that take place between different systems, and demonstrates how, if the family courts are truly to respond to the challenges posed by children's uncertain futures, the answer cannot be found in symbolically motivated reform and expedient solutions that serve neither grandparents nor grandchildren. Instead, the only meaningful pathway available is closer scrutiny of the particular grandparent–grandchild relationship in each individual case, unfettered by general pronouncements on the importance of grandparents to children and an untested faith in the protective role they can play in children's lives.

II. Autopoietic Theory and the Challenge of Future Uncertainty for Family Law

Deciding which family members are best positioned to promote children's welfare is inherently difficult within family law, because this rests upon an assessment of each individual child's welfare in a future setting that, by definition, has yet to take place.[16] Despite this uncertainty, judges cannot decline to deliver a judgment when faced with conflicting accounts of how to promote children's welfare by the parties to the dispute.[17] The legal system has had to find a way, through its autonomous and self-referential existence, to be 'based on certainty, or at least have an air of certainty', since it cannot 'tie itself to an unknown, uncertain future'.[18]

Autopoietic theory, by framing the legal system as self-referring and closed,[19] is able to explain how the family courts attempt to overcome the challenge of future uncertainty and 'decide who is right and who is wrong and then how to justify that decision in ways that appear cogent and convincing'.[20] The legal system is 'cognitively open' but 'normatively closed', meaning that it will 'admit' or 'recreate' information, but that information does not automatically change the approach taken within the legal system, with that system retaining control over its own interpretations of the information.[21] Any 'reconstruction' of the

---

Committee within the House of Lords; see at https://committees.parliament.uk/committee/581/children-and-families-act-2014-committee/.

[16] King (n 1).
[17] ibid 542.
[18] ibid.
[19] ibid. More generally, see N Luhmann, 'The Third Question: The Creative Use of Paradoxes in Law and Legal History' (1988) 15(2) *Journal of Law and Society* 153; Newnham (n 8).
[20] King (n 1) 523.
[21] Newnham (n 8) 429.

information entering the legal system will take place 'only on terms that make sense within law'.[22] Family law thus structures its specific communications on '*present futures* rather than *future presents*',[23] with the family courts reaching their judgments in individual cases through their own 'internally reconstructed version of reality'[24] of 'what is best for children upon the facts (as perceived by law) *of the existing situation* – the present child-parent relations, the wishes of the children, their response to separation etc'.[25] By doing so, it becomes possible to '[tie] together past, present and present futures'.[26] It has been acknowledged that this is a 'selective, restrictive and ... necessarily biased account of children's welfare', but that, crucially, it is this autonomy and self-reference that 'allows the legal system to construct and apply its conditional programmes and so avoid exposing the paradoxical nature of its own being'.[27]

The application of an autopoietic understanding to the private family law's treatment of grandparents is important, since it focuses our attention on the potential tensions between policy intentions, the statutory framework, the courts' interpretation of that framework and the understanding of the law possessed by families themselves,[28] rather than assuming that they exist in harmony. 'Legality', therefore, is what 'the law decides ... is lawful',[29] but there is no guarantee that this understanding of legality will be easily transferred outside of the legal context into, for example, grandparents' understanding of the law. As this chapter will argue, it is this process of reinterpretation and retranslation that warns against both the use of the law for symbolic purposes to promote the involvement of grandparents in children's lives, and the expedient reliance on grandparents as a protective force in cases involving domestic abuse. Both risk significant unintended consequences that undermine, rather than promote, children's welfare.

III. Symbolic 'Solutions' and the Calls for Statutory Reform: The Removal of the Leave Requirement and the Extension of the Statutory Presumption of Parental Involvement

The law has frequently been identified within arguments for reform as part of the solution to the perceived problem that grandparents are missing out on

---

[22] L Smith and L Trinder, 'Mind the Gap: Parent Education Programmes and the Family Justice System' (2012) 24(4) *Child and Family Law Quarterly* 428, 447.

[23] King (n 1) 542 (original emphasis).

[24] Newnham (n 8) 428.

[25] King (n 1) 542 (emphasis added).

[26] ibid.

[27] ibid. See also Newnham (n 8) 426.

[28] Newnham (n 8) 426–27.

[29] ibid 427. See also N Luhmann, 'Law as a Social System' (1989) 83(1&2) *Northwestern University Law Review* 136, 141–142; J Priban, 'Beyond Procedural Legitimation: Legality and Its "Infictions"' (1997) 24(3) *Journal of Law and* Society 331, 335-336; King, '"Being Sensible"' (n 10) 252; King (n 1)

relationships with their grandchildren,[30] despite relatively few grandparents taking their cases to court.[31] This section first outlines the calls for statutory reform and then uses an autopoietic understanding to explore the significant risks that are likely to attach to pursuing such reform.

A. The Calls to Remove the Leave Requirement

Grandparents in England and Wales can apply for a section 8 order within the Children Act 1989 to spend time with their grandchildren. Grandparents are not, however, given direct access to proceedings, having first to seek leave from the court.[32] At this leave stage, and unlike at the substantive stage of deciding if an order will be made for the grandparent to spend time with the grandchild, the welfare of the child is not the court's paramount consideration. Instead, the court will have 'particular regard' to a range of factors in determining if leave should be granted, including: 'the nature of the proposed application for the section 8 order'; 'the applicant's connection with the child'; and 'any risk there might be of that proposed application disrupting the child's life to such an extent that he would be harmed by it'.[33] If leave is granted, there is no presumption that the grandparent's application for a child arrangements order will go on to be successful.[34]

At the core of the arguments that the leave requirement is unjustified is the belief that grandparents are in a 'special position regarding their grandchildren' in comparison with other non-parental relatives and non-relatives who may have a relationship with the child.[35] Grandparents Plus, for example, has argued in relation to the leave requirement:

> A grandparent's relationship to a child is different and special but the law treats them like any other adult when they are trying to establish contact with their grandchildren. We believe this should change and do not accept the argument that the court system would be overrun with applications if this requirement were removed.[36]

It has also been argued that the leave requirement creates an unjustified barrier to grandparents' access to the courts,[37] giving rise to delay and cost by increasing the

---

525; Teubner, Nobles and Schiff (n 11) 905. And more broadly, see King, 'Child Welfare Within Law' (n 10).

[30] See, eg, the arguments in Family Justice Review Panel, *Interim Report* and *Final Report* (n 7) and House of Commons (n 7).

[31] L Cusworth et al, *Uncovering Private Family Law: Who's Coming to Court in England?* (London, Nuffield, Family Justice Observatory, 2021) 9.

[32] Unless they fall into one of the limited categories in which leave is not required (see further Children Act 1989, s 10(5)).

[33] Children Act 1989, s 10(9).

[34] See, eg, *Re W (Contact: Application by Grandparent)* [1997] 1 FLR 793.

[35] See, eg, G Douglas and N Ferguson, 'The Role of Grandparents in Divorced Families' (2003) 17(1) *International Journal of Law, Policy and the Family* 41, 63.

[36] Family Justice Review Panel, *Final Report* (n 7) para 4.43.

[37] See, eg, the discussion in KR Pritchard and K Williams, 'The Rights of Grandparents and Other Family Members in Relation to Children – From Both a Domestic and International Perspective' (2018) 4 *International Family Law* 281.

length of time grandparents have to spend within proceedings.[38] From a policy perspective, however, the leave requirement has never been 'designed to be an obstacle to grandparents'.[39] Instead, it is intended to act 'as a filter to sift out those applications that are clearly not in the child's best interests'.[40]

The leave requirement for grandparents was most recently formally considered within the Family Justice Review,[41] and within both its *Interim Report* and *Final Report*, the conclusion was that the leave requirement should be retained,[42] which was accepted by the then Coalition Government.[43] Influential in shaping the Family Justice Review's conclusion was that it was 'not convinced that the courts are refusing leave unreasonably or that seeking leave is slow or expensive for grandparents'.[44] This point has been more recently echoed in Parliament, with Lucy Frazer MP (the then Parliamentary Under-Secretary of State for Justice) stating that 'experience shows that grandparents do not usually experience any difficulty in obtaining permission when their application is motivated by a genuine concern for the interests of the child'.[45] It also remains the case that grandparents can apply for permission at the same time as applying for the child arrangements order itself, and they do not need to pay two sets of fees, one for the leave application and another for the substantive application.[46] As it stands, therefore, it is difficult to see how removing the requirement to seek leave would bring meaningful benefits to grandparents, save for differentiating them at a symbolic level from other non-parental relatives and non-relatives who might have a relationship with the child. The cost and disruption arising from the child arrangements proceedings themselves are likely to constitute the more significant barrier to grandparents' engagement with the court system, a barrier that would continue to exist whether the leave requirement is removed or not.[47]

---

[38] ibid. See also the discussion in Dickson (n 3) 1093.

[39] Child Arrangements Orders: Grandparents, Question for Ministry of Justice, UIN 20478, tabled on 16 December 2015.

[40] ibid.

[41] This Review commenced in March 2010, during the time in office of the Labour Government, and was taken forward by the subsequent Coalition Government. An earlier Green Paper consultation on whether to remove the leave requirement ran until April 2010 (Department for Children, Schools and Families, *Support for All: The Families and Relationships Green Paper* (Cm 7787, 2010)), but the Labour Government then lost the May 2010 General Election. The new Conservative–Liberal Democrat Coalition Government declined to take the Green Paper forward, making the Family Justice Review the next time the leave requirement was formally reviewed.

[42] Family Justice Review Panel, *Interim Report* (n 7) para 5.82; Family Justice Review Panel, *Final Report* (n 7) para 4.48.

[43] Ministry of Justice and Department for Education, *The Government Response to the Family Justice Review: A System with Children and Families at its Heart* (Cm 8273, 2012) 22.

[44] Family Justice Review Panel, *Interim Report* (n 7) para 5.84; Family Justice Review Panel, *Final Report* (n 7) para 4.46. See also J Herring, *Older People in Law and Society* (Oxford, Oxford University Press, 2009) 246–47.

[45] Lucy Frazer, HC Deb 2 May 2018, vol 640, col 184WH.

[46] Gov.uk, 'Form C100: Apply for a Court Order to Make Arrangements for a Child to Resolve a Dispute About Their Upbringing' at www.gov.uk/government/publications/form-c100-application-under-the-children-act-1989-for-a-child-arrangements-prohibited-steps-specific-issue-section-8-or-der-or-to-vary-or-discharge. See also Frazer (n 45).

[47] Douglas and Ferguson (n 35) 63.

Of more significance, therefore, is the argument also advanced in favour of removing the leave requirement that this removal would '"focus the minds" of parents' and 'compel' them to 'think twice before refusing contact'.[48] This argument rests heavily upon the assumption that legal reform can shape the behaviour of the non-legal actors to the dispute in a predictable way. This same assumption also drives the most recent push for reform to extend the statutory presumption of parental involvement to include the importance to children of grandparents' involvement in their lives.

B. The Calls to Extend the Existing Statutory Presumption of Parental Involvement to Include Grandparents

There have been recent calls to extend the statutory presumption of parental involvement in section 1(2A) of the Children Act 1989 to include grandparents.[49] Section 1(2A) directs the court that, in the absence of evidence to the contrary, it should be presumed that the involvement of each parent in the child's life will further the child's welfare.[50] The main driver for this extension of the statutory presumption of parental involvement has not been that the courts are unduly denying grandparents time with their grandchildren in individual cases.[51] Instead, the assumption is that, by including grandparents within the statutory presumption, parents will be less likely to stop grandparents from spending time with their grandchildren, both in cases that reach court and those that do not.[52] That the law is being viewed as the 'solution' to problems that emanate from outside the legal system can be clearly seen here in the development of policy recommendations for reform. In expressing his support for an extension of the statutory presumption to include either the words 'and extended family' or 'and any grandparents', Nigel Huddleston MP, for example, said that 'changing the law also changes the culture so that deliberately restricting the access of one family member to another becomes socially unacceptable'.[53] The claim is that by extending the statutory presumption to include grandparents, this would 'avoid the need for people to go to court in the first place'.[54] The belief, therefore, is that the law can shape behaviour in a controlled way, performing a culture-changing function by setting a standard on what is, and is not, acceptable, which will then be dutifully observed by the parties involved in disputes, regardless of whether they access the court system or not.

---

[48] As discussed in Dickson (n 3) 1093. See also Stather (n 9).

[49] See n 7.

[50] 'Involvement' can be direct or indirect, and the presumption does not guarantee 'any particular division of a child's time': Children Act 1989, s 1(2B).

[51] See, eg, the arguments advanced for reform in House of Commons (n 7).

[52] See, eg, Huddleston (n 9).

[53] ibid cols 173WH–174WH. See also Deuchars and Loudoun (n 7); Stather (n 9).

[54] Michael Tomlinson MP, HC Deb 2 May 2018, vol 640, col 184WH.

This faith in the law's capacity to bring about predictable behavioural change is more than familiar within private family law.[55] The most recent iteration of this argument heavily influenced the introduction of the statutory presumption of parental involvement.[56] As this chapter explores, the assumption that the law can change behaviour in a predictable way is flawed, and the legal framework has an important 'censoring' role that warns against the removal of the leave requirement and the calls to extend the statutory presumption.

C. Are Grandparents 'Special'? The 'Censoring' Role of the Legislative Framework

An autopoietic understanding of the law as autonomous and self-referential demonstrates how the legislative framework within the family justice system can act as a 'censor' on the 'entry into legal decision-making' of information, including 'science-generated notions of what is good, healthy or less risky for children' arising from existing research evidence.[57] In response to children's inherently uncertain futures, the Children Act 1989 exerts some control over this uncertainty by setting the criteria by which family members are deemed 'closest' to the child, through both the leave requirement and the statutory presumption of parental involvement.[58] Judges are then charged with making assessments in individual cases on whether particular grandparents will promote children's welfare within that legal framework. The extent to which the legal system can, and should, reflect the broader research evidence base on children's welfare is a complex issue.[59] This issue does not form the focus of this chapter, save for considering the extent to which the 'censoring' process that constructs the legislative framework has resulted in a legal position that is aligned with the existing research evidence.

The involvement of grandparents in children's lives can undoubtedly be of great importance to children (see chapter 2 of this volume for further discussion),[60]

---

[55] For further discussion of the way in which the Children Act 1989 has previously been deployed for symbolic ends, see, eg, PG Harris and RH George, 'Parental Responsibility and Shared Residence Orders: Parliamentary Intentions and Judicial Interpretations' (2010) 22(2) *Child and Family Law Quarterly* 151; Kaganas (n 8); Newnham (n 8).

[56] See, eg, the discussion in Kaganas (n 8); J Harwood, 'Presuming the Status Quo? The Impact of the Statutory Presumption of Parental Involvement' (2021) 43(2) *Journal of Social Welfare and Family Law* 119.

[57] King (n 1) 532.

[58] In relation to the leave requirement, see Children Act 1989, s 10(1). In relation to the statutory presumption of parental involvement, see s 1(2A).

[59] For discussion of the relationship between the law and research evidence bases, see, eg, Newnham (n 8) 431–33. See further F Kaganas and C Piper, 'Shared Parenting: A 70% Solution?' (2002) 14(4) *Child and Family Law Quarterly* 365; A Barnett, 'Family Law Without Lawyers: A Systems Theory Perspective' (2017) 39(2) *Journal of Social Welfare and Family Law* 223; King and Piper (n 10) 43.

[60] See further the discussion in M Purnell and B H Bagby, 'Grandparents' Rights: Implications for Family Specialists' (1993) 42(2) *Family Relations* 173, 174–75; J Eekelaar, *Family Law and Personal Life* (Oxford, Oxford University Press, 2007) 70; M Murch, *Supporting Children when Parents Separate* (Bristol, Policy Press, 2018) 51, 55–56, 59–60 and 87.

particularly in relation to adolescent children.[61] Reviews of the available research evidence with relevance to private family law cases, however, have found that whilst this importance can exist in individual cases, there is currently a lack of evidence, overall, that grandparents are sufficiently different from other non-parental relatives to merit being given a blanket privileged legal status.[62] It has been shown that grandparents' relationships with their grandchildren are not uniform,[63] and the emphasis within existing research is on the quality of the relationship in individual cases, rather than on its mere existence.[64] Grandparents who enjoyed a meaningful relationship with their grandchildren when the parental relationship was intact have also been shown to be unlikely to lose that relationship following parental separation,[65] meaning that the cases that engage the private family court system are likely to be those where this meaningful relationship is lacking and/or there is high conflict between grandparents and parents. Overall, there are also limited studies conducted in the United Kingdom, and the studies that exist tend not to cover the higher-conflict cases that result in court action.[66]

This is again not to downplay the important role grandparents can play in grandchildren's lives. Instead, it is to suggest that any removal of the leave requirement, or any extension of the statutory presumption of parental involvement on the basis of grandparents' enjoyment of a 'special' relationship with their grandchildren, would represent more of a symbolic attempt to translate a perceived societal importance of grandparents within families into the legal framework than a firm rooting in the available evidence. As it stands, the current legal framework in acting as a 'censor' is broadly aligned with this evidence, with no special legal status being given to grandparents through either the non-existence of a leave requirement or the extension of the statutory presumption of parental involvement to include them.

---

[61] See, eg, S Attar-Schwartz and A Buchanan, 'Grandparenting and Adolescent Well-being: Evidence from the UK and Israel' (2018) 13(2) *Contemporary Social Science* 219. More generally, see A Buchanan and A Rotkirch, 'Twenty-First Century Grandparents: Global Perspectives on Changing Roles and Consequences' (2018) 13(2) *Contemporary Social Science* 131.

[62] See, eg, Douglas and Ferguson (n 35) 62–63; Kaganas and Piper (n 7) 189–91. See also N Ferguson et al, *Grandparenting in Divorced Families* (Bristol, Policy Press, 2004) 72–74 and 140–41. For further discussion of the empirical evidence base, see F Kaganas and C Piper, 'Grandparents and the Limits of the Law' (1990) 4(1) *International Journal of Law, Policy and the Family* 27, 32–34; F Kaganas, 'Grandparents' Rights and Grandparents' Campaigns' (2007) 19(1) *Child and Family Law Quarterly* 17, 26–28.

[63] Douglas and Ferguson (n 35) 45–49 and 63; Kaganas and Piper (n 7) 191.

[64] Ferguson et al (n 62); Douglas and Ferguson (n 35); A Buchanan and E Flouri, *Involved Grandparenting and Child Well-being*, UK Data Archive Study No 6075, 2007; Kaganas and Piper (n 7) 191.

[65] Ferguson et al (n 62). This finding was influential in the Family Justice Review's interim review (n 7) para 5.83.

[66] For further discussion, see Kaganas and Piper (n 7) 189–91.

D. Is There a Place for Symbolic Reform to Promote the Involvement of Grandparents in Children's Lives?

The issue, then, is whether there is any role for the law in relation to grandparents to be used for symbolic ends to attempt to shape the behaviour of the parties involved in disputes. There are significant parallels between the introduction of the statutory presumption of parental involvement through the Children and Families Act 2014, and the calls to remove the leave requirement and to extend the statutory presumption to include grandparents. When explored through an autopoietic perspective, there are important lessons to take from the introduction of the statutory presumption of parental involvement that warn against the adoption of both of these reforms.

The articulated policy intention behind the introduction of the statutory presumption of parental involvement was to address public perceptions of bias against fathers within the family justice system,[67] set a standard at the 'societal level' on the importance of parents' joint responsibility for their children's upbringing[68] and, by doing so, encourage parents to reach agreements on contact without reliance on the court.[69] The government at the time was emphatic that the statutory presumption was never intended to change the courts' practice,[70] which was important since there was no empirical evidence of any actual bias against fathers, or any indication that judges were unduly restricting contact when sought by a parent.[71] The assumption was, therefore, that parents would receive the message from the legislative framework that both parents should be involved in their children's lives post-separation, process that message in the way intended at the policy level, and then change their behaviour to stop the denial of contact and shift, instead, to reaching amicable agreements without court assistance.[72]

There was significant doubt expressed prior to the introduction of the statutory presumption of parental involvement that this 'message-sending' function of the reform would achieve these intended objectives,[73] and the available evidence

---

[67] The emphasis was on remedying a *perception* of bias, since no bias had been found to exist within the courts' practice: M Harding and A Newnham, *How Do County Courts Share the Care of Children Between Parents?* (London, Nuffield Foundation, 2015). See also Harwood (n 56). For a more general discussion of the impact of perceptions of bias, see also Newnham (n 8) 434 and 439.

[68] Department for Education and Ministry of Justice, *Consultation: Co-operative Parenting Following Family Separation: Proposed Legislation on the Involvement of Both Parents in a Child's Life* (London, Department for Education and Ministry of Justice, 2012) para 3.2.

[69] ibid para 4.3.

[70] See, eg, Secretary of State for Education, *Children and Families Bill 2013: Contextual Information and Responses to Pre-Legislative Scrutiny* (Cmnd 8540, 2013).

[71] Harding and Newnham (n 67).

[72] Department for Education and Ministry of Justice (n 68).

[73] See Kaganas (n 8). See also Justice Committee, *Fourth Report of Session 2012–13: Pre-Legislative Scrutiny of the Children and Families Bill* (HC 739, 2012); M O'Grady, 'Shared Parenting: Keeping Welfare Paramount by Learning from Mistakes' (2013) 43(Apr) *Family Law* 448; F Kaganas, 'Parental Involvement: A Discretionary Presumption' (2018) 38(4) *Legal Studies* 549.

on its impact post-implementation suggests that it is indeed unlikely that those objectives are being achieved.[74] As autopoietic theory explains, this is due to the 'well known' understanding 'that changes sought by one system are rarely straight-forwardly achieved in the other'.[75] Each system has its own 'internal logic'.[76] As a result, the 'second system will not respond as required [by the first system], as it "obeys a different internal logic"'.[77] It cannot, therefore, be assumed that parents will respond to legislative change in the way intended at the policy level, since parents inhabit their own normative systems and will interpret the legal frame-work through their own 'internal logic', if they are even aware of the legislative change in the first place. Indeed, it has consistently been argued that parents 'feel justified in disobeying legal pronouncements where these conflict with their inter-nal moral codes'.[78] As a result, parents' perception of the legal framework depends on what they 'can understand and process and what they want to hear'.[79]

It is similarly unlikely that introducing a further symbolic gesture into the stat-utory framework by extending the statutory presumption to include grandparents will have any meaningful impact on the behaviour of the parties to a dispute, at least not in the way intended at the policy level.[80] The belief that removing the leave requirement will make parents 'think twice'[81] before refusing contact is also misplaced. When understood from an autopoietic perspective, the more likely outcomes of an extension of the statutory presumption, and the removal of the leave requirement, are unintended consequences, both in increasing grandparents' dissatisfaction and in introducing a risk of unpredictable change to the courts' approach in cases involving allegations of harm that could undermine children's welfare.

i. Unintended Consequences – Increasing Grandparents' Dissatisfaction

In theory, neither the removal of the leave requirement nor the extension of the statutory presumption of parental involvement to include grandparents should significantly alter the courts' practice. The removal of the leave requirement for grandparents should not materially change the final outcomes the courts reach, since the courts' decisions on whether to grant leave are separate, and involve

---

[74] See, eg, Kaganas, 'Parental Involvement' (n 73) 564–65; Kaganas and Piper (n 7) 188.

[75] Newnham (n 8) 438.

[76] Teubner (n 13) 22. For further discussion, see, eg, Newnham (n 8).

[77] Newnham (n 8) 438.

[78] Newnham (n 8) 438. See also F Kaganas and S Day Sclater, 'Contact Disputes: Narrative Constructions of "Good" Parents' (2004) 12 *Feminist Legal Studies* 1; K Laing, 'Doing the Right Thing: Cohabiting Parents, Separation and Child Contact' (2006) 20(2) *International Journal of Law, Policy and the Family* 169.

[79] Newnham (n 8) 426 (quoted) and 426–27.

[80] For further discussion of possible broader unintended consequences, see Kaganas and Piper (n 7).

[81] Dickson (n 3) 1093. See also Huddleston (n 9).

different considerations, from the decisions on whether to allow grandparents to spend time with their grandchildren, as discussed previously. If the existing statutory presumption were to be extended to include grandparents, it is most likely that it would operate in the same way as the presumption that currently applies to parents: it would become one of the factors for the court to consider when determining if an order should be made for the grandparent to spend time with the grandchild. The Explanatory Notes to the Children and Families Act 2014 frame the statutory presumption not as a strict legal presumption but, instead, as one of the factors for the court to 'weigh in the balance ... along with the other considerations in section 1 of the Children Act 1989, subject to the overriding requirement that the child's welfare remains the court's paramount consideration'.[82] This is significant, since anything stronger than this in steering the courts' decision making is likely to encounter incompatibility with the paramountcy of the welfare principle.[83] In common with the original introduction of the statutory presumption of parental involvement,[84] therefore, it is unlikely that the policy intention behind any extension to include grandparents will be to change the courts' practice in individual cases, or to detract from the paramountcy of the welfare principle.

In practice, however, the reinterpretations and retranslations of meaning that take place between different systems point to the unpredictability of reform. One outcome of removing the leave requirement and extending the statutory presumption of parental involvement is that there will indeed be no material change to the courts' approach. If this is the case, the risk then arises that, rather than placating those arguing for reform, the reform itself could bring about further dissatisfaction. Since grandparents will interpret the statutory reform using their own 'internal logic',[85] there is no guarantee that this logic will be aligned with the policy intention behind the reform, or the application of the statute by judges. In particular, once grandparents realise the limited practical impact of the removal of the leave requirement and the extension to the statutory presumption of parental involvement, and in particular that neither guarantees that any order to spend time with their grandchild will be made, their dissatisfaction with the legal framework is likely to become more, rather than less, entrenched.[86] This speaks again to the limits of using the law for symbolic purposes, as autopoietic theory reveals. Once the law fails to fulfil its expected objectives, as interpreted through the specific perspectives of the particular actors involved, renewed dissatisfaction then opens the door to further arguments for reform.[87]

---

[82] Children and Families Act 2014, Explanatory Notes, 109.

[83] Children Act 1989, s 1(1). For further discussion, see A Bainham and S Gilmore, 'The English Children and Families Act 2014' (2015) 46(3) *Victoria University of Wellington Law Review* 627; Kaganas, 'Parental Involvement' (n 73).

[84] Secretary of State for Education (n 70).

[85] Teubner (n 13) 22.

[86] For discussion of this risk in relation to previous attempts to utilise the law for symbolic purposes, see, eg, Newnham (n 8) 441.

[87] N Luhmann, *Essays on Self-Reference* (New York, Columbia University Press, 1990) 240. See also the discussion in Newnham (n 8) 440.

ii. Unintended Consequences – Changing Decision Making in High-Risk Cases Involving Allegations of Harm

Owing to the unpredictability of reform, an alternative outcome is that statutory reform changes the courts' approach, which is likely to impact particularly negatively the higher-risk cases, such as those involving domestic abuse. The risk is that contact would be promoted in cases in which it does not, in practice, serve the welfare of the child. Judges may '[obey] a different internal logic'[88] to the legislation itself and, again, as a result, the 'second system will not respond as required [by the first system]'.[89] Even if the policy intention is not to change the courts' practice, therefore, it cannot be guaranteed that the courts' practice will remain unchanged in individual cases.

A material change to the courts' practice is more likely in relation to an extension of the statutory presumption of parental involvement than the removal of the leave requirement, since the former concerns the substantive application for the child arrangements order itself. That said, the removal of the leave requirement, and its 'censoring' function in particular, could still undermine the level of safeguarding the court can provide. The policy intention behind any removal of the leave requirement would never be to encourage grandparents who pose a risk of harm to gain access to substantive hearings to argue to spend time with their grandchildren. However, there is an ever-present and well-established risk that domestically abusive parents' parents attempt to secure contact 'through the back door'.[90] This suggests that there is a need, therefore, for verification on a case-by-case basis that the grandparents seeking to use the court system to secure time with their grandchildren are not those who would pose a risk of harm to either children or parents who have been subject to domestic abuse. The retranslations that take place between different systems, here in relation to the removal of the leave requirement from the statutory framework and the courts' resolution of cases in practice, could have the unintended consequence of taking away the additional layer of protection available to the courts, contrary to any policy intention underpinning the leave requirement's removal.

Without a leave requirement, judges would have more limited scope to verify that the grandparents entitled to apply for contact are not those who would risk putting parents and children who have experienced domestic abuse into positions where their safety and well-being may be at risk. The leave requirement also provides the opportunity to assess the risk of intergenerational abuse, with grandparents potentially at risk of abuse themselves, as well as to safeguard against grandparents' involvement in the perpetration of abuse. Support for the retention

---

[88] Teubner (n 13) 22.
[89] Newnham (n 8) 438.
[90] For discussion more generally, see Dickson (n 3) 1092.

of the leave requirement to perform this protective role has been expressed by Women's Aid for this reason:

> While many grandparents can provide a vital positive role, in our experience this can sometimes be negative or harmful if it exacerbates and intensifies existing disputes or risks. We have seen some examples of cases where grandparents perpetuate or collude in abuse against a child and their non-abusing parent, especially if they are facilitating contact between the child and the abusive parent.[91]

This risk, in cases involving domestic abuse, of undermining the protective power of the court is even greater at the substantive hearing stage, and there are lessons that should be learned again here from the introduction of the statutory presumption of parental involvement that warn against its extension to include grandparents. The existing evidence on the impact of the statutory presumption suggests, overall, that, as intended at the policy level, it is indeed not having a material impact on the courts' approach.[92] There is, however, some evidence that the reinterpretations and retranslations of meaning that take place between the statutory legal framework and judges' applications of that framework in individual cases, are resulting in the misinterpretation of the statutory presumption as a direction that contact should always take place.[93] This speaks more generally to the problems inherent in the use of presumptions within family law, namely that they can 'inhibit or distort the rigorous search for the welfare solution', in particular since they can be relied upon 'as an aid to determination when the individual advocate or judge feels either undecided or overwhelmed'.[94] The evidence here suggests that the statutory presumption could be undermining the courts' duty to give paramount consideration to each individual child's welfare, by being used not simply as one of the factors for the courts to 'weigh in the balance'[95] but rather as a direction that children always 'need' the involvement of both of their parents in their lives.

Owing to the level of concern about misinterpretation, and its negative impact on the courts' practice,[96] a major expert review into the family courts' treatment of harm to children and parents in private law disputes recently concluded that a follow-up review into the operation of the presumption was 'needed urgently in order to address its detrimental effects'.[97] At the time of writing, this review

---

[91] Family Justice Review Panel, *Interim Report* (n 7) para 5.84.

[92] Harwood (n 56); House of Lords, Children and Families Act 2014 Committee, *Corrected Oral Evidence: Children and Families Act 2014* (Monday, 4 April 2022, 4.15pm).

[93] For further discussion, see Harwood (n 56).

[94] *Re L (A Child) (Contact: Domestic Violence); Re V (A Child) (Contact: Domestic Violence); Re M (A Child) (Contact: Domestic Violence); Re H (Children) (Contact: Domestic Violence)* [2001] Fam 260, 295 (Thorpe LJ).

[95] Children and Families Act 2014, Explanatory Notes (n 82). See further see Kaganas, 'Parental Involvement' (n 73).

[96] See also the concerns raised in *F v L* [2017] EWHC 1377 [11] (Russell J); and Kaganas, 'Parental Involvement' (n 73) 563.

[97] Ministry of Justice (n 6) 9.

process has commenced but not concluded.[98] There remains a real possibility that the outcome will be one of 'legislation [inciting] legislation',[99] with the Children Act 1989 needing amendment to remedy the risks that came into existence with the initial introduction of the statutory presumption.

Additional risks of misinterpretation arguably exist even more in relation to grandparents than parents. In relation to parents, it was well-established prior to the introduction of the statutory presumption that the courts already navigated the challenge of future uncertainty through the imposition of their self-referential legal knowledge that what is 'best' for children is to maintain a relationship with both parents post-parental separation, since both are seen to be of 'equal psychological importance to a child's present and future well-being'.[100] The statutory presumption therefore put on the statute book the approach the courts were already following in practice, with an assumption,[101] or even non-statutory presumption, in favour of contact being in existence prior to the reform.[102] This is not the case in relation to grandparents. The case law suggests that while judges are willing to recognise the potential benefits to children of spending time with grandparents,[103] they have also been clear that grandparents do not stand in the same position in relation to children as parents.[104] As Thorpe LJ said in *Re B (Transfer of Residence to Grandmother)*, 'Manifestly grandparents are not on equal footing with parents. ... Inevitably there are disbenefits for a child to be brought up by an adult of a different generation to either of her parents.'[105]

As a result, the courts have been less willing to assume the benefits to children of a relationship with their grandparents than they have been to children's relationships with parents,[106] and there is neither an assumption nor a presumption in favour of a relationship between grandparents and their grandchildren within the existing case law.[107] Any unintended change in the courts' approach through the mistranslation of the statutory presumption into judicial practice by leading judges to promote contact with grandparents, in cases in which it would not previously have been promoted, is likely to give rise to significant questions about the

---

[98] A broader inquiry into the Children and Families Act 2014 is also being undertaken by the House of Lords, Children and Families Act 2014 Committee (n 15).

[99] Luhmann (n 87) 240.

[100] King (n 1) 526.

[101] *Re L; Re V; Re M; Re H* (n 94) 294–95 (Thorpe LJ). See also *Re P* [2008] EWCA Civ 1431 [38] (Ward LJ).

[102] For discussion, see Harwood (n 56). See also A Barnett, 'Contact at All Costs? Domestic Violence and Children's Welfare' (2014) 26(4) *Child and Family Law Quarterly* 439.

[103] See, eg, *Re W (Contact: Application by Grandparent)* (n 34) 795 (Hollis J); *Re J (Leave to Issue Application for Residence Order)* [2003] 1 FLR 114 [19] (Thorpe LJ); *CW v TW* [2011] EWHC 76 (Fam) [31] (Sir Nicholas Wall). See further the discussion in Kaganas and Piper (n 7) 182–83.

[104] See, eg, *Re A (Section 8 Order: Grandparent Application)* [1995] 2 FLR 153, 157 (Butler-Sloss LJ); *Re W (Contact: Application by Grandparent)* (n 34) 795–98 (Hollis J).

[105] *Re B (Transfer of Residence to Grandmother)* [2012] EWCA Civ 858 [13] (Thorpe LJ).

[106] See, eg, *Re A* (n 104). More broadly see, eg, *Re G (A Child)* [2018] EWCA Civ 305.

[107] See, eg, *Re A* (n 104); *Re K (Mother's Hostility to Grandparent's Contact)* [1996] CLY 565, Case Digest. See further the discussion in Kaganas and Piper (n 7) 182–83.

presumption's interruption of the courts' proper application of the welfare principle. In response to the calls both to remove the leave requirement and to extend the statutory presumption to grandparents, therefore, it would be advisable to listen, this time, to the earlier warning by the Family Justice Council in relation to the statutory presumption of parental involvement:

> *Rather than introducing a provision that creates problems and then adding a fix for those problems, it would be far more sensible not to introduce the problem-creating provision in the first place.*[108]

Instead, there needs to be a more sustained focus on individual grandchild-grandparent relationships, unimpeded by general pronouncements on the importance of grandparents to children, along with greater sensitivity to the risk of unintended consequences that can attach to reform.

IV. Expedient 'Solutions': The Deployment of Grandparents to Play a Protective Role in Domestic Abuse Cases

The questions raised by the application of an autopoietic understanding of the legal status of grandparents explored thus far also provides a framework for the interrogation of the later stages of parties' progression through the family court, and in particular the uncertainty of the outcomes arising from the expedient deployment of grandparents to play a protective role in domestic abuse cases. An autopoietic understanding focuses attention again here on the way in which the law gives itself legitimacy in navigating the challenge of future uncertainty, as well as the way in which the closed and autonomous nature of legal and non-legal systems means that they do not necessarily work harmoniously with each other. In common with the risks that attach to the use of the law for symbolic ends, risks are revealed here too that the expedient use of grandparents can threaten the safety and broader welfare of children, principally owing to the misinterpretations and mistranslations that can take place between judicial intentions and grandparents' application of those intentions in practice.

The challenge of future uncertainty is particularly acute when the decision is whether a child should spend time with a domestically abusive parent. These cases involve the additional layer of unpredictability of how the parent will behave and the precise level of risk they pose. Judges, however, are bound to reach a decision in these contested cases. Future uncertainty is overcome by basing judicial decisions on 'present futures', namely, the information and resources available to judges at the time of hearing the case, interpreted through their own self-referential

---

[108] Family Justice Review Panel, *Final Report* (n 7) para 4.39 (original emphasis).

framework.[109] There is some evidence that a judicial solution to future uncertainty has been the temporary designation of maternal or paternal grandparents as the protectors of the child during the time the child spends with a parent who has perpetrated domestic abuse.[110]

The practical need for reliance on grandparents has arisen in part due to the lack of resourcing for supervised contact centres.[111] The courts have faced the dilemma of accepting significant delay to the resumption of contact or refusing contact altogether, or, alternatively, calling upon relatives to perform a protective role. By calling upon grandparents, the courts are relying on the self-perpetuating judicial perception that the priority in promoting children's welfare is maintaining children's relationships with both parents wherever possible,[112] and that this can be made 'safe' by asking loving grandparents to step in to monitor contact.

How widespread the practice of relying on grandparents is remains unclear. Evidence was, however, given to the All-Party Parliamentary Group on Domestic Violence that 'very unsafe or inappropriate' contact arrangements were being made involving supervision conducted by grandparents, including in cases such as the following:

> He applied for contact, and at the first hearing they granted supervised contact but the supervision was to take place at his parents' home and his parents would do the supervision – his parents had two weeks before watched him smash my head through a wall and refused to tell the police what had happened ... [They] (the court) never met the parents. BO[113]

The existence of these arrangements was also evidenced in the author's qualitative empirical study involving interviews with judges, barristers, solicitors, CAFCASS practitioners and representatives from domestic abuse organisations.[114] Forty-one semi-structured interviews were conducted within one county in England between February 2016 and April 2017. Interviewees were not asked specifically about grandparents, but some, nevertheless, pointed to this practice. One of the barristers explained that in some cases, including those involving threats to life, the court might arrange for 'some friendly granny to come along' to monitor the time spent between the domestically abusive parent and the child. Other interviewees pointed to variations in judicial practice, with some judges being more in favour of reliance on grandparents than others. Another barrister, for example, spoke of experiences with one circuit judge who 'thinks grandparents are the best thing ever'.

---

[109] King (n 1) 542.

[110] See, eg, All-Party Parliamentary Group on Domestic Violence (n 5).

[111] See, eg, J Harwood, 'Child Arrangements Orders (Contact) and Domestic Abuse – An Exploration of the Law and Practice' (PhD thesis, University of Warwick, 2018) 282–87.

[112] King (n 1) 526. See also Barnett (n 102).

[113] All-Party Parliamentary Group on Domestic Violence (n 5).

[114] Harwood (n 111). The particular findings discussed in this chapter have not previously been published elsewhere.

The autonomous and self-referential nature of different systems allows for misalignment between the courts' intentions in finding 'solutions' to the challenges posed by limited resources, and the implementation of those intentions by grandparents charged with performing the protective role in the high-risk cases. Whilst the judicial intention behind the temporary designation of grandparents as protectors of the child may be well-meaning, based on perceptions of grandparents as being 'friendly' and 'loving', there is no guarantee that, when translated outside of the legal framework into practice, grandparents will have either the impartiality or the skills needed to safeguard children. There is also the associated risk of the involvement of the grandparents themselves in the perpetration of abuse post-separation.[115] One of the representatives from the domestic abuse organisations within the author's empirical research, for example, was particularly concerned about the practice of calling upon grandparents to perform a protective role, in particular in relation to paternal grandparents:

> And that is something that has come up a lot with regards to survivors, where someone in the perpetrator's family is meant to supervise contact and where, actually, they feel that that is really unsafe and they don't feel they can trust that person who is in the supervisor role to actually ensure that contact is happening in a safe way ... And I think the level of anxiety that that gives to women [is significant, with survivors] feeling that the supervision is really inadequate.[116]

These risks are being amplified by the move away from post-order reviews, with limited information on the way in which contact is progressing being fed back into the legal system. In the place of post-order reviews, there is evidence that judges have instead increasingly been using staggered orders, in which the court sets out a map for the relaxation of the restrictions on the time spent by a domestically abusive parent over time with their children, without directly overseeing this relaxation.[117] The onus then falls on the non-abusive parent to monitor the relaxation of contact, and to bring the case back to court if deemed necessary.[118] In practice, therefore, it is possible that orders for grandparents to monitor contact are being made, with contact progressing to an unsupervised level without further judicial oversight.[119]

An autopoietic understanding enables assessments of possible solutions to overcome these risks, here by drawing attention to the importance of the feeding of information back into the legal system. Due to the circularity in the law's construction of meaning, information entering the legal system on how contact is progressing post-order, such as from parents, will be reprocessed into a format understood by judges on their own terms.[120] However, it remains crucial that

---

[115] See, eg, Family Justice Review Panel, *Interim Report* (n 7) para 5.84.
[116] Harwood (n 111) 284.
[117] ibid 199–203.
[118] For further discussion, see ibid; Ministry of Justice (n 6) 145–46.
[119] Harwood (n 111) 199–203; Ministry of Justice (n 6) 145–46.
[120] King (n 1) 525; Newnham (n 8) 427–28.

this information is at least entering the legal system. Without this, contact risks progressing when there might be significant threats to children's safety and welfare. The expedient deployment of grandparents to perform a protective role should not, therefore, be an outcome reached without careful scrutiny; and in the cases where this role is performed, it becomes imperative that the court maintains greater oversight of the way in which contact is progressing through post-order reviews.

This autopoietic understanding is particularly significant now, since the resistance to post-order reviews was identified as a problem within the Ministry of Justice's recent expert review.[121] One of the recommendations was that there should be greater court involvement post-order to monitor how contact is progressing.[122] While there are major disadvantages to prolonging children's involvement in the court system, this call for post-order reviews should be welcomed as a practical tool to support the courts in navigating the challenge of future uncertainty. There are significant problems with passing responsibility, in practice, to a parent who has experienced domestic abuse to manage this uncertainty by monitoring the relaxation of the restrictions on contact over time, including the impact of domestic abuse on that parent's safety, well-being and parenting capacity.[123]

V. Conclusion

This chapter has explored how well-intentioned attempts to promote the involvement of grandparents in children's lives through the use of symbolic and expedient 'solutions' give rise to significant risks of unintended consequences that threaten children's welfare, and ultimately do not serve grandparents. Both in the formation of the statutory framework and in its application to individual cases, the risk of unintended consequences arises since, at the time decisions are taken, there is no way of predicting with certainty how those decisions will play out in practice in relation to the specific children subject to the dispute.[124] From an autopoietic perspective, any statutory reform, or indeed any judgment given by the court, can give rise to unpredictable results within children's uncertain futures, owing to the reinterpretations and retranslations of meaning that take place between different systems. While this unpredictability will always exist, given that symbolic reform and the expedient deployment of grandparents are very unlikely to serve either grandparents or grandchildren, taking this risk of unpredictable results is one that is not merited, and different solutions are needed.

At the heart of resistance to statutory reform to remove the leave requirement and to extend the statutory presumption of parental involvement to include

---

[121] Ministry of Justice (n 6) 145–46.
[122] ibid 147.
[123] ibid 145–47; Harwood (n 111) 199–203.
[124] King (n 1).

grandparents should be an understanding, informed by the insights provided by autopoietic theory in this context, that there can be no guarantee that the intended impact of reform will be achieved neatly in practice. Lessons should be learned here from previous, failed attempts to deploy the law for symbolic means, and most recently from the problems arising from the introduction of the statutory presumption of parental involvement. Generalised presumptions, while convenient, have never sat easily within family law, given the diversity of the issues at stake, and they also give rise to significant risks of undermining the paramountcy of each individual child's welfare. Neither the removal of the leave requirement, nor the extension of the statutory presumption to include grandparents is likely to enjoy success in positively shaping the behaviour of the parties to any dispute. These non-legal actors will reinterpret legal reform from their own perspectives since they inhabit their own normative systems, based on how they can, and want to, interpret the legal framework, with no guarantee that this will align with policy intentions. The more likely outcomes are unintended consequences, including renewed dissatisfaction and the introduction of a risk that the courts will unduly promote contact in inappropriate cases.

The reliance on grandparents later in the private family court process as 'protectors' to monitor the time spent between domestically abusive parents and children again gives rise to risks of harmful unintended consequences, here through mistranslations of the courts' intentions for grandparents to safeguard children into grandparents' capacity to actually do so in practice. The importance of the feeding of information back into the court system on how contact is progressing through post-order reviews is also highlighted here, albeit with the acknowledgement that this information will be re-processed into judges' own terms once it enters that system.

In progressing debates in this space, the framework provided by the application of autopoietic theory has contributed to an understanding of the real risks that attach to reliance on symbolic and expedient solutions. It has also shone light on the pathway that needs to be taken to find more meaningful solutions. Within the court system, these solutions cannot involve reference to generalised statements on the benefits grandparents can bring to children, or an untested reliance on the protective role they can play. Instead, there has to be a true examination of the particular grandchild–grandparent relationship in each individual case. More careful scrutiny of where any problem with grandparents' relationships with their grandchildren actually lies is also needed, which should involve an acceptance that there are significant limits to the deployment of the law to solve problems with grandparents' relationships with their grandchildren that originate from outside the legal system itself.

8

A Socio-Legal Analysis of Grandparents' Rights in Iran

SAHAR MARANLOU AND FATEMEH KEYHANLOU

I. Introduction

In the Civil Code of the Islamic Republic of Iran, grandparents who are defined as the fathers of the fathers, also known as paternal grandfathers (*jad*), are considered legally responsible vis-à-vis their grandchildren.[1] Grandparents' rights and responsibilities in the Iranian legal system stem from the Islamic concept of guardianship in the *Shia* tradition. This chapter focuses on *Shia* or Twelvers Islamic juristic discourse,[2] especially in modern Iran, as well as in post-revolutionary court practice. The traditional jurists and modern codification of Islamic law are compared with contemporary issues around gender and the best interests of the child. This discourse examines overall themes relating to guardianship of grandparents, as well as tensions between classical Islamic law, gender and child-centred international standards.

Classical Islamic jurisprudence makes a clear distinction between 'custody', which means generally the nurturing of children, and 'guardianship', which is defined as caring for the child's property and education. The concept and conditions of grandparents' guardianship over grandchildren are closely related to custody, and both have been codified within family law in classical Islamic legal doctrine. In modern statutory legislation, the dynamic between custody and guardianship of grandparents has not changed as much, and no contemporary concept of guardianship has been codified within the civil law tradition to which Iran adheres. Here, it is important to understand to what extent the courts in Iran have deviated from applying the classical Islamic law of *wilayat* (guardianship) where grandparents are involved.

---

[1] The Civil Code of the Islamic Republic of Iran, 1935, Art 1194.

[2] Also known as *Ithna Ashariyyah* or *Immamya*, it is the official religion of Islamic Republic of Iran as stated in the 1979 Constitution.

Section II examines the historical development of the concept of *wilayat*[3] in Iranian family law, especially regarding grandparents. In section III, post-revolutionary legislation is examined to understand the nature of grandparents' rights in Iran. That section also reviews the main provisions concerning the best interests of the child principle in relation to grandparents.

II. Historical Overview of Guardianship Law in Iran

In Islamic juristic debate in the pre-modern period, before the early nineteenth century, there was a clear distinction between rights and responsibilities, which in Western legal tradition are known as 'physical custody' and 'legal custody'.[4] Physical custody refers to nurturing a child, having custody and managing the child's property, and legal custody refers to caring for a child's education and guardianship. It seems that the child's most basic needs, such as access to adequate food, shelter and health, have been prioritised over the child's best interests.[5]

The concept of natural guardianship, as it is known today, had been widespread among Arabian tribes before the rise of Islam. Post-Islam, the concept was endorsed by Muslim jurists, but still, there is no information about who first referred to natural guardianship.[6] Among others, Ibn Junaid Eskafi, a jurist of the fourth century, spoke of the guardianship of fathers and grandfathers.[7] Paternal grandfathers are the guardians of their grandchildren in the absence or death of the fathers. Ali added that guardianship is the absolute right of the father, allowing him to intervene in any of his children's affairs, including their right to life.[8] It seems that, in the case of the death or absence of fathers, the same authority could be attributed to grandfathers.

The Iranian Civil Code, governing personal status law (*ahwal shakhsiyya*), was first codified in 1934–35 based on the *Shia* jurisprudential school (as the official religion of the country[9]) and the modern legal system (French Civil Code). These

---

[3] Guardianship.

[4] A Ibrahim, *Child Custody in Islamic Law: Theory and Practice in Egypt since the Sixteenth Century* (Cambridge, Cambridge University Press, 2018).

[5] Muslim scholars define custody as the action of raising, educating and taking care of a minor's basic needs, such as housing, food, clothes and body care. More examples of domestic laws about the best interests of the child can be found in this interesting comparative study: N Yassari, L-M Möller, and I Gallala-Arndt (eds), *Parental Care and the Best Interests of the Child in Muslim Countries* (The Hague, TMC Asser Press, 2017).

[6] Some jurists believe that the term 'natural guardianship' has not been used in *Shia* jurisprudence and that its first use dates to the adoption of the Civil Code of the Islamic Republic of Iran in 1935. H Safaii and A Emami, *A Concise Family Law* (Tehran, Mizan, 1997) 371.

[7] Recited in H Sadeqi, *A New Approach to Compulsory Guardianship of Children in Jurisprudence and Civil Law (with the views and opinions of Imam Khomeini)* (Tehran, Research Institute of Imam Khomeini, 2002) 64.

[8] J Ali, *The History of The Arabs Before Islam*, vol 5 (Beirut, Dar El Ilm Lilmalayin, 1970) 528.

[9] Constitution of the Islamic Republic of Iran, 1979, modified in 1989, Art 12.

two important resources played different roles in drafting the Iranian Civil Code. While the French Civil Code has been applied to the structure, chapters and articles of the Iranian Code, the contents were founded on the *Twelvers*[10] Jurisprudence or *Shia*. Thus, the legal relations of grandparents and grandchildren have their roots in *Immamya* and Twelver Shia, or the *Twelver Ja'fari* school (*Ithna 'Ashariyyah*) as the principal branch of the Shia school of thought. The followers of other recognised religious groups, such as the Sunny Muslims, Shia Muslims belonging to the Zaydi sector as well as Zoroastrian, Jewish and Christian Iranians, are allowed to have certain and common rules and customs of their sectors applied to them in all matters about their personal status, such as marriage, divorce, inheritance, wills, etc.[11] This system is based on the Islamic law notion that non-Muslim citizens of the 'Islamic state' (*dhimmiyyīn*) enjoy autonomy in their religious and personal affairs.[12] In the Civil Code, the term 'natural guardian', as in the common law tradition, refers to a presumptive guardian (*wali*). This assumption of male power in natural guardians as *wali* and the concept of *qayyem* or judicial designation used by jurists show that male-dominated guardians have variable powers over the child. For example, in all matters about the estate and the civil and financial concerns of the child, *wali* is his or her legal representative.[13]

III. Family and Guardianship

There is no specific definition of 'family' in Iranian law and its codified legislation. One common understanding is that family is a union of people who, because of kinship, are dependent on each other. Kinship is created by marriage or blood. This definition is based on the Iranian Civil Code, especially the law on inheritance,[14] which enumerates a group of persons who inherit from each other and includes the following categories: (i) father, mother, children and their children; (ii) grandparents, sibling, and their children; (iii) uncles, aunts and their children.[15]

The definition of family is limited to a heterosexual marital union and does not apply to cohabitation outside marriage. Therefore, in legal terms, family is usually

---

[10] *Imamya* Jurisprudence, also known as *Shia*, is a school of thought following the descent of divine revelation through Prophet Muhammad's family line over accounts of his life and teachings as passed down by his companions. The Islamic Law sources in *Shia* jurisprudence are the Qur'an (divine revelation as recited to the Prophet), Sunnah (the customary example of the Prophet), Hadith (reports of what he said), Consensus (agreement between the jurists) and the intellect (wisdom).

[11] Constitution of the Islamic Republic of Iran, Arts 12 and 13.

[12] J Moussa, 'Egypt' in N Yassari (ed), *Parental Care and the Best Interests of the Child in Muslim Countries*, (Asser Press, The Hague, 2017) 4.

[13] The Civil Code of the Islamic Republic of Iran, 1935, Art 1183.

[14] ibid Art 1032.

[15] N Katouzian, *Civil Law: Family Law*, vol I (Tehran, Ganje Danesh Press, 1999) 1–2.

understood as including the husband and wife, and children if they are under the protection and guardianship (*wilayat*) of their father. By including guardianship in the above definition based on Iranian laws, the definition should be construed in a way to cover paternal grandparents as well.[16] According to the Iranian Civil Code, 'grandchildren are under their fathers and paternal grandparents' guardianship'. This definition of grandparenthood is deep-rooted in Islamic law kinship norms. In Islamic law, the family is considered a social unit and is something more than the group of people who form it; members of a family are responsible for each other in different ways, such as through providing for economic needs, providing education, etc.[17]

The concept of the family in Iran has also been considered by sociologists. Some claim that this concept is under the influence of social development.[18] Social development is, in their view, a process of transition from traditional societies to modern ones. Urbanisation, the higher education of women and increased employment of women are among the indicators of this development.[19] For example, regarding higher education and the employment of women, statistics show that Iranian women are more willing to go to university.[20] It means that, nowadays, many mothers are more educated than their husbands, let alone their parents or parents-in-law. This fact, on its own, could have positive effects on the raising of children. However, it may cause legal problems when it comes to a court's deciding who, rightfully, ought to be the natural guardian of a child. According to Iranian Civil Law, along with fathers, paternal grandparents are the natural guardians of their grandchildren. They are preferred to mothers, irrespective of any priority a mother might have based on her education or social position.[21]

Among the results of this social development is the transformation of family structures, with statistics showing a decline in the more traditional extended family and the emergence of a variety of nuclear families.[22] Nevertheless, grandparents, especially maternal grandparents, may still play a vital role in bringing up and looking after their grandchildren, especially where both parents go out to work.[23] Public legal culture recognises grandparents as 'family pillars' or 'stabilisers', especially during times of family crisis such as parents' divorce or death.

---

[16] ibid 3–4.

[17] ibid 8.

[18] S Mohammadi, 'Preference of Mother Guardianship to Grandfather Guardship' (2017) 98 *Legal Justice* 179. In Persian.

[19] ibid.

[20] Studies show that 'Overall, this increase in women in higher education has contributed to the rise of Islamic feminism and an intrinsic movement of Iranian women pursuing the advancement of their legal and social status'; see, eg, MK Winn, 'Women in Higher Education in Iran: How the Islamic Revolution Contributed to an Increase in Female Enrollment' (2016) 10 *Global Tides* 10.

[21] Art 1183 Civil Law.

[22] H Sarai, 'Family and evolution in the context of the demographic transition in Iran' [2007] *Journal of Population Association of Iran* 37.

[23] A Tavassoli, 'Investigating the degree of dependence of the nuclear family on paternal and maternal families among students' (2018) 7 *Sociology of Education* 12.

The rights and relationships of grandparents on divorce, however, are contro-versial, especially with the rise in the divorce rate among women.[24] Culturally speaking, societal disapproval of divorce is often embodied by grandpar-ents, leading to disruption of grandparent–grandchild relations. According to formal statistics, in 2020 there were 183,193 divorces, while a year earlier there were 176,814.[25] Informal statistics show that in by the Spring of 2021 alone, the divorce rate had increased by 16.4 per cent in comparison with the same time in 2020.[26] According to the Iranian Civil Code, in divorce, parties cannot deprive the other of visitation rights.[27] Discussion of the nature of grandparent visitation rights is included in section III.A following.

A. The Nature of Grandparents' Rights

The exercise of guardianship of grandparents over a child can be analysed from two perspectives: financial and non-financial concerns. As mentioned earlier, in all matters regarding the estate and financial concerns of the child, the guardian will be his or her legal representative. Accordingly, all of the guardian's actions with regard to, and transactions of, the estate of the ward are considered valid if they conform with the best interests (*maslehat*) of the child.[28] That is, the guardian should act in the interests (well-being) of the child.[29] Nevertheless, some believe that although the guardian's legal transactions need not be profitable, it should not result in a loss to the ward (*massage*). This requirement[30] is also inferred from the wording of Article 1184 of the Civil Code, which provides if the guardian does not respect the interests of the child, he will be dismissed. Moreover, a uniform judicial precedent provides in this respect that a person such as a father or pater-nal grandfather who acts on behalf of a ward should reasonably respect the ward's benefits and interests. This precedent not only makes it clear that the powers of natural grandparents are limited to the interests and benefit of the child,[31] but

---

[24] S Jaberi et al, 'Iranian Women's Divorce Style: A Qualitative Study' (2022) 61(1) *Family Process* 436.

[25] Published in the Statistical Centre of Iran as the main organisation for statistics in Iran at www.amar.org.ir/ (accessed 10 May 2022).

[26] More figures are available at www.imna.ir/news/547856/ (accessed 5 May 2022).

[27] Art 1174 Civil Code.

[28] H Emami, *Civil Law*, vol V (Tehran, Eslamiyeh, 1992) 213.

[29] According to a consultative opinion of the Judiciary's Legal Department, *qebte* means the material benefit or the interests of the ward in administrating his or her property and related contracts (*Civil Law Revision Collection*, (Tehran, Deputy for compiling, revising and publishing laws and regulations, 2020)357.) Also see M Langroodi, *Legal Terminology* (Tehran, Ganj-e Danesh, 1993) 487; Emami (n 28) 213.

[30] A Helli, *TahrireAhkam e Shariie ala mazhabeEmamaya*, vol 1 (Qom, Aal al-Bayt Institute, 2000) 220.

[31] Revocation of title deed due to non-observance of minor benefits by the natural guardian, Minutes of the Judicial Session, Bojnoord, Khorasan, 27 November 2007, at www.neshast.org/Home/GetPublicJ SessionTranscript/8aa5a8a7-78d6-4e21-96d3-08d601ea40a4 (accessed 10 March 2022).

indicates that both terms have an identical meaning.[32] In summary, guardians can sell, rent or change the property of the child, or transact business on behalf of the child, if those actions are deemed to be in the favour of the ward. They are also responsible for ensuring that the ward has appropriate living conditions. To this end, and to manage the child's property, guardians are allowed to engage nurses, maids or even employees. They can even pay a fee to themselves from the child's accounts or belongings.[33] The only area in which both maternal and paternal grandfathers and grandmothers are involved is in maintenance. It is an enforceable[34] legal obligation of close relatives towards each other, by which well-off relatives provide maintenance for poor ones.[35] The obligation to provide maintenance is subject to the existence of kinship, the financial resources of one relative and the indigence of the other.[36] To determine the available financial resources of a family member, his obligations and his manner of life must be taken into consideration.[37] To establish indigence, the family member should not be able to find an appropriate normal job.[38] According to the definition, maintenance consists of the provision of a dwelling, clothing, food and furniture to the extent regarded as covering the bare necessities, and is subject to the means of the person providing the maintenance.[39]

A consensual legal provision[40] in this regard states that relatives by blood in the direct line (ascending or descending) are under a reciprocal obligation to provide maintenance for each other.[41] As far as the present discussion is concerned, the following order should be applied with regard to providing maintenance: for a child whose father is dead or unable to maintain him or her, this duty devolves to the paternal grandfather, the nearest male next of kin.[42] In the absence of a paternal grandfather, or in the event of his incapacity, the duty of maintenance devolves to the mother. If the mother is dead or is also unable to maintain the child, the duty

---

[32] The majority holds that 'benefits' and 'interests' have an identical meaning. However, some argue that a child's benefit is different from his or her interests. In their view, a benefit is not a requirement; and for the legal transactions of guardians to be valid, the interests of the ward are the only requirement. According to this view, non-profitable transactions that are also contrary to the interests of the ward are invalid, but non-expedient and non-harmful ones remain valid. Ayatollah Naraqi, *Javaher-al-Kalam* [*Theological Jewels*], vol 22, 322.

[33] This is inferred from Art 1246 of the Iranian Civil Code, which allows *qayyem* to ask for fees for the fulfilment of his duties, and is *a fortiori* applied to natural guardians. Although the above-mentioned view is supported by some jurists, there are lawyers who argue that the guardian is not allowed to receive fees from the ward's property because it is against his social duties *via-à-vis* his children or grandchildren (the only exception in this regard is relatives maintenance, which will be discussed further below). See N Katouzian, *Civil Law: Family Law*, vol II (Tehran, Ganje Danesh Press, 1999) 229.

[34] The Civil Code of the Islamic Republic of Iran, Art 1205.

[35] See N Katouzian, *Civil Law: Family Law*, vol II (Tehran, Ganje Danesh Press, 1999) 330.

[36] ibid 333.

[37] The Civil Code of the Islamic Republic of Iran, Art 1198.

[38] ibid Art 1197.

[39] ibid Art 1204.

[40] Emami (n 28) 228.

[41] The Civil Code of the Islamic Republic of Iran, Art. 1196.

[42] ibid Art 1199.

will be taken on by any maternal grandfathers and grandmothers and paternal grandmothers who are sufficiently wealthy to provide maintenance, giving preference to the nearest next of kin of the children's father. If several of the grandparents are similar in degree of kinship, the expense of maintenance must be paid by them in equal shares.[43] As may be seen, here the paternal grandfather is in the same line as the maternal grandfathers and the grandmothers.

The expense of maintaining parents, however, must be paid by the nearest related children or grandchildren (either the daughter or son) in the order of kinship. So, if a child is unable to maintain his or her parents, the duty falls to the grandchildren in descending order. If the relatives who are to be maintained are numerous and the supporter cannot pay for all of them, as Article 1202 provides, the maintenance of the children and grandchildren in the descending direct line will be given priority over grandparents in the ascending direct line. This is in opposition to the view of *Shia* jurists, who consider that grandparents in an ascending direct line should be preferred.[44]

The other most significant office is non-financial guardianship. Although Article 1183 of the Civil Code exclusively refers to the responsibility of the guardian for the financial concerns of the ward, some other articles provide for the guardian's duties regarding non-financial issues. Marriage is of utmost importance in this regard. According to Article 1041 of the Civil Code, the marriage of a girl under the age of 13 or a boy under the age of 15 is subject to the permission of the guardian and conditional on taking into consideration the child's best interests under the supervision of competent courts.[45] The marriage of boys is thus merely subject to the permission of guardians up until the age of 15, unless their immaturity or mental unfitness continues past their minority. The marriage of the girls, however, remains at the discretion of guardians for a longer time.[46] In addition to the permission of their guardians for marriage of girls aged under 13, which is a consensual requirement, *Shia* jurists believe that to assure benefit, the marriage of virgin, mentally mature girls, irrespective of their age, should be done only with the consent of the guardians.[47] 'Virgin', in this context, connotes a girl who has not lost her virginity through lawful sexual intercourse.[48] This discriminatory gender rule has been included in the Article 1043 of the Iranian Civil Code, which provides that 'the marriage of a virgin girl is dependent on the permission

---

[43] The Civil Code of the Islamic Republic of Iran, Art 1199.

[44] Emami (n 28) 230–31.

[45] For years after the adoption of the Iranian Civil Code in 1928, marriage before the age of maturity was allowed by the permission of the guardian and was conditional on taking into consideration the ward's interest (Note to Art 1041). This Note was omitted in 1991.

[46] Boys are presumed to be mentally mature after 15 unless any contrary fact is established.

[47] A Soltani, 'A study of the jurisprudential principles of the father and paternal grandfather in the marriage of a virgin girl' (2015) *The Second International Congress of Religious Thought and Research* 13.

[48] H Al Taha, 'Guardianship in marriage from *Shia's* jurisprudence point of view and the law' (2017) *The Second International Congress of Islamic Sciences and Humanities* 2.

of her father or her paternal grandfather even if she has reached the full age of maturity.'[49]

The discriminatory permission requirement can be removed if: (i) both guardians are dead;[50] (ii) both guardians have been disqualified from exercising guardianship.[51] No other permission, whether from the mother or maternal grandparents, is legally required as a prerequisite to marriage.[52] The guardians' permission is replaced by the Court's permission for the marriage if: (i) the father or the paternal grandfather is not present and obtaining their permission is impossible;[53] or (ii) the guardians withhold the permission without any justifiable reason.[54] According to a Uniform Judicial Precedent, marriage celebrated without any of these permissions is void.[55]

In order to understand grandparents' rights in a plural legal system such as Iran's, a useful discussion to have is to analyse some of the eligibility requirements for being a guardian and see how they impact on the best interests of the child. Such a discussion follows in section III.B.

B. The Competence of Natural Guardians

According to Article 1183 of the Civil Code, in all matters regarding the estate and financial concerns of the child, the guardian will be the child's legal representative. Accordingly, in case of doubt, natural guardians are recognised as the legal representatives of their wards and the courts or attorneys-general are not allowed to intervene.[56] Although this article refers to financial concerns, natural guardianship is not limited to these. The guardians' status also extends to non-financial concerns, unless expressly barred by law.[57]

---

[49] See also Uniform Judicial Precedent No 126-31/2/1363. There is even a belief that the method of losing virginity may affect the authenticity of the marriage. For example, if virginity is lost as a result of a medical operation, the girl is considered a virgin for the purpose of marriage. The same rule applies to a girl who divorces before any sexual intercourse with her husband has taken place. However, a girl who has lost her virginity because of adultery is not considered a virgin and will no longer be under guardianship for marriage (Al Taha (n 48)) According to the Uniform Judicial Precedent of 29/1/1363, sexual intercourse, whether legal or illegal, removes the necessity for the guardians' permission. *Civil Law Revision Collection* (Tehran, Deputy for compiling, revising, and publishing laws and regulations, 2020) 263, 62/62.

[50] Inferred from the contrary argument of The Civil Code of the Islamic Republic of Iran, Art 1044.

[51] M Langroodi, *Family Law* (Tehran, Ganj-e Danesh, 1997) 25, 28.

[52] H Emami, *Civil Law*, vol IV (Tehran, Eslamiyeh, 1992) 287.

[53] The Civil Code of the Islamic Republic of Iran, Art 1044.

[54] ibid Art 1043.

[55] Uniform Judicial Precedent of 18 April 1984; see also Judiciary's Legal Department Opinion, No 1.2261, 1999/3/14, *Civil Law Revision Collection* (Tehran, Deputy for Compiling, Revising and Publishing Laws and Regulations, 2020) 263.

[56] N Katouzian, *Civil Law: Family Law*, vol II (Tehran, Ganje Danesh Press, 1999) 215.

[57] ibid, 217.

By recognising fathers and paternal grandfathers as natural guardians, a question may arise regarding the priority of each in exercising guardianship over the ward. Some jurists have envisioned situations in which fathers and paternal grandfathers are in the same line and are independently responsible for exercising their guardianship (*Wilayat*) over a ward and administering their property.[58] Other than this, jurists assumed that natural guardians act alone; therefore, if the father is alive, the paternal grandfather should be forbidden from exercising guardianship. They argue that the nearer next of kin excludes the remoter next of kin, thus the guardianship of the father should be given priority.[59] Yet the Civil Code's preference is for the first view, where the father and paternal grandfather may exercise their guardianship rights and duties independently of one another.[60] This is a view that is not in conformity with current social customs, according to which, while the father is alive, not only society but also paternal grandparents do not consider themselves allowed to intervene in matters relating to the grandchildren. Grandparents' guardianship starts once the father is prevented from exercising guardianship, either by death or by a legal cause.[61] There is even a consultative opinion of the Judiciary's Legal Department that says the father's natural guardianship continues until the ward's age of maturity.[62]

Accepting the first view may also cause conflict in cases where the legal transactions of natural guardians are concurrent.[63] For example, where they sell the same property to different persons at the same time. To determine which transactions must be given priority, three different solutions may be proposed: (i) the invalidity of both transactions; (ii) the validity of the paternal grandfather's transactions; and (iii) the validity of the father's transactions. Despite disagreement surrounding the conflict in such cases, some consensual views of jurists imply that in each case the legal transaction is preferred that is most for the benefit of the child, and in case of any doubt the Court (*Hakem*) will resolve the dispute by applying the principle of caution.[64] Some jurists, however, consider the father's transactions to have priority, in accordance with what was said earlier; the paternal grandfather is not customarily considered a member of a family.[65]

---

[58] *Javaher-al-Kalam* [*Theological Jewels*], vol 26, 322.

[59] Allama al-Hillī, *Sharāyi' al-Islām* [*Islamic Law*], vol 7, 116.

[60] See Art 1180 Civil Code.

[61] N Katouzian, *Civil Law: Family Law*, vol II (Tehran, Ganje Danesh Press, 1999) 212.

[62] Consultative Opinion of the Judiciary's Legal Department, No 518, 7 February 1989.

[63] H Masjedsaraie, 'Paternal Guardianship in Islamic Jurisprudence' (2016) 13 *Journal of Islamic Law & Jurisprudence Researches* 169.

[64] ibid no 63.

[65] ibid no 61, vol II, 214.

Having discussed the competence of natural guardians, we can now turn to assess the qualification of natural guardians as grandparents.

C. The Qualification of Natural Guardian

According to the Iranian Civil Code,[66] natural guardians should be mentally mature. Once a guardian becomes *alieni juris* (for any reason), his legal guardianship will cease and his responsibilities will be conferred on the other guardian.[67] This is consensual legal opinion between different school of thought, but in the event that the incapacity of the guardian is as a result of insanity, the prominent view is that only permanent insanity forbids guardians from exercising guardianship. A guardian suffering from periodic insanity is allowed to exercise his guardianship when he is not so suffering.[68] The definition of mental health for guardians – especially for grandparents – is an important issue regarding the best interests of the child. There are no statistics as to how much regular child care grandparents provide in Iran, or how many children are raised by their grandparents. Grandparents are often involved with their grandchildren's lives, though. Although cultural values promote the benefits for grandparents' and grandchildren's well-being and health, the relationship between grandparents' mental health and the best interests of children in Iran is surprisingly overlooked within academic discourse.

There are international studies investigating whether grandparenting can improve well-being by being involved in their grandchildren's lives.[69] A counter-hypothesis, however, takes the stance that caring for young children is challenging, particularly for older adults with limited reserves of strength.[70] According to this perspective, active grandparenting could overburden older adults and lead to grandparents' decreased health and well-being. Poverty and sanctions increase the weight of the burden on Iranian grandparents, as recent figures suggest that more than 60 per cent of the population live below the poverty line.[71]

---

[66] Arts 1184–1188 Civil Code.

[67] The Civil Code of the Islamic Republic of Iran, Art 1185. If the natural guardian of the child becomes incapacitated, the Public Prosecutor is obliged to appoint a guardian for the child according to the regulations governing the nomination of guardians.

[68] Kh Moradi, 'The Consequences of Violation by the Natural Guardian from the Viewpoints of Jurists of Different Islamic Denominations and the Civil Code of Islamic Republic of Iran' at http://fiqhemoqaran.mazaheb.ac.ir/article_51380.html?lang=en (accessed 20 June 2022).

[69] See, eg, K Mahne and O Huxhold, 'Grandparenthood and Subjective Well-Being: Moderating Effects of Educational Level' (2015) 70(5) *The Journals of Gerontology: Series B, Psychological Sciences and Social Sciences* 782.

[70] See LA Baker, M Silverstein and NM Putney, 'Grandparents Raising Grandchildren in the United States: Changing Family Forms, Stagnant Social Policies' (2008) 28(7) *Journal of Sociology and Social Policy* 53. Also ME Hughes et al, 'All In the Family: The Impact of Caring for Grandchildren on Grandparents' Health' (2007) 62(2) *The Journals of Gerontology: Series B, Psychological Sciences and Social Sciences* S108–119.

[71] The Parliament Research Centre Report for 2018/2019 indicates that the essential goods poverty line has increased in the last seven years rising from 15% to over 18%. See N Bozorgmehr, 'Spiraling Poverty in Iran Adds to Pressure on Regime' *Financial Times* (Tehran, 25 January 2021).

Another important issue is religion. The guardian should be Muslim. In fact, the common requirement found in all jurisdictions is religion. A non-Muslim paternal grandfather has no right of guardianship over his Muslim grandchildren. This is inferred from a Quranic verse that says, 'God has never put the Muslims under the domination and control of non-believers'.[72] The Civil Code is silent on this matter but provides that a Muslim guardian cannot appoint a non-Muslim guardian for his ward.[73] Lawyers argue that this article also, *a fortiori*, covers the apostasy of guardians. However, Christians, those of the Jewish faith and Zoroastrians are governed by their own religious personal status laws. This is known as the 'plurality of laws'[74] in many Muslim-dominant countries, granting relative legislative and judicial autonomy to non-Muslims in their status such as guardians and as regards 'grandparents' rights'. The other important issue that is also related to the best interests of the child is that the guardian must be just. This means that the paternal grandfather should be fair in his legal transactions regarding the property of the ward. This requirement is rather controversial, as some jurists consider the legal transactions of an unjust paternal grandfather as invalid; yet others believe that, irrespective of whether they are fair or not, all legal transactions of guardians are legally binding. Since the Iranian Civil Code is silent on this issue, lawyers suppose fairness is not a condition for guardians.[75] Along with fairness, however, the importance of the child's best interests, emphasised in the United Nations Convention on the Rights of the Child (UNCRC),[76] is the foundation of the grandparents' rights over the child, as can be seen from the visitation rights discussed in section III.D.

D. Visiting Rights of Grandparents

The Family Protection Law gives grandparents the right to be heard in court when custodial parents do not allow visitation.[77] It does not give grandparents an exclusive right to visit grandchildren. Grandparent visitation statutes vary from one family court to another, but there are some common elements. The new Family Protection Law provides general guidelines about how the courts should decide whether to grant visitation privileges. The legal visitation rights are applicable only when certain events, such as divorce or the death of a parent, have occurred, or when children have lived with their grandparents.

---

[72] Quran, Nesa 141.

[73] The Civil Code of the Islamic Republic of Iran, Art 1192.

[74] See MH Fadel, 'Political Liberalism, Islamic Family Law, and Family Law Pluralism' in J Nichol (ed), *Marriage and Divorce in a Multicultural Context: Multi-Tiered Marriage and the Boundaries of Civil Law and Religion* (New York, Cambridge University Press, 2012) 184.

[75] M Haghkhah, 'Unauthorized Transactions by Natural Guardians on The Property of The Ward' (2013) 57 *Family Law and Jurisprudence Journal* 115.

[76] Art 12 UNCRC.

[77] Art 41.

The right to visit belongs to the parent who does not have custody of the child. It applies where the parents of the child do not live in the same house because of divorce or for any other reason.[78] According to a consultative opinion of the Judiciary's Legal Department, this right belongs to parents exclusively and does not extend to maternal or paternal grandparents.[79] Yet there are judgments in which the courts have recognised the right of visitation of grandparents, whether paternal or maternal, by referring to the best interests of the child as mentioned in the UNCRC. In one case, for example, the court, when referring to Articles 3–4 UNCRC, held that depriving an 8-month-old girl of visits with her paternal grandparents was against her best interests as, due to the death of her mother, it might cause her physical and mental suffering or lead to her forgetting them.[80] In another case, extending the paternal grandfather's visiting time with a 5-year-old girl whose father was killed in a car accident was affirmed by the Court of Appeal. The Court argued that visiting the paternal grandfather was not only in compliance with the best interests of the child, but also conformed with his position as the child's natural guardian.[81]

There is a need to conduct more research into grandparent visitation rights in law and practice in Iran. It would be very interesting to view court proceedings in such cases. Also, more research is needed to see how parents may benefit from grandparent visitation rights granted by law and the courts, because they require them to uphold contact with their children's grandparents (their own parents) beyond cultural norms.

With this argument, it is important to examine the end of *Wilāya*, loss and revocation of guardianship in Iranian legislation that distinguishes between 'guardianship over property' and 'guardianship over the ward'. The issues of eligibility, loss and revocation of guardianship are governed by several legal provisions as discussed in section III.E.

E. When a Grandparent Stops Being a Guardian

The court, on the application of any interested person or of its own motion, may remove a guardian or revoke a guardianship order in the following circumstances:

1.   As soon as a child reaches the age of maturity, he or she will cease to be under wardship.[82] Immature or insane children whose immaturity or mental

---

[78] The Civil Code of the Islamic Republic of Iran, Art 1174.
[79] Judiciary's Legal Department Opinion, No 7.3744, 3 April 2004, *Civil Law Revision Collection* (Tehran, Deputy for Compiling, Revising and Publishing Laws and Regulations, 2020) 352.
[80] Mazandaran Province, Court of Appeal No 13.
[81] Mazandaran Province, Court of Appeal No 12.
[82] The Civil Code of the Islamic Republic of Iran, Art 1193.

unfitness continues past their minority,[83] and virgin, mentally mature girls, as discussed in section III.A, are exceptions. To ensure the maturity of the child, identity documents are determinative. A grandparent must prove the claim if he asserts that the child has not reached maturity.[84]

2. If the court finds that the grandparents do not act in accordance with the child's best interests, the court may terminate the guardianship and appoint another competent person (as a *qayyem*).[85]

In the following cases, grandparents are not barred from guardianship but, due to their mental or physical condition, a trustee may be attached to them by the order of a competent court:

1. *Guardian's incapacity.* Where the guardian of the ward is unable to administer the ward's estate owing to old age or sickness or similar reasons, the court may dismiss him and prohibit him from administering the ward's estate, appointing another competent person (*Amin*) in his stead.[86]

2. *Guardian's absence or imprisonment.* If the only natural guardian of a child cannot administer the estate of his ward owing to absence or imprisonment for any reason, and if he has not nominated anyone else to represent him, the court will provisionally appoint a trustee (*Amin*) on the proposal of the Public Prosecutor to take charge of the estate and attend to all matters regarding it.[87]

In both cases, the guardianship is transferred to the other natural guardian if he is alive and able to perform the necessary duties.

As the Civil Code does not provide examples of how the termination of guardianship may affect the best interests of the child, jurists have suggested three main situations, including: (i) disadvantageous transactions of the guardian are not legally binding (effective) unless the child approves them after maturity;[88] (ii) disadvantageous transactions of the guardian are valid if concluded reasonably with due care to the interests of the child; and[89] (iii) disadvantageous transactions of the guardian are void if they cause loss and the guardian is considered to be aware of this result.[90] In practice, it seems that the court has applied the last of these approaches. For example, in an Appeal Judgment, it was held that transferring a child's financial right to a third person, which the guardian admitted was not

[83] ibid Art 1180.

[84] Uniform Judicial Precedent No 518-7, February 1989, *Civil Law Revision Collection* (Tehran, Deputy for Compiling, Revising and Publishing Laws and Regulations, 2020) 354.

[85] The Civil Code of the Islamic Republic of Iran, Art 1184.

[86] The Civil Code of the Islamic Republic of Iran, Art 1184.

[87] ibid Art 1187.

[88] Emami (n 52) 213.

[89] However, the guardian should compensate the losses of the ward (ibid no 15, vol II, 224, 226).

[90] Haghkhah (n 75).

in the child's best interest, was voidable and could be declared void at the request of the child.[91] A recent judicial precedent holds that guardians should reasonably consider the benefit to the child in their transactions, or they will be void.[92]

The limitations of grandparents' rights in their relationships with their grand-children have many similarities to those applying to parents. For example, if the dishonesty of a guardian is strongly proved in respect of the estate of the ward, the court may appoint another competent person (as a *qayyem*).[93] The court considers several factors when assessing whether a relationship falls within the category of 'deceitfulness', but jurists argue that proving the guardian's deceitful intention is not required and evidence of his negligence will be satisfactory.[94] Consequently, the guardian will be dismissed if he exceeds the permissible use of the ward's property, fails in his duty of care or causes loss.[95] Again, debates over the validity of the legal transactions of a dishonest guardian have resulted in different views. The well-established view is that these transactions are considered unauthorised (ineffective) by the time of the maturity of the child, when he or she can confirm or reject them. In practice, however, a judicial precedent implies that the dishonesty of a guardian makes his transactions void. The case was about a guardian who had sold the property of a child (a shop) to cover his study expenses in the UK. The child had inherited the shop from his maternal grandfather, with a condition that the property was not to be sold until he reached maturity. The Supreme Court declared this transaction was void.[96] In doing so, the Court reiterated its protection of the best interests of the child.

IV. Concluding Remarks

The starting point of this chapter was to show the historical development of grand-parents' rights in understanding the concept of guardianship. This was achieved by reviewing grandparents' rights in the current Iranian family structure and examining the nature of grandparents' rights. It is important to mention that there are other aspects of grandparents' rights that have not been discussed in this chapter, such as the permission of guardians that is required for any medical operation of children aged under 18[97] or the rights of guardians in Islamic criminal law.[98]

---

[91] Observance of financial expediency against acknowledging the rights of others, No 44 Tehran's Appeal Court, 9109970224400781, 29 October 2012 at dadrah.ir/danesh (accessed 10 May 2022).

[92] Revocation of title deed due to non-observance of minor benefit to the natural guardian, Minutes of the Judicial Session, Bojnoord, Khorasan, 27 December 2007 at www.neshast.org/Home/GetPublicJ SessionTranscript/8aa5a8a7-78d6-4e21-96d3-08d601ea40a4 (accessed 15 May 2022).

[93] The Civil Code of the Islamic Republic of Iran, Arts 1184 and 1186.

[94] L Asadi, 'The Capacity of the Islamic Government and the Necessity of the Mother Guardianship' (2007) 35 *Quarterly Journal of Women's Socio-Cultural Council* 56.

[95] Moradi (n 68).

[96] ibid no 95.

[97] Islamic Penal Code of the Islamic Republic of Iran, Art 158(f).

[98] For example, the guardian is not subject to the punishment exactly defined by Sharia (*Hudud*) if he steals from his grandchildren.

What we learn from the foregoing analysis of guardianship is that paternal grandparents, traditionally and in *Shia* jurisprudence, are regarded as parents and often accorded priority in connection with guardianship over their grand-children. One major difficulty in court cases involving grandparents is the determination of what is in the child's best interests. 'Best interests' are not defined in the Iranian Civil Code. Only a handful of *Shia* jurisprudential principles have described specific criteria for determining best interests. It seems that *Shia* jurists' conception of *gebte* is quite like the 'best interests of the child' expressed in the UNCRC. Jurists have suggested different explanations of best interests. Some have considered it literally to mean the opposite of loss, such that loss is the cause of imbalance and best interests are a cause of stability and fairness. From this perspective, guardianship is provided in order that the interests of the child may be protected.[99] Accordingly, guardians should act in the way required by the interests of their wards.

Perhaps one reason for the lack of clarity on a definition of best interests is the shortage of research examining the best interests of children involved in grand-parent disputes. A critical research-based analysis of grandparents' rights can provide a case-law analysis to assist in understanding how judges apply criteria for determining best interests regarding grandparents' rights. In Iran, as in many other jurisdictions, judges rely on their personal values, culture and conception of the family to reflect on grandparents' rights in the family structure.[100] As shown, the judge enjoys inclusive discretionary powers to assess the best interests of the child in light of the circumstances and the evidence presented for or against the grandparents.

The reality is that civil law does not include comprehensive principles covering the entirety of grandparents' rights in Iran. Important areas such as grandparents' visitation rights, for example, are not explicitly regulated in the law. In addition, because the law is silent regarding the conditions governing the loss and revocation of grandparents' rights, courts have mainly applied the principles of guardianship in *Shia* jurisprudence. As the legislative provisions on grandparents' rights are based on the *Shia*-derived notion of *wali*, the significant impact that Islamic law has had on grandparents' rights is unlikely to change any time soon. First, much of the existing law on financial guardianship has been measured against the child's interests. The law on the revocation of guardianship does not clearly mention the best interests of the child principle. However, it does provide a list of cases in which guardianship can be suspended or removed, with considerable discretion given to the judge to deprive the *wali* of guardianship rights. Second, aspects of civil law

---

[99] See, eg, legal opinion of Iran's Supreme Leader on guardianship at https://farsi.khamenei.ir/treatise-content?id=138#1514 (accessed on 10 June 2022).

[100] See R Brown, 'Grandparent visitation and the intact family' (1991) 16 *Southern Illinois University Law Journal* 133. Also M Purnell and BH Bagby, 'Grandparents' Rights: Implications for Family Specialists' (1993) 42(2) *Family Relations* 173.

have supplemented the visitation rights of parents. The law does not stipulate that the court may limit visitation rights where it is in the child's best interests to do so. Finally, by understanding the continued change in family structure in Iran, it can at best be described as a sign that although grandparents' rights have a strong hold on Islamic law, judicial practice is evolving to include the best interests of the child in such cases.

9

A French Perspective on Grandparents and Private Law

The Right of the Child to Maintain Personal Relationships

LAURE SAUVÉ

I. Introduction

The position of grandparents in their grandchildren's lives was once described by Jean Carbonnier, a well-known French jurist of the twentieth century, as follows: 'Grandparents, especially grandmothers, transmitters of traditions of all kinds, contribute usefully to the cohesion of a society, but their critical visits can be the bearer of conflicts.'[1] Indeed, national jurisdictions have reacted differently to the question of personal relationships between grandparents and their grandchildren, showing that it may be difficult to reach a balance between the benefits that grandparents can bring to their grandchildren and to society, and the conflicts that grandparents can generate when they raise their voices against the parents. This difference of perceptions is well illustrated by the comparison between England and Wales and other Western jurisdictions,[2] and especially by the comparison between England and Wales and France. In many European countries, the child and the grandparent have a 'right to contact', which may be defined as a child's right or as a grandparent's right.[3] For instance, Spain recognises a right of communication and visitation between grandparents and grandchildren (Article 94 II Spanish Civil Code) and Italy a right of grandparents to maintain a significant

---

[1] J Carbonnier, 'Ve bis Famille, Législation et quelques autres' in *Mélanges offerts à René Savatier* (Paris, Dalloz, 1965) 135.
[2] See J Sosson and G Willems, 'The Future of Legal Relationships between Adults and Children: Complex Issues and Hybrid Solutions' in G Motte (ed), *Adults and Children in Postmodern Societies* (Cambridge, Intersentia, 2019) 825.
[3] ibid.

relationship with their grandchildren (Article 317-bis Italian Civil Code). Only a few jurisdictions, however, go as far as establishing a statutory presumption in favour of contact between grandchildren and grandparents: it appears that such a presumption exists only in Belgium, France and Quebec.[4] French law, which has influenced the Belgian and Quebecois systems,[5] gives to children a special right to maintain personal relations with their grandparents. This special right is based on the presumption that maintaining personal relations with their grandparents is in the children's interest.[6] The situation differs radically from that in England and Wales, and this chapter aims to analyse the French law system to offer to English readers a new perspective on this topic.

In England and Wales, there are no specific provisions for grandparents who want to maintain personal relationships with their grandchildren but cannot do so because they are facing parental opposition. In such circumstances, grandparents must seek a child arrangement order under section 8 of the Children Act 1989, and in order to do that, they must first get the leave of the court.[7] In addition, there is no automatic leave requirement for grandparents under section 10 of the Children Act 1989. Therefore, grandparents do not benefit from any specific regime and there is no presumption that grandparents should succeed when they apply for a child arrangement order. Hence, in *Re A (Section 8 Order: Grandparent Application)*,[8] it was stated that 'there cannot be a presumption that a grandmother who gets leave is entitled to contact unless it can be shown by cogent reasons that she should not have it'[9] and that grandparents are not in a 'special position'.[10] The consequence is that some grandparents might not get contact with their grandchildren, because it will not be deemed to be in children's best interests due to conflict with parents.

The absence of specific legal provisions for grandchildren and grandparents in England and Wales has led to the creation of dedicated organisations promoting grandparents and grandchildren's rights[11] (for a critical analysis of the English system, see chapters 2 and 7 of this volume). Some of these groups have called for a legal presumption in favour of grandparents' spending time with their

---

[4] D Goubeau, 'Le droit des grands-parents aux relations personnelles avec leurs petits-enfants: une étude comparative des systèmes québécois, français et belge' (1991) 32(3) *Les Cahiers de droit* 557.

[5] ibid.

[6] Art 371-4 para 1 of the French Civil Code, see section II.

[7] Applications for permission to start proceedings are governed by the Family Procedure Rules 2010 (FPR 2010) (SI 2010/2955), pt 18 and the corresponding FPR 2010, PD18A.

[8] *Re A (Section 8 Order: Grandparent Application)* [1995] 2 FLR 153.

[9] ibid 157.

[10] ibid. See also *Re K (Mother's Hostility to Grandmother's Contact)* [1996] CLY 565, Case Digest; and *Re A (A Minor) (Contact Application: Grandparent)* [1995] 2 FLR 153. Cases all quoted by F Kaganas and C Piper, 'Grandparent contact: another presumption?' (2020) 42(2) *Journal of Social Welfare and Family Law* 176.

[11] To name but a few: Kinship (previously known as Grandparents Plus), The Grandparents Association, Grand Parents Apart UK (GAUK).

grandchildren.[12] For instance, Jane Jackson, founder of the Bristol Grandparents Support Group, proposes the following changes: the removal of the leave requirement; the introduction of a particular presumption; and more rigorous enforcement of orders against parents.[13] The partisans of these proposals consider that creating a presumption in England according to which grandparent contact is desirable would change the national culture: as the personal relationship between the child and the grandparents would be presumed as beneficial to the child, it would render illegitimate any opposition of the parents.[14] However, some academics have noted that there is already an extra-legal norm that grandparents should have contact with their grandchildren.[15] As this social norm has become generally accepted, the establishment of a presumption in favour of contact for grandparents may be perceived as unnecessary, especially as the majority of disputes over contact are settled between the parents and the grandparents with no intervention of the court.[16]

Taking into consideration the demand from some of the grandparents' support groups, the House of Commons debated in May 2018 on 'Access Rights to Grandparents'.[17] During the debates, Nigel Huddleston criticised the current process as being 'time-consuming' and 'costly', due to the fact that grandparents must take the additional step of seeking permission from the court before applying for a child arrangement order.[18] To address these current issues, some proposed the possibility of enacting a presumption that the involvement of a grandparent in the life of the child will further the child's welfare, unless the contrary is shown,[19] while Dr Matthew Offord suggested looking at the specific procedure that already exists in France, stating that 'we can learn from that country'.[20] Indeed, considering the provisions of other jurisdictions helps to identify the possible need and consequences of law reform in England and Wales. Studying the rationale behind the French rules, as well as analysing their consequences, helps the English lawmaker to reflect on the possible enactment of a special children's right to maintain personal relationships with their grandparents and on a statutory presumption

---

[12] Groups such as the Grandparents Association and the Grandparents Action Group have argued in favour of a 'pro-grandparent' government policy and have tried to increase the media exposure of grandparents. See J Herring, *Older People in Law and Society* (Oxford, Oxford University Press, 2009) 239. However, Kaganas and Piper 'point out that not all grandparent groups now campaign for changes regarding contact', and mention that Grandparents Plus 'deals neutrally with the issue of contact': Kaganas and Piper (n 10) 178.

[13] J Jackson, 'Judiciary stand up and take action' (Bristol Grandparents Support Group, 2020).

[14] HC Deb 25 April 2017, vol 624, col 492, 'Grandparents' rights: access to grandchildren'.

[15] F Kaganas, 'Grandparents' Rights and Grandparents' Campaigns' (2007) 19 *Child and Family Law Quarterly* 17. On this point, see Herring (n 12) 248.

[16] N Ferguson et al, *Grandparenting in Divorced Families* (Bristol, Bristol University Press, 2004) ch 12. See Herring (n 12) 248.

[17] HC Deb 2 May 2018, vol 640, col 170, 'Access Rights to Grandparents'.

[18] ibid col 173.

[19] T Loughton, ibid col 172; N Huddleston, ibid col 174.

[20] ibid col 174.

in favour of contact with grandparents. This chapter therefore aims to critically examine the French system to offer a new perspective of reflection to the English experts in this field.

In France, any child has a special right to maintain personal relations with his grandparents, based on the presumption that maintaining personal relations with his grandparents is in the child's interest.[21] By defining the right to access as a child's right, rather than as a grandparent's right, French law puts the child at the heart of the system. However, this statutory presumption does not mean that the French courts will not play a substantial role when it comes to deciding whether a child could obtain contact with his grandparents. First, it is possible to rebut the legal presumption by demonstrating that contact between the child and his grandparents will not be in the child's interest. This leads to the necessity for the courts to define the child's interest, especially as there is no statutory framework equivalent to the English welfare checklist. It means that despite the statutory presumption, the opinion of the courts is essential when interpreting what is in the child's interest. Second, the legal possibility for a child to see his grandparents usually emerges when there is a disagreement between the child's parents and grandparents. Indeed, when there is no disagreement, the legal presumption is unnecessary: in such a case, the relation between the child and his grandparents will be spontaneous and will not lead to any specific legal difficulties. On the contrary, it is when the parents refuse any contact between the child and his grandparents that the statutory presumption is considered. In such a situation, there are various interests at stake: the child's interest, but also those of the parents and the grandparents. Again, it is the role of the courts to assess how the statutory presumption should be applied in this scenario.

This chapter aims to explain the justifications behind the French statutory presumption in favour of child's right to maintain personal relations with his grandparents, and to consider critically the challenges that occur in France because of the application of this presumption. Despite these difficulties, the chapter argues that the French statutory presumption provides a satisfactory solution. Therefore, the aim of this chapter is to analyse the French approach, to provide the English readers with some comparative elements of reflection within the context of potential reform to grandparents' rights in England and Wales.

This chapter is divided into four further sections. Section II examines the evolution of the right to maintain personal relations between children and grandparents, while the sections following concentrate on the three main issues arising from this evolution. As such, section III considers critically the transformation of the grandparents' right into a 'child's right', section IV calls into question the originality of the grandparents' position in comparison with other non-parents

---

[21] Whilst French law refers to the 'child's interest' (*l'intérêt de l'enfant*), and not to the 'child's best interests', the concept does present many similarities with the English one. In this chapter, I refer without distinction to the 'child's interest' or 'best interest'.

claiming access to the child, and section V discusses the pertinency of a statutory presumption as the best tool to interpret the child's interest. The chapter concludes that the existence of a statutory presumption in France plays the role of a 'guideline' for the courts, and that courts retain some important discretionary powers of appreciation.

II. The French Statutory Presumption: The Child's Right to Maintain Relations with His Grandparents

Under the French Civil Code, 'Any child has a right to maintain personal relations with his ancestors …'.[22] In other words, French law allows the courts to impose upon parents the enforcement of their child's right to maintain a relationship with his grandparents. The child has his own 'personal relations right', which restricts the authority of his parents because the latter cannot deprive their child of relations with his ascendants.[23] This section examines the content of the child's right, the arguments in favour of the statutory presumption and the evolution of the legal provision.

A. Content and Scope of the Child's Right

The right to 'maintain personal relations' is conceived of extensively and could allow the child to correspond with his grandparents or to visit them, but also to stay at their place of residence (for example, a weekend every month or during a portion of the child's holidays).[24] The judge can also decide that the child will meet his grandparents in a 'neutral place', and may order that a professional childhood worker mediates at the meetings between grandparents and child.[25] For example, this option was favoured in a case where there was a risk that the grandparents would have used the child's right to put their grandchild and their own son (the child's father) in contact, where the latter had been deprived of any access rights due to his violent behaviour.[26] Therefore, case law often refers to 'contact', 'visitation' or 'access' rights, and this chapter will use similar terms.

The child's right is in relation to *all* his ancestors and includes not only his grandparents but also his great-grandparents. This expansion of the provision to

---

[22] Art 371-4 of the French Civil Code, para 1.
[23] F Evano, 'Les grands-parents et l'autorité parentale [Première partie]' (2001) 1 *Revue juridique de l'Ouest* 21; F Evano, 'Les grands-parents et l'autorité parentale [Deuxième partie]' (2001) 2 *Revue juridique de l'Ouest* 215.
[24] A Gouttenoire, *Répertoire civil* (Paris, Dalloz, 2020–2021) 'Autorité parentale', 329.
[25] Cass Civ 1re, 13 June 2019, 18-12.389, D 2019. 1284.
[26] Agen, 21 February 2008, n° RG 07/00779.

all the ancestors was introduced by the legislator in 2002[27] and had followed an outcome already established by the courts.[28] This change may be explained not only by an ageing population, but also by a willingness to reinforce the ties of kinship and the links of parenthood.[29] For this purpose, grandparenthood would be defined biologically, and an ancestor would be a person from whom one is descended. The only exception would be for adoptive ancestors, who will be in the same position as biological ancestors, as plenary adoption severs all the child's legal links with his blood family and confers on the child a new filiation, which is substituted for his original filiation (see Article 356 of the French Civil Code).

B. The Arguments behind the Presumption

The implementation of a specific statutory provision in favour of the ancestors aims to reinforce the links between the child and his grandparents, and may be explained by various elements: first, ancestors do play a major role in their grandchildren's life; second, the right is framed as a child's right, and as such emphasises the benefits for the child; third, the right to maintain personal relationships is implemented in a legal system that does confer several legal rights and duties on grandparents. These three elements are considered in the following paragraphs.

First, on a sociological level, several elements highlight the increasing role played by grandparents within the family, a phenomenon that Marie-Thérèse Meulders-Klein described in 1965 as 'the spring of grandparents'.[30] Thanks to longer life expectancy, there are more grandparents than ever before: this does not seem balanced out by the possibility of having children later in life, as in 2011 there were 2.5 million more grandparents than in 1999.[31] In addition, grandparents may occupy a major position in their grandchild's life. Even when the parents are living together, grandparents often see their grandchildren regularly. When the children are young, grandparents sometimes act as informal carers, whose services are free and often more flexible than those provided by professional carers.[32] For instance, two-thirds of children under the age of 6 are occasionally looked after by their

---

[27] Loi n° 2002-305 du 4 mars 2002 relative à l'autorité parentale [Law n° 2002-305 of 4 March 2002 on parental authority].

[28] TGI Paris, 3 June 1976, D. 1977. 303, comments by Cazals.

[29] A Etienney de Sainte Marie, 'Le droit de l'enfant d'entretenir des relations personnelles avec ses grands-parents' in M Bourassin et C Coutant-Lapalus (eds), *Les droits des grands-parents, Une autre dépendance?* (Paris, Dalloz, 2012) 107, 111.

[30] M-T Meulders-Klein, 'Le printemps des grands-parents et le droit' in *Mélanges en l'honneur de Jacques-Michel Grossen* (Bâle, Helbing & Lichtenhahn, 1992) 165.

[31] In 2011, there were just over 15.1 million grandparents in France, which represents 2.5 million more than in 1999. N Blanpain and L Lincot, '15 millions de grand-parents' (2013) *Insee Première*, n° 1469 at www.insee.fr/fr/statistiques/1281390 (accessed 28 June 2021).

[32] J Hauser, 'Les grands-parents, subsidiaires, autonomes ou indépendants?' in M Bourassin and C Coutant-Lapalus (eds), *Les droits des grands-parents, Une autre dépendance?* (Paris, Dalloz, 2012) 3.

grandparents.[33] After a parental separation, case law demonstrates that grandparents may act as a 'support network',[34] helping the residential parent (the mother in most cases) to look after the child.[35] As such, the child's right to maintain personal relations with his grandparents is positive not only for the child and for the grandparents, but also for the broader society, as it strengthens the unity of the family by maintaining its cohesion.[36]

The involvement of grandparents in the lives of their grandchildren is often described as a manifestation of the affection that most grandparents have for their grandchildren, grandparenthood being defined as a 'presumption of reciprocal and caring affection'.[37] One can only think of the marvellous poem by Victor Hugo, celebrating the specificities of grandparental love:

> In seeing them one believes to see himself born;
> Yes, to become a grandfather is to re-enter the dawn.
> The joyous old man mixes himself with the triumphant marmot.
> We are shrinking ourselves into small children.[38]

In addition to affection, grandparents are often described as 'transmitters', passing on the family heritage.[39] Thanks to the grandparents, the child is part of a lineage and becomes part of a transgenerational story.[40] From this specific bond arises inter-generational solidarity, and grandparents may sometimes feel morally bound to take care of their grandchild. Therefore, French law considers that grandparents have a genuine place in parenthood as an integral part of parents' lives.[41] However, this sociological reality may be difficult to translate into legal terms. Indeed, creating a legal framework to regulate the relationship between the child and his grandparents involves a delicate balance as this relationship is often based on affection, a concept that French law mainly ignores. Rather than referring to the 'social grandparents', French law clearly refers to 'biological' ancestors.[42]

---

[33] M Kitzmann, 'Les grands-parents: un mode de garde régulier ou occasionnel pour deux tiers des jeunes enfants' (2018) *Drees, Etudes et Résultats*, n° 1070.

[34] Goubeau (n 4) 564.

[35] For international studies on this question, see, eg, E Marcus, 'Over the Hills and Through the Woods to Grandparents House We Go: Or do We, Post-Troxel?' (2001) 43 *Arizona Law Review* 751; G Douglas and N Ferguson, 'The Role of Grandparents in Divorced Families' (2003) 17 *International Journal of Law Policy and the Family* 41.

[36] P Guilho, 'Essai d'une théorie générale du droit de visite', JCP 1952. I. 963.

[37] G Sutton, 'Le droit des grands-parents aux relations avec leurs petits-enfants', JCP 1972. I. 2504.

[38] V Hugo, 'L'autre' in *L'Art d'être grand-père* (1877) tr R Lowrie.

[39] J-C Roehrig, 'La famille du troisième millénaire' in *Des concubinages, Droit interne, Droit international, Droit comparé, Études offertes à Jacqueline Rubellin-Devichi* (Paris, Litec, 2002) 316; P Murat, 'Couple, filiation, parenté' in *Des concubinages, Droit interne, Droit international, Droit comparé, Études offertes à Jacqueline Rubellin-Devichi* (Paris, Litec, 2002) 53.

[40] M Lasbats, 'Les grands-parents dans notre société', *Actualité Juridique famille* 2008, 147.

[41] T Garé, *Les grands-parents dans le droit de la famille* (Paris, CNRS, 1989).

[42] Gouttenoire (n 24). On the position of step-grandparents, see C Le Tertre, 'Les relations intergénérationnelles dans la famille recomposées de fait?' in S Moisdon-Chataigner (ed), *Les grands-parents et leurs descendants: quelles relations juridiques?* (Paris, LexisNexis Litec, 2009) 143. Step-grandparents or social grandparents will be considered as 'third persons' and will benefit from the provision of Art 371-4, para 2 (see section IV).

Under French law, parenthood is largely based on biological relationships,[43] and non-biological family constellations (such as step-families[44]) are often regulated differently than the blood family.[45] This approach is shared by many jurisdictions who 'base parenthood on the biological link with the child'[46] (for instance, Australia, Canada, England and Wales, Ireland, Romania).[47]

In 1857, the Cour de cassation, in a less poetic way than Victor Hugo, stressed the specificities of the grandparenthood relationship: '[B]etween children and their … ancestors there is a reciprocity of interests and ties, of rights and duties, which have their principle in nature and their sanction in civil law itself.'[48] Since then, the judiciary and the legislature alike have presumed the conformity of these links with the best interest of the child. Due to the bond of kinship and affection between children and their grandparents, it is presumed that it is in the children's interest to maintain relations with their ancestors.[49] The strength of grandparenthood seems particularly valuable as the family bond is indissoluble: children have a right to learn about their ancestry and about their own genetic identity.[50]

A second justification is that French law does confer a right on the child, not on the grandparent, and consequently is in conformity with the 2003 Council of Europe Convention on Contact concerning Children.[51] The French provision's rationale would then be 'the interest of the child'. Such an argument has been developed since the 1960s, as expressed by Geneviève Viney:

> We could no longer speak of the right to maintain personal relationships with a child, but of the right of the child to maintain relationships with others. The 'visitor' … would then be the debtor of an obligation of which the child would be a creditor.[52]

In other words, the starting point must be the child's interest: it is because these relations are presumed to be in the child's interest that the child has a right to maintain them. The child is the 'creditor', that is, the person to whom the personal relationships are due, the person who can claim enforcement of this right. The grandparents, on the other hand, are only perceived as the persons who have to fulfil these obligations: they cannot make any claim in their own names. However, we will see in the next section that such a statement must be nuanced.[53]

---

[43] Even if socio-affective links are also taken into account to restrict any attempt to rebut legal paternity (especially via the 'possession of status'): see P Murat, *Droit de la famille* (Paris, Dalloz Action, 2020–2021).

[44] On step-families, see L Sauvé, *Le beau-parent en droit français et anglais* (Paris, LGDJ, 2014).

[45] Murat (n 43).

[46] J Sosson and G Willems, 'Parentage, parenthood and parental responsibility in traditional families' in J Sosson, G Willems and G Motte (eds), *Adults and Children in Postmodern Societies* (Cambridge, Intersentia, 2019) 726, 756.

[47] ibid.

[48] Cass Civ, 8 July 1857, S 1857, I, 721, for further details see n 60.

[49] Garé (n 41) para 286.

[50] Etienney de Sainte Marie (n 29) 111. The United Nations Convention on the Rights of the Child has adopted a similar approach: on this question, see ch 6 of this volume.

[51] Council of Europe, Convention on Contact concerning Children, 15 May 2003, ETS No 192.

[52] G Viney, 'Du droit de visite', *Revue trimestrielle de droit civil* (1965) 225, 232.

[53] See section III for further details.

A third explanation for the existence of a statutory presumption is that, on a domestic level, French law confers an important role on grandparents in various aspects of the child's life. While this chapter focuses on the right to personal relations, it is important to stress that under French family law, the grandparents occupy a special position in relation to many key aspects of their grandchild's life. To name but a few: grandparents have the power to oppose the adoption of their grandchild;[54] when the child's parents are dead, grandparents can oppose their grandchild's marriage (even when their grandchild is over 18)[55] and they must give their consent to their minor grandchild's marriage.[56] In private law, the relationship between a child and his ancestors leads to various legal consequences: they have a reciprocal maintenance obligation,[57] and similarly they may have inheritance rights and duties towards each other.[58] All of these elements show the particularity of the grandparents' (or ancestors') position in French law and may explain the presumption of Article 371-4 of the French Civil Code.

C. The Evolution of Access Rights for Grandparents

Historically, the demand for grandparents' access to their grandchildren has emerged in conflictual situations, placing grandparents and their own children in opposition, where the latter have refused to grant access to their grandchildren to the former. The Cour de cassation's[59] first famous decision dates from 1857.[60] At that time, the question was framed in term of limits to paternal authority, as fathers were the only parents who could exercise their 'authority' over children. The

---

[54] Art 345-1 of the French Civil Code.

[55] Art 173 of the French Civil Code. This provision allows the parents (or the grandparents, where the parents are dead) to register their opposition to the child's future marriage when they believe that the marriage will not comply with all the legal requirements (because, for instance, their child's consent will not be given freely).

[56] Art 150 of the French Civil Code. Marriage can only be celebrated if the future spouses are over 18 (Art 144, Civil Code), but the marriage of a minor can be authorised by the public prosecutor for 'serious reasons'(Art 145, Civil Code). It does require, however, the consent of at least one of the parents. When both parents are dead, the grandparents will take the deceased parents' place and at least one of them will have to give consent to their minor grandchild's marriage.

[57] Art 205 of the French Civil Code: 'Children owe support to their father and mother or other ascendants who are in need.' Art 207, para 1, French Civil Code: 'The obligations resulting from these provisions are reciprocal.' For the English translation of the French Civil Code provisions, see D Gruning et al, 'Traduction du Code civil français en anglais, version bilingue' (2015) at https://halshs.archives-ouvertes.fr/halshs-01385107 (accessed 8 September 2021).

[58] See Art 734 of the French Civil Code: 'In the absence of a spouse who is called to the succession, relatives are called to succeed as follows: 1° Children and their descendants; 2° The father and mother; brothers and sisters and the descendants of these; 3° Ascendants other than the father and mother; 4° Collaterals other than brothers and sisters and the descendants of these. Each of these four categories constitutes an order of heirs that excludes the following.' (English translation as in n 57.).

[59] The 'Cour de cassation' is the highest court in the French judiciary. Its role is to control the correct application of law by the courts of first instance and courts of appeal, thus ensuring a uniform interpretation of law. See at www.courdecassation.fr/en.

[60] Cass Civ, 8 July 1857, S 1857, I, 721. See H Capitant, F Terré and Y Lequette, *Les grands arrêts de la jurisprudence civile*, vol 1 (Paris, Dalloz, 2015) 61–62.

question submitted to the Cour de cassation was whether paternal authority would allow the child's parents to override the natural rights of grandparenthood invoked by the grandparents? The Court decided that the grandparents could succeed if they provided evidence that the refusal of access was abusive. In other words, the father's refusal was perceived as an abuse of his paternal authority. Later, the judges abandoned the concept of a parental abuse of rights and acknowledged a right for the grandparents. In circumstances where parents had refused any contact right to grandparents without any serious reasons, the courts were inclined to protect the existing relationship of a child with his grandparents.[61]

In 1970, the legislator enshrined the case law solutions into law by introducing a new Article 371-4 into the Civil Code.[62] The original provision was as follows:

> The father and mother cannot, except for serious reasons, obstruct the personal relations of the child with his grandparents. In the absence of agreement between the parties, the terms of these relations are settled by the court.

This did not give a right to the grandparents but acknowledged the importance of personal relations between a child and his grandparents, and it was soon interpreted by the Cour de cassation as creating a presumption in favour of rights of access for grandparents. For instance, in a case brought in 1982, the Cour de cassation indicated that 'article 371-4 of the Civil Code presumes that is in the child's interest to maintain personal relations with his grandparents, unless serious reasons prevent it'.[63] Since the enactment of this provision, it is for the parents opposed to the recognition of any personal relations between their child and his grandparents to demonstrate that there are serious reasons likely to hinder these relations.[64]

Later, Article 371-4 was reformulated by Law 2002-305 of 4 March 2002; it now expressly stated that the right to personal relations was a right of the child:

> The child has the right to maintain personal relations with his ancestors. Only serious reasons can prevent this right.

This new provision placed the child at the heart of the court process by conferring a right on the child. The judge had discretionary powers to take into account any 'serious reasons' preventing the implementation of this right. In other words, the 2002 Law presumed that it would be in the child's interest to maintain a personal relationship with his grandparents, unless this relationship might cause serious disruption to the child's life (for example, because of serious disputes between the grandparents and the parents, or because of a child's refusal[65]).

---

[61] Capitant, Terré and Lequette (n 60) 61–62.

[62] Loi nº 70-459 du 4 juin 1970 relative à l'autorité parentale [Law nº 70-459 of 4 June 1970 on parental authority].

[63] Cass Civ 1re, 1 December 1982, Bull civ I, n° 346, 81-14.627.

[64] Cass Civ 1re, 15 July 1999, 97-17.497. The Cour de cassation held that 'Ms X [the mother] did not prove the existence of serious reasons likely to impede this relationship.'

[65] See section V for more details on such exceptions.

The provision was amended one more time in 2007,[66] and since then Article 371-4, paragraph 1 of the Civil Code has stated:

> Any child has a right to maintain personal relations with his ancestors. Only the interest of the child can impede the exercise of such a right.

The amendment of the text concerns the possibility of restricting the child's right: where previously only 'serious reasons' could overturn the presumption, the new provision refers to 'the child's interest'. The aim of the reform was to prevent the child from being confronted with family conflicts: 'the new wording of paragraph 1 of article 371-4 invites the lower courts to assess the opportunity for the child of a relationship with his grandparents, and not the conflict between them and his parents'.[67] However, as the next section explains, Article 371-4 may still be perceived as conferring more of a right to the grandparents than to the child.

III. The French Statutory Presumption: A Child's Right or a Grandparent's Right?

Some academics have criticised the 2002 and 2007 Laws as having only changed the wording of the legal provisions without having introduced any substantial amendments.[68] It seems that despite the reforms, the child does not have any right per se, while the grandparents can still introduce a claim to gain contact with their grandchild.

A. The Child's Right: A Fake Right

By conferring a right on the child, the 2002 Law implies that the child himself should initiate a legal claim to develop or maintain a relationship with his grandparents. In practice, this seems unlikely to happen, as in most cases the parents – who could act as the child's representatives – are opposed to this measure. The only option would then be for the child to nominate an 'ad hoc administrator' (an individual designated by the court to represent the interests of the child) to act on his behalf, which supposes that the child will be sufficiently mature to do so.[69]

---

[66] Loi n° 2007-293 du 5 mars 2007 réformant la protection de l'enfance [Law n° 2007-293 of 5 March 2007 reforming child protection].

[67] P Eudier, commenting on Cass Civ 1re, 18 January 2007, 06-11.357, NP, RRJ, 2007-4, 29, quoted by A Gouttenoire 'Autorité parentale : définition, sources, nature et attributs' in P Murat (ed), *Droit de la famille* (Paris, Dalloz Action, 2020–2021) 966, 978.

[68] J Hauser, commenting on Cass Civ 1re, 27 May 2010, *Revue trimestrielle de droit civil* 2010. 548; D Fenouillet, C Goldie-Genicon and F Terré, *La famille*, (Paris, Précis Dalloz, 2018), para 926; Capitant, Terré and Lequette (n 60) 386–87.

[69] See Art 383 of the Civil Code. According to this article, the Public Ministry or the child can request in court the nomination of an 'ad hoc administrator'.

It means that, despite the formulation of the 2002 Law, the child will not initiate the claim.[70] In practice, the claim will be made by the grandparents themselves, although, according to the text, they should in principle ask the Public Ministry to act on behalf of the child.[71] As such, the new text is misleading, since the grandparents will often act on their own behalf and such action introduced on behalf of the child will be rare.

Moreover, even if the child could make a claim, in practice he will not be able to force his grandparents to maintain relations with him.[72] We saw earlier that the child has sometimes been considered as the 'creditor' of an obligation to maintain a personal relationship imposed on the grandparents.[73] However, the child seems to be a theoretical creditor only, who does not have any means of enforcing his legal right. Indeed, the child cannot oblige his grandparents to maintain relations with him. The purpose of the right is to oblige the parents not to prevent access to the grandparents. Therefore, whilst the law is phrased in terms of positive protection for children, it imposes certain obligations upon parents. In situations where parents deny any personal relations between their children and the grandparents, the court may intervene to enforce this obligation upon parents.

B. The Genuine Right: A Reciprocal Right?

Despite the 2002 and the 2007 reforms, grandparents are still allowed to claim a right to personal relations with their grandchild. The Court of Appeal of Lyon, in its 20 September 2004 judgment, held that the right to maintain personal relations should not be interpreted as an exclusive right of the child and not of the ancestors. Reserving this right to the child would render the text ineffective, because the grandparents require this right when there is a disagreement with the parents, and because the child himself must wait until a certain age to express the need to maintain personal relations with his grandparents.[74] The Court refers to grandparents' rights but would nevertheless have to consider the child's interest, as any decision must be in the interest of the child. Therefore, it may be said that the grandparents can claim access to their grandchild, but that rights of access would only be granted based on the child's interest. This analysis is consistent with the European outcomes, which confer a right to

---

[70] P Roth, 'Droit de visite et d'hébergement des grands-parents: pour deux réformes textuelles', *Actualité Juridique famille* 2010, 430.

[71] In France, one of the roles of the Public Ministry is to defend the interests of society and of the application of law in civil litigation. In particular, one of the Public Ministry's missions is to protect the child's interest.

[72] A Gouttenoire, 'Le droit de l'enfant d'entretenir des relations personnelles avec ses grands-parents', *Actualité Juridique famille* 2008, 138.

[73] Viney (n 52). See section II for more details.

[74] Lyon, 20 September 2004, BICC, 15 December 2006, n° 2442.

both grandparents and children. Hence, even if the 2003 Council of Europe Convention on Contact concerning Children implemented a right to contact for the child,[75] the Convention has also acknowledged in its Preamble the importance for some adults to maintain relations with the child.[76] The European Court of Human Rights has even considered that the need to preserve the link between both grandparents and their granddaughter falls within the scope of the grandparents' right to respect for their family life guaranteed by Article 8 of the European Convention on Human Rights (ECHR).[77] In *Manuello and Nevi v Italy*,[78] the Court condemned the violation of the right to respect for family life of grandparents who were banned from maintaining a personal relationship with their granddaughter due to an allegation that their son had committed a sexual offence against his daughter. Similarly, in *Mitovi v the former Yugoslav Republic and Macedonia*,[79] the Court held that the national authorities must make all the necessary efforts to guarantee this right.

Despite the phrasing of Article 371-4 of the Civil Code, the right to personal relations seems, therefore, to be more a reciprocal right than a right of the child.[80] This is reflected by case law, as courts sometimes refer to the child's right and at other times to the grandparents' right.[81] Although the 2002 Law reformulated the right as being exclusively a child's right, it seems that there is a right both for the child and for the grandparents, as in practice the action would be brought by the grandparents, but the decision would always be based on the child's best interest.

C. Enforcement of the Orders

Parents may be reluctant to obey a court's decision conferring rights of access to grandparents. The child has no means of enforcing the visitation or access orders, and for this reason, as discussed earlier, the child may appear to be only a 'theoretical creditor' of a right to maintain personal relations. Therefore, despite

---

[75] Council of Europe (n 51).

[76] ibid, Preamble: 'Agreeing on the need for children to have contact not only with both parents but also with certain other persons having family ties with children and the importance for parents and those other persons to remain in contact with children, subject to the best interests of the child …'.

[77] *Marckx and Marckx v Belgium* App no 6833/74 (ECtHR, 13 June 1979), [1979] ECHR 2, (1980) 2 EHRR 330, IHRL 22: 'The Court considered that "family life" within the meaning of art 8 includes at least the ties between near relatives and that "respect" for family life so understood implies an obligation for the State to act in a manner calculated to allow these ties to develop normally.'

[78] *Manuello and Nevi v Italy* App no 62198/11 (ECtHR, 20 January 2015), *Actualité Juridique famille* 2015, 101, comments by E Viganotti.

[79] *Mitovi v the former Yugoslav Republic and Macedonia* App no 53565/13 (ECtHR, 16 April 2015), *Actualité Juridique famille* 2015, 340, comments by E Viganotti.

[80] D Bourgault-Coudeville, 'Les relations de l'enfant avec d'autres personnes que ses père et mère', *Droit et patrimoine*, 2001, n° 85, 71; N Rexand-Pourias, 'Les relations entre grands-parents et petits-enfants depuis la loi du 4 mars 2002 sur l'autorité parentale', *JCP* 2003. I. 100.

[81] See section V for some examples.

a court order, it may be difficult for the child to see his grandparents. However, French law provides remedies in circumstances where parents fail to allow access to the child to the grandparents despite a judicial decision. Under Article 227-5 of the Criminal Code, parents can be found guilty of the criminal offence of 'non-representation of a child', punishable by one year's imprisonment and a fine of up to €15,000. In addition, grandparents potentially would have further recourse to the European Court of Human Rights, where the Italian authorities were recently condemned for a breach of Article 8 ECHR because they were not deploying sufficient means to allow the execution of a grandmother's access rights with regard to her granddaughter.[82] In the future, this judgment could be a precious tool for grandparents, who could claim that there is breach of Article 8 ECHR when their national authorities do not give them efficient measures to obtain the enforcement of the judicial decision.

It seems easier for the grandparents to obtain enforcement of a contact order than it is for the child. As explained previously, the child who would like to maintain a personal relationship with his grandparents would not be able to compel his grandparents to see him. In addition, in some cases, the child has to be forced to maintain a relationship with his grandparents, even though he does not want to.[83] Therefore, the right to maintain personal relationships is never an exclusive right of the child; it is rather a reciprocal right of the grandparents and the child, based on what the judge would consider as being in the interest of the child.

The 2002 Law has reformed Article 371-4, paragraph 1 by transforming the right to personal relations into a reciprocal right for the child and for his grandparents. In addition to this, the 2002 legislator has extended the child's right to contact in relation to other 'non-parents', such as step-parents. The next section examines whether this provision challenges the special position of grandparents.

IV. The French Statutory Presumption and the 2002 Law: Is There Still a Special Place for Grandparents within the Child's Life?

In 2002, the French legislator introduced a second paragraph into Article 371-4 of the French Civil Code, as follows:

> If the interest of the child so requires, the judge for family matters fixes the modes of the personal relationship between the child and a third person, relative or not.

---

[82] *Terna v Italy* App no 21052/18 (ECtHR, 14 January 2021).
[83] See section V.

The current text, amended by the 17 May 2013 Law (*Loi n° 2013-404 ouvrant le mariage aux couples de même sexe*), goes on to be more precise, stating that the judge will assess

> in particular when this third person has resided in a stable manner with [the child] and with one of his parents, has seen to his education, his support, or his establishment, and has built durable emotional bonds with him.

This provision gives the child a right to personal relationships with adults with whom he has created a bond of affection. The article must be noted as being a particularly original provision in French law as it refers to 'emotional bonds' ('*liens affectifs*' in the French version). Affection is a factual concept, requiring the judge to analyse the quality of the relationship between the child and the adult. Reference to a broadly defined concept such as 'affection' is not common in France, and French law usually uses well-identified categories such as 'parenthood' instead.[84] As such the vagueness of the new paragraph 2 of Article 371-4, which refers to 'a third person' who 'has built durable emotional bonds' with the child, contrasts with paragraph 1 and its clear reference to the biological 'ancestors', a category that is easily identified.

Jean Hauser has described this provision of paragraph 2 as calling into question the special position of the grandparents.[85] As the child may have rights of access to any 'third person', the particularity of the grandparent's situation seems to have disappeared. Indeed, the two provisions are shaped around the 'child's interest'. In both cases, the necessary condition is that the contact must be in the child's interest. Despite the presumption in favour of a child's contact with his ancestors, the judges have discretionary powers in the two situations when establishing whether the claimed contact is in the child's interest. In addition, by opening Article 374-1, paragraph 1 to all the 'ancestors' and not only to grandparents, the 2002 Law has increased the number of potential applicants. Since 2002, the adults who may bring a claim to get contact with the child on the basis of Article 374-1, paragraphs 1 and 2 are numerous: up to 12 ancestors, the extended members of the child's family (aunt, uncle ...), a former step-parent, a former same-sex partner of a parent acting as a social parent, etc. This seems to demonstrate that a grandparent is only one adult amongst many others who can play an important role in the child's life. The 'kinship bond' itself does not necessarily put the grandparents in a special position, as Article 374-1, paragraph 2 is also applicable to other family members, such as the child's aunt or uncle. In fact, when comparing, for instance, the claim of a great-grandparent with the claim introduced by the aunt of a child, it appears that the kinship bond is the same in the two situations: why, therefore, should we give a specific consideration to the ancestor of a child? The presumption in favour of the ancestors is thus more difficult to justify. This idea is also illustrated by two cases where a de facto grandparent obtained a right to contact

---

[84] See section II.
[85] Hauser (n 32) 5.

on the basis of Article 374-1, paragraph 1 (and not on the basis of paragraph 2).[86] The grandmother made a joint application with her husband, who was not the biological grandfather of the children. In the two cases, the court did not make any distinction between the grandmother and the 'step grandfather', which may call into question the biological definition of 'ancestors' and reinforce the argument according to which the key element should be the child's interest. It can be argued that the absence of any distinction between the 'biological grandparent' and the 'social grandparent' illustrates a new conception of grandparenthood. More than mere genetical connections and the right of the children to know their origins, Article 374-1 paragraph 1 would have at its primary purpose the reinforcement of the emotional bond existing between children and their grandparents.

However, to counterbalance Jean Hauser's opinion, it can be argued that there is at least an important symbolic difference between grandparents and 'other' third persons. Symbolically, grandparents are still the beneficiaries of a special provision, exclusively reserved to them. Their mere quality of being grandparents is the basis of a presumption in favour of a right of access to the child. On the other hand, step-parents, same-sex social parents, aunts or uncles, etc all fall within the same broadly defined category: they are 'third persons'. Their qualities as step-parents, social parents, or as members of the extended family, are never sufficient in themselves to give them access rights. In relation to grandparents, the bond of kinship gives rise to a presumption of affection, while the third person must demonstrate that there is a bond of affection uniting them to the child.[87] Formally, the choice of the legislator to opt for two separate paragraphs within Article 371-4 reflects a willingness to maintain a distinction between the ancestors and the other third persons.[88]

In addition to this, the differences in phrasing between paragraph 1 and paragraph 2 of Article 371-4 may direct the courts to recognise more easily the relation between the child and his grandparents than the relations between the child and another third person. First, the category of third persons is subdivided between those individuals who have resided with the child in a stable manner and others. When it comes to grandparents, having shared a common residence with the child will not be – in itself – a prerequisite, nor a 'priority element'. Second, paragraph 2 makes a distinction between the relatives and the non-relatives. It also provides a list of guidelines for the courts: Has the third person provided for the child's education? For his support or establishment? Has the third person built a durable emotional bond with him? By contrast, the ancestor – whoever he or she is – will be able to make a claim, even in situations where the child has had limited personal relations with that ancestor in the past.[89] Third, despite the 2007 reform,

---

[86] Cass Civ 1re, 18 January 2007, 06-11.357, NP; RRJ 2007-4. 29, comments by F Eudier; Cass Civ 1re, 12 February 2014, n° 13-13.674, RJPF 2014-5/34.
[87] Etienney de Sainte Marie (n 29) 111.
[88] Rexand-Pourias (n 80).
[89] For example, Cass Civ 1re, 13 June 2019, 18-12.389, D. 2019. 1284.

the spirit of paragraph 1 has not changed, and it still aims to protect the relations of the child with his ancestors. As regards his grandparents, the child benefits from a presumption in favour of personal relationships (leading to a contact or a visitation order for instance), whereas there is no similar presumption in connection to the other 'third persons'. This means that an application for a contact order for a child in relation to a third person can be made, but it will be necessary to demonstrate that the interest of the child requires this contact. The principle that relationships with grandparents are in the best interest of the child, and that it is up to the father and mother, who claim the contrary, to provide some evidence of that fact, remains.[90]

V. Reversing the Statutory Presumption: How French Courts Define the Child's Interest in Relation to Article 371-4 of the French Civil Code

In 2007, the 'interest of the child' replaced the previous criterion of 'serious reasons'.[91] Textually, it seems easier for the judge to refuse to accede to the grandparents' claim as the judge is no longer required to qualify a 'serious reason'. However, some decisions prior to 2007 had already anticipated the reform.[92] Thus, in 2005 the Cour de cassation refused to give a right to contact to grandparents in a case where the relations between the parents and the grandparents were highly conflictual, and where the child, a young girl named Sybille, was at risk of being placed at the centre of these disputes. The Court based its judgment on the 'child's interest', stating that 'the organisation of forced meetings with her grandparents would be harmful to the stability of young Sybille and contrary to her interest'.[93]

While looking at the child's interest, the judge will have to balance two key elements: on one hand, the child may benefit from knowing his origins and the grandparents can be seen as providing him with family roots; on the other hand, the child needs stability in his daily life, and the development of access rights with his ancestors may be an obstacle to this stability. There are some clear similarities with the English criteria, as section 10(9) of the Children Act 1989 provides:

> Where the person applying for leave to make an application for a section 8 order is not the child concerned, the court shall, in deciding whether or not to grant leave, have particular regard to … any risk there might be of that proposed application disrupting the child's life to such an extent that he would be harmed by it …

This provision applies to grandparents claiming for a child arrangement order, meaning that the child's stability seems to be a limit to access rights in the two

---

[90] Gouttenoire (n 72).
[91] Loi nº 2007-293 du 5 mars 2007 (n 66), modifying Art 371-4 of the Civil Code.
[92] On judgments referring to the child's interest before 2007, see Rexand-Pourias (n 80).
[93] Cass Civ 1re, 8 November 2005, 03-17.911.

systems. However, this is not the only limit. It seems that there are three main categories of cases where the French judge will consider that personal relations with grandparents will be against the child's interest.

A first possible scenario is one where the child is strongly opposed to any contact with his grandparents. Courts will consider the child's opposition when the child is old enough and sufficiently mature, making it an important element in deciding whether maintaining relations with his grandparents is against the child's best interest.[94] In some judgments, courts have decided that personal relations should not take place because of the child's opposition. For instance, the Court of Appeal of Rennes took into consideration the willingness of two children of 14 and 16 to deny any access rights to their grandparents.[95] Similarly, in a case where the children were reluctant to stay at their grandparents' place of residence, the Court of Appeal of Paris granted a right of visitation to the grandparents, taking place exclusively at the parents' house.[96] As such, when the child is old enough and sufficiently mature, his opinion will certainly be an important element in appreciating what is in his best interests. However, this appreciation is always factual and may also differ from one judge to another: for instance, the Court of Appeal of Montpellier granted the grandparents a right to visit their 16-year-old grandson despite the latter's opposition. The Court argued that the 16-year-old boy was unable to understand fully what was in his own interest and justified its decision on the grounds that 'it is important to maintain the child/grandparent relationship to ensure the continuity of the family group and the transmission of values'.[97] When the child is younger or less mature, it may be even more difficult to consider his wishes and to apprehend his genuine interest. As noted by Anne Etienney de Sainte Marie, children are naturally vulnerable, and may be easily influenced by their parents or by their grandparents. The author denounces the ambiguity of the child's right: how could the child know what is in his best interest when he lacks sufficient maturity to do so?[98]

The second category of scenarios encompasses the cases where the parents' refusal is based on an objective element, providing clear evidence that it would be against the child's interest to maintain a relation with his grandparents because the child would be in danger (the grandparent being violent, or an alcoholic, or a drug addict, etc). The child must not be exposed to a grandparent whose behaviour could represent a risk to his safety, his morality or his education.[99] When the child's safety is at risk, the court may reject the grandparents' request.

---

[94] See, eg, Bourges, 30 September 2002, Juris-Data n° 2002-190324; Nancy, 6 July 2009, n° 07/01650; Dijon 3 December 2009, n° 09/00450; Dijon, 3 November 2011, n° 10/02450.

[95] Rennes, 18 July 1995, Dr fam 1997, comm n° 58, note P Murat.

[96] Paris, 30 August 2000, Juris-Data n° 2000-123689.

[97] Montpellier, 19 March 2002, Juris-Data n° 2002-176964. See S Moisdon-Chataigner et al, 'L'intérêt de l'enfant dans le contentieux de l'article 371-4 du Code civil (étude analytique de décisions)' in S Moisdon-Chataigner (ed), *Les grands-parents et leurs descendants : quelles relations juridiques?* (Paris, LexisNexis Litec, 2009) 171, 181–83.

[98] Etienney de Sainte Marie (n 29) 114.

[99] Moisdon-Chataigner et al (n 97) 179.

For instance, in one case the suppression of personal relations with the maternal grandparents was justified as there was a risk that the grandparents would have put their granddaughter in contact with her mother who refused the psychiatric care she needed.[100] Similarly, a court refused access rights to alcoholic and violent grandparents.[101] Following moral standards is also essential, and judges denied any visitation rights to grandparents in a case where they suspected an incestuous family climate.[102]

The third category includes cases where the relation between the parents and the grandparents is so conflict-ridden that the dispute in itself is perceived to be an obstacle. The courts must then find a balance between the child's protection, the child's welfare and respect for the parents' rights. Disputes around grandparents' contact with a child may bring a parent and his or her own parents, or a parent and his and her parents-in-law, into opposition; it may be a post-divorce or a post-separation case, where the parents disagree about the grandparents' access to the child, or it could emerge after the death of one of the parents, when the surviving parent refuses to maintain links with his or her former parents-in-law. On one hand, French courts consider the necessity for the child to maintain personal relations with his grandparents. On the other hand, courts consider the risk that the child may find himself at the centre of the dispute. Therefore, in a 28 February 2006 decision, the Cour de cassation held that

> if the disagreement between the grandparents and the parents does not in itself constitute a serious reason to refuse access rights, it is only on the condition that this disagreement does not spill over into the child and does not present any risk for him.[103]

In this particular case, the Court of Appeal noted that, should access have been given to the claimant grandfather, 'the girl would ... find herself at the centre of a conflict', as the grandfather was criticising and discrediting the education the parents had chosen for the child in a virulent manner.[104] Hence, the necessity to preserve the psychological and emotional balance of the child may justify a rejection of the grandparents' request when the conflict is such that it could disrupt this balance.[105] If there is a sharp conflict between the grandparents and the parents, the court may decide that it is not in the child's interest to maintain personal relation with the grandparents.[106] Similarly, in a recent case, a grandmother's claim was rejected due to her animosity towards her daughter-in-law and because of her attempt to denounce the allegedly violent behaviour of the parents towards the child to the Public Ministry. The grandmother's attitude led the parents to

[100] Riom, 27 March 2001, Juris-Data n° 2001-140925.
[101] Dijon, 6 November 2003, Juris-Data n° 2003-229951.
[102] Dijon, 29 October 2002, Juris-Data n° 2002-194086.
[103] Cass Civ 1re, 28 February 2006, n° 05-14.484, NP.
[104] Cass Civ 1re, 28 February 2006, n° 05-14.484, NP.
[105] Cass Civ 1re, 13 December 1989, 87-20.205, P I, n° 389.
[106] Cass Civ 1re, 5 January 1999, 97-13.613.

bring a complaint of slanderous denunciation. The Court held that, in this context, the behaviour of the paternal grandmother could only be prejudicial to the child.[107]

This approach – consisting of measuring the impact of the conflict upon the child – has been systematically followed by the courts. For instance, in a judgment of 14 January 2009, the Cour de cassation confirmed that the disagreement per se does not constitute a reason to refuse rights of access. In this case, the grandparents had shown the ability to make a clear distinction between the conflictual relationship they had with their own child and their ties with their grandchildren. That was evidenced by the grandparents' behaviour, by which they had shown a willingness to not insult the children's parents in front of the children.[108]

Sometimes, the Court will reject the grandparents' claim for a mixture of reasons. For instance, the Court of Appeal of Paris refused the visitation right requested by a grandmother on the basis that the 16-year-old child did not want to see his grandmother, that the grandmother did not have the material conditions to accommodate the child, that the psychological context was anxiety-provoking for the child, and that the grandmother had adopted an attitude of disparagement towards the child's father.[109]

The courts are especially inclined to maintain a child's relations with his grandparents where the child is deprived of one of his parents, because this parent has passed away or because this parent does not show any interest in the child. In such circumstances, maintaining personal relations with the grandparents allows the child to get to know their branch of the family.[110] In a case where the child's father was absent from the child's life, the Court of Appeal of Lyon granted to the child a right to maintain personal relations with the paternal grandmother, despite a disagreement the grandmother had with the child's mother.[111] Similarly, another Court of Appeal judged that

> the bond uniting the granddaughter and the grandmother is qualified as vital when the child is placed in an establishment, when her mother shows little interest in her, when her father has been sentenced for sexual assault on her daughter, the grandmother ensuring that father–daughter encounters do not take place.[112]

In another case, the paternal grandparents obtained a right to visit their granddaughter, despite the fact that the child's father had been sentenced for the attempted murder of the child's mother, and despite the lack of contact between the child and her grandparents for several years. Taking into account the grandparents' desire to maintain a relationship with their granddaughter, the Court considered that the alleged lack of empathy shown by the grandmother towards her ex-daughter-in-law was not a 'sufficiently serious reason' to prevent any

---

[107] Cass Civ 1re, 26 June 2019, 18-19.017.
[108] Cass Civ 1re, 14 January 2009, 08-11.035, P I, n° 2.
[109] Paris, 8 January 2015, n° 13-08469.
[110] Cass Civ 1re, 11 June 2008, 07-11.425, NP.
[111] Lyon, 9 September 2008, RG n° 07/08184.
[112] Besançon, 30 July 2002, RG n° 02/00016.

relationship between an 11-year-old child and her grandparents.[113] In a similar case, the Court of Appeal of Riom held that a grandmother should not be penalised for the actions of her son, sentenced to 10 years of criminal imprisonment for the attempted murder of his wife, while there was no risk that the children would meet their father at their grandmother's home.[114] These cases illustrate the importance of distinguishing between the parents' and grandparents' behaviour. Thus, if the grandparents themselves do not represent a danger to the child (by not putting the child in contact with a dangerous parent, for example), it is presumed that right of access would be in the child's interest.

In contrast, when there is a good reason to believe that the grandparents will denigrate the child's parents or will intervene in the child's education in a way of which the parents would disapprove, the courts will consider that the child is at risk of suffering from the disagreement and will deny access rights to the grandparents. For example, the Court of Appeal of Lyon rejected a claim brought by the paternal grandparents of a child after the death of his father, on the basis that the grandparents were disrespectful towards the child's mother and represented a risk of intruding into the mother-and-child relationship.[115] Giving access rights to grandparents may have some impact upon the parent's exercise of parental authority: therefore access rights do not have to be granted if the stability and the well-being of the child are threatened.[116] The well-being of the child could be at risk, for instance, if his grandparents are likely to exert pressure on him. In a case where the child's father was imprisoned for sexually touching the child, the Court refused to give access to the paternal grandmother on the grounds that the grandmother did not believe the child and could exert pressure on him.[117]

Overall, there are three categories of cases where the courts will be reluctant to apply the presumption in favour of ancestors: when the child does not want to maintain personal relations with his grandparents; when the grandparents represent a danger for the child or are unable to take care of him; and when the disagreement between the parents and the grandparents is such that it puts the child's stability or well-being at risk. The discretionary powers of the courts are essential to appreciate the 'child's interest' and can be perceived as limiting the scope of the statutory presumption. The French system here is quite like the statutory presumption of parental involvement introduced in England and Wales in 2014 by section 1(2A) of the Children Act 1989.[118] There is a statutory presumption in favour of parental involvement in the child's life, but this presumption may

---

[113] Lyon, 10 September 2012, RG n° 11/02956.
[114] Riom, 20 February 2001, RG n° 00/01424, *Lexbase* n° A9846ITT.
[115] Lyon, 21 February 2017, RG n° 15/02574.
[116] See, eg, Nimes, 22 May 2002, Juris-Data n° 2002-177769.
[117] Dijon, 6 February 2003, RG n° 02/00885, *JCP* 2003. IV. 2673.
[118] 'A court, in the circumstances mentioned in subsection (4)(a) or (7), is as respects each parent within subsection (6)(a) to presume, unless the contrary is shown, that involvement of that parent in the life of the child concerned will further the child's welfare.'

be rebutted by the courts if this involvement is shown to be damaging to the child's welfare. As explained by Kaganas:

> [D]espite the operation of a presumption that contact is best for the child, and despite a lack of evidence to rebut it in any particular case, the court is at liberty, by, for example, applying the s1(3) welfare checklist, to decide that contact is not in the child's best interests.[119]

The French courts seem to benefit from a similar liberty when deciding that contact with grandparents is not in the child's interest.

Despite the French statutory provision and the presumption in favour of the grandparents, in practice French courts play a major role when deciding whether the child can maintain a personal relationship with his grandparents. The French Cour de cassation leaves the qualification of the 'child's interest' to the sovereign appreciation of the lower courts,[120] as indeed the flexibility of the concept of the 'child interest' necessarily leads to judicial discretion. Therefore, the 'child's interest' is often described as an elusive or abstract notion.[121] The use of a statutory presumption in favour of the grandparents has therefore been criticised as being inappropriate to an essentially factual question. For instance, Michelle Gobert has insisted on the necessity to appreciate the factual circumstances and the unsuitability of a rigid tool such as a statutory presumption.[122] Despite the French statutory provision and the presumption in favour of the grandparent(s), French courts will in practice be the ones to decide when the child's best interest calls for a refusal to grant the grandparent(s) access rights. The flexibility of the 'child's best interest' concept necessarily leads to judicial discretion. Giving the grandparents an almost automatic access right to their grandchild despite a disagreement with the child's parents may alter the consistency of direction and education that any child needs to have. The author has a strong preference for the flexibility provided by case law and criticises the crystallisation of the solutions laid down by the legislator.[123] Similarly, Etienney de Sainte Marie argues that in such a matter, the judge's discretionary powers have a key role to play. Despite the statutory presumption, in practice, it seems that the power of decision is mostly delegated to the judges, because the necessity to assess the facts deprives the legal presumption of its substance.[124] In any case, the judge must check that granting contact rights to

---

[119] F Kaganas, 'Parental involvement: a discretionary presumption' (2008) 38(4) *Legal Studies* 549, 556.

[120] Cass Req, 6 November 1939, DH 1940, p 28; see also, on grandparents' rights, Cass Civ 1re, 13 December 1989, 87-20.205, P I, n° 389.

[121] In the context of grandparents' visitation rights, see Moisdon-Chataigner et al (n 97) 181. For a more general study on this question, see esp J Carbonnier, *Droit civil*, vol 2: *La famille, l'enfant, le couple* (Paris, PUF, 2002) 85.

[122] M Gobert, 'L'enfant et les adultes (à propos de la loi du 4 juin 1970)', *JCP* 1971. I. 242, n° 12.

[123] ibid.

[124] Etienney de Sainte Marie (n 29) 108.

the grandparents is in the child's interest, which led Rexand-Pourias to state that the statutory presumption is much weaker than the child's interest criteria.[125]

An alternative to these criticisms is to consider the presumption and the best interest as being complementary. French courts will use the statutory presumption as a starting point when qualifying what is in the child's best interest. The statutory presumption is not only symbolic; it plays the role of an essential guideline for the courts. The courts do not have to establish what is the child's best interest *ab initio* but are guided by the principle that maintaining a relationship with grandparents *is* in the child's interest. However, this principle is not a rigid one and may be overturned by an exception broadly conceived: the child's interest. This seems to offer a welcome balance between the security offered by the legal provision and the flexibility provided by the court's control.

VI. Conclusion

The English family law system is sometimes described as giving 'weak statutory guidance', as opposed to the French system, which is based on 'extended statutory guidance'.[126] In France, 'the law remains particularly important, as it provides guidelines to almost all aspects of relationships between adults and children';[127] while England belongs to the 'least legal-centric group of jurisdictions',[128] where 'family law is not based on a very strong idea of what a family should look like and how family members should behave'.[129] These differences may explain the variance in approach between English and French law when it comes to considering the personal relations between a child and his grandparents. In France, the starting point is a statutory presumption providing the child with a right to maintain personal relations with his grandparents. In England and Wales, the starting point is judicial discretion. However, despite using two completely different starting points, both jurisdictions consider the child's interest as a key element in appreciating the legal question of the child and grandparents' personal relations, and both leave it to the discretion of the judiciary to define it. Therefore, if a statutory presumption similar to the French one is established in England and Wales, its role will probably be limited: the courts will keep their current discretionary powers to assess whether or not the presumption has to be rebutted to protect the child's best interest. The study of French case law demonstrates the importance of the role played by the courts in such a matter, and reveals that the introduction of a statutory presumption in England and Wales may have little impact.

---

[125] Rexand-Pourias (n 80).
[126] See Willems and Sosson (n 2) 844.
[127] ibid 845.
[128] ibid 847.
[129] ibid.

In addition, the influence of the French statutory presumption on the national culture and the perception of grandparents' role in the family is not clearly established. In France, the number of claims related to visitation rights by grandparents is low. In 2018, there were 1,679 judgments relating to the child's right to contact, including not only claims by the grandparents but also those by other third persons.[130] However, there is no evidence that this small number of applications results from the statutory presumption. One could argue that knowing that the courts will recognise personal relations between children and their grandparents, the children's parents are more likely to accede to grandparents' demands. It has been argued, however, that there is already a similar social norm in England and Wales, according to which grandparents should have contact with their grandchildren.[131] Therefore it is difficult to appreciate what the practical impact of the introduction of a statutory presumption could be: it may neither reduce nor increase the number of applications, and may have very little impact on the way the courts deal with these questions.

The existence of Article 371-4 of the French Civil Code mainly contributes to the general idea that grandparents should play a role in their grandchildren's lives. This idea goes beyond a right for the child to maintain personal relations with his grandparents, as in French law a grandparent has many duties and rights.[132] In order to keep the coherence of the English system, the best way to consider a reform may be to examine the figure of the grandparent as a whole, and not only via the spectre of the right to maintain personal relations.

---

[130] Of these, 918 claims were accepted and 411 refused. See Ministère de la Justice (2018) at www.justice.gouv.fr/art_pix/Annuaire_ministere-justice_2018_CHAPITRE_1.pdf (accessed 8 September 2021).

[131] See the references in nn 15 and 16.

[132] See section II for some examples.

10

The Impact of Culture on Grandparents' Rights: Laws and Social Practices in Nepal

SNEHA SHRESTHA

[I]n the non-Western world, traditions of gender hierarchy, kinship and property ownership have promoted the higher social status of grandparents within the family and society.[1]

I. Introduction

Nepal is a relatively small country, landlocked between 'the behemoths'[2] of India and China. It is viewed as a 'quiet jewel among the clouds',[3] 'rich in geographic, climatic, demographic, and cultural diversity'.[4] Nepali culture is collectivistic: relationships with members of the family, and the community at large, are at the heart of everyone's identity. Like many South Asians, Nepali families have practised the norm of a joint family system for centuries, where several generations and extended family members live under the same roof.[5]

In subsistence economies like Nepal, grandparents and other family members tend to form close alliances.[6] One's family life is very much the business of one's extended family and the social group (often determined by caste) to which one belongs. Hence, the country and its people are mainly governed by culture and norms, as opposed to the by law and the state. From observation, this could be

---

[1] Z Hossain, G Eisberg and DW Shwalb, 'Grandparents' Social Identities in Cultural Context' (2018) 2 *Journal of the Academy of Social Sciences* 275, 275.

[2] J Aiken, 'Lessons from Nepal: Partnership, Privilege, and Potential' (2003) 2 *Washington University Global Studies Law Review* 391, 391.

[3] ibid.

[4] BP Mishra, *Rebuilding Nepal* (Bhrikuti, Academic Publications, 2007) 3–4.

[5] Hossain, Eisberg and Shwalb (n 1) 280.

[6] ibid 276.

largely due to a weak and unstable state; the government cannot be relied upon for any meaningful system of support (ie social welfare system). Nepal is one of the poorest countries in the world and the 20th largest receiver of remittances.[7] The situation is, no doubt, deteriorating due to Covid-19.[8]

The assumed protection stemming from social practices means there is little legal protection of the grandparent–grandchild relationship in Nepal. Thus far, grandparents' rights ('*baje-bajai ko adhikar*') do not appear to be a topic of concern in the Nepali context. Grandparents are important in Nepal; the relationship they share with their grandchildren is arguably even more special than in the west because they are much more likely to be actively involved in raising their grand-children from birth. Perhaps that is why their roles have not been challenged in the social domain and, since the law generally follows social convention/practice,[9] grandparents' rights have been non-existent in the legal domain. However, increas-ing awareness of legal rights, and other factors (discussed in section V) such as the dramatic rise in divorce and modernisation in general, has transformed the traditional family structure in Nepal. Changing social dynamics could lead to less grandparent involvement and the greater likelihood of conflict between parents and grandparents about contact with their grandchildren. There is now a potential danger that the law will start to lag behind social change, hence there is a need for greater support from the state to provide legal mechanisms to ensure that grand-parents' and grandchildren's interests are protected.

The expression 'legal rights of grandparents' understandably bewilders common and learned Nepali individuals alike. Sources on grandparents' 'rights' are limited in the context of Nepali legislation; most legislation on grandparents stems from senior citizens' property rights, which are not the focus of this chapter. The aim of this chapter is to put grandparents' rights into their Nepali context and initiate meaningful dialogue among policymakers, lawyers, academics and other stakeholders about how best to protect relationship rights between grand-parents and grandchildren in Nepal. This chapter will draw on an understanding of grandparent–grandchild relationships in other Asian countries to shed light on the situation in Nepal and, where appropriate, highlight the contrast with the United Kingdom's (UK's) legal system – a system addressed in detail by others in this collection. This approach will suggest ways in which grandparents' rights may potentially be protected in Nepal.

Furthermore, legal rules and decisions must be understood in context since '[l]aw is not autonomous, standing outside of the social world, but is deeply

---

[7] See at data.worldbank.org/indicator/BX.TRF.PWKR.CD.DT?locations=NP.
[8] See at blogs.worldbank.org/endpovertyinsouthasia/covid-19-will-hit-south-asia-hard-we-are-fighting-back; and at www.worldbank.org/en/news/press-release/2020/04/03/world-bank-fast-tracks-29-million-for-nepal-covid-19-coronavirus-response.
[9] *See generally* HLA Hart, *The Concept of Law* (Oxford, Clarendon Press, 1961); SL Roach Anleu, *Law and Social Change*, 2nd edn (Thousand Oaks, CA, Sage Publications, 2009) 1–13.

embedded within society'.[10] In light of this, this chapter will begin with a brief history of Nepal, which is integral to understanding the setting within which our discussion is based (section II). It will then explore the social norms and roles of grandparents in Nepal (section III), followed by an examination of relevant Nepali laws in place and recommendations (section IV). As this research is the first step toward discussing grandparents' rights in Nepal, the raison d'être for protecting grandparents' rights will need to be considered (section V). The chapter will then end with possible next steps toward addressing grandparents' rights in Nepal (section VI).

II. Nepali History: Rana Rule, Civil War and the Earthquake

Communities emerging from conflict often must rebuild their economic infrastructure, political system, and social institutions. Nations recovering from major natural disasters must similarly rebuild from the ground up. Countries such as Nepal – which experienced both of these challenges simultaneously – face overlapping effects, presenting significant challenges but also major opportunities for regrowth and recovery.[11]

The historical origins of Nepal have had a significant impact on the development of laws and culture. Nepal is the birthplace of the Buddha, hence it is often referred to as 'a land of peace'[12] and spirituality. Yet paradoxically this land has experienced the 'ruthless violence of the struggles for power ... at several junctures in its history'.[13] Nepal was controlled by a ruling dynasty, the 'Ranas', for over a century, during which time the civilians were treated as a source of revenue[14] as opposed to rights-bearing citizens.[15] The oppressive feudal monarchy is claimed to be the origin[16] of socio-economic backwardness, rampant corruption,[17] profound inequality and widespread poverty[18] in Nepal; the root causes for the civil war, known as the 'People's Movement'.[19] Despite the aim of the conflict's being to

---

[10] L Mather, 'Law and Society' in RE Goodin (ed), *The Oxford Handbook of Political Science* (Oxford, Oxford University Press, 2011) 289, 289.

[11] B Mawby and A Applebaum, *Rebuilding Nepal: Women's roles in political transition and disaster recovery* (Georgetown Institute for women, Peace and Security, 2018) Foreword.

[12] M Hutt (ed), *Himalayan 'People's War' – Nepal's Maoist Rebellion* (London, Hurst & Company, 2004) 2.

[13] ibid.

[14] Mishra (n 4) 159.

[15] Hutt (n 12) 2.

[16] See generally S Tamang, 'Legalizing State Patriarchy in Nepal' (2000) 5(1) *Studies in Nepali History and Society* 127.

[17] D Sapkota, *Ten years of Upheaval – Reportage of the Decade long Maoist People's War in Nepal* (Kathmandu, Revolutionist Journalist Association, 2010) 41; Mishra (n 4) 30.

[18] J Whelpton, *History of Nepal* (Cambridge, Cambridge University Press, 2005) 202.

[19] Sapkota (n 17) 21.

bring 'real democracy',[20] the people endured a decade of violence from the 'Royal Nepalese Army' and the Maoists.[21] The conflict ended in 2006 with the signing of the 'Comprehensive Peace Agreement', ushering in the phase of 'transitional justice' in Nepal.[22]

To add to this backdrop, Nepal was struck by a devastating, 7.8 magnitude earthquake on 25 April 2015. Thousands of lives were lost, and poverty escalated in a country already fighting extreme poverty:[23] 80–90 per cent of rural homes belonging to low-income families were destroyed[24] and there was damage estimated at $5.17 billion.[25] This was exacerbated by state corruption regarding foreign aid.[26] The intersecting challenges (post-conflict *versus* post-disaster reconstruction) took the country back into despair and instability. The aftermath of the earthquake further shattered the social fabric of Nepal, thereby causing a lack of leadership and legal infrastructure to protect basic human rights, such as freedom of expression, justice for civil war victims, etc.[27] This explains why legal reform on grandparents' rights might not be on the agenda, let alone a priority.

Despite Nepal's unfortunate history, the current transitional phase presents opportunities to recover and redevelop. As an example, the earthquake catalysed the drafting of a new constitution, which was promulgated in less than five months (20 September 2015).[28] Accordingly, it seems an appropriate time to instigate discussions on grandparents' rights in Nepal.

III. Social Norms and Grandparents in Nepal

To classify Nepal as a patriarchal society alone would be an oversimplification: 'Nepal is a patriarchal, patrilineal and patrifocal society.'[29]

---

[20] ibid 23.

[21] L Friedman, *Conflict in Nepal, A Simplified Account* (Kathmandu, Shtrii Shakti, 2005) 1.

[22] See generally S Shrestha, 'The Curious Case of Colonel Kumar Lama: Its Origins and Impact in Nepal and the United Kingdom, and Its Contribution to the Discourse on Universal Jurisdiction' (2017) *Transnational Law Institute Think! Paper 2/2018*.

[23] Mawby and Applebaum (n 11) 10.

[24] ibid; Government of Nepal Ministry of Finance, *Economic Survey Fiscal Year 2014/15* (Kathmandu, Government of Nepal, 2015) 280.

[25] Asian Development Bank, 'Recent Significant Disasters in the Asia and Pacific Region' (27 September 2016) at www.adb.org/news/infographics/recent-significant-disasters-asia-and-pacific-region.

[26] P Bhagat, 'An Earthquake Exposes Nepal's Political Rot' (30 April 2015) at www.foreignpolicy.com/2015/04/30/an-earthquake-exposes-nepals-political-rot/.

[27] Human Rights Watch, 'Nepal Event of 2020' at www.hrw.org/world-report/2021/country-chapters/nepal.

[28] Global Legal Monitor, 'Nepal: New Constitution approved' (1 October 2015) at www.loc.gov/law/foreign-news/article/nepal-new-constitution-approved/.

[29] Asha Nepal, 'The impact of Hinduism and Patriarchy on women in Nepal' (14 July 2019) at www.asha-nepal.org/news/impact-hinduism-and-patriarchy-women-nepal.

A. Typical Nepali Families

Like other Asian countries such as Myanmar, Thailand and Vietnam, in Nepal there is a culture of reciprocal intergenerational obligations;[30] co-residence of older persons and adult children is still a common phenomenon, unlike in the west. Despite a gradual decline over time, 'extended or intergenerational families are still more prevalent in Asia than any other region globally'.[31] In Nepal, the word 'family' refers to a wide network of extended relationships. The Asian culture values 'commitment to protecting one's family',[32] hence families often combine their assets to ensure all members are economically secure. A child's education, through to their marriage[33] (and beyond), falls on their parents and their extended family. Nepali households have a structured hierarchical environment as respect for elders is a long-standing tradition.[34] Younger household members customarily 'serve, respect and defer'[35] to their elders. Grandparents conventionally assume the position at the head of the family, without the need for legal recognition.

B. The Impact of Gender Bias and the Persistence of Patriarchy in Grandparent–Grandchild Relationships

Nepal is characterised by unequal and gendered power relations.[36] A daughter born into a family is considered a temporary member of the household. The living pattern is patrilocal as women, to this day, formally move into their husband's home after marriage, which may comprise his parents, siblings, and often their wives and children. The patrilineal culture dictates that the lineage is traced through the father and inheritance moves strictly from father to son within all communities in Nepal. Accordingly, son preference[37] has historically been prevalent amongst parents,[38] as has grandson preference for paternal grandparents.

---

[30] J Knodel and MD Nguyen, 'Grandparents and grandchildren: care and support in Myanmar, Thailand, and Vietnam' (2015) 35 *Ageing & Society* 1960, 1960.

[31] S Kim, 'Grandparenting: Focus on Asia' at www.un.org/development/desa/family/wp-content/uploads/sites/23/2020/06/EGM2020.Grandparenting-in-Asia.SK_.pdf, 1.

[32] ibid.

[33] See BR Acharya, 'Sociological Analysis of Divorce: A Case Study from Pokhara, Nepal' (2006) 1 *Dhaulagiri Journal of Sociology and Anthropology* 6: 63% of divorce cases in the study were arranged marriages.

[34] This is enshrined in the law, see Senior Citizens Act, s 3: 'It shall be the duty of all to respect senior citizens'; Civil Code, s 122: 'Every son or daughter shall treat his or her mother, father with honour and respect.'

[35] MC Goldstein and CM Beall, 'Family chance, caste, and the elderly in a rural locale in Nepal' (1986) 1 *Journal of Cross-Cultural Gerontology* 305, 305.

[36] J Baniya et al, 'Gender and Nepal's transition from war' *Accord Spotlight* (September 2017) 16.

[37] See generally YB Karki, 'Sex preference and the value of sons and daughters in Nepal' (1998) 19(3) *Studies in Family Planning* 169.

[38] EA Jennings, 'Family composition and marital dissolution in rural Nepal, 1945–2008' (2017) 71(2) *Population Studies* 229, 233.

In some families, women are expected to keep giving birth, 'waiting for a boy to come',[39] and some husbands remarry if their first wife does not bear a son.[40] Traditionally in-laws expect daughters-in-law to conceive soon after marriage,[41] affording paternal grandparents' immense control[42] and rights over grandchildren. This reveals the issue of prospective grandparenthood in Nepal, where there is an anticipation of 'rights' or 'interest' from the beginning of a relationship. Thus, grandparents' rights, in a Nepali family context, are assumed even though they lack legal recognition/regulation as such.

According to Hindu scriptures, only a son can perform a parent's funeral rites[43] to ensure a smooth transition to the next life.[44] Consequently, patriarchy has been enforced in the home for centuries, leading to the transmission of patrifocal values and norms from grandparents and parents to children and grandchildren.[45] These norms and deeply entrenched traditions tend to place women on a lower pedestal than men.[46] This context is relevant in understanding the roots of patriarchal norms and laws in Nepal, which differentiate between maternal and paternal grandparents rights, as will be clear in the remainder of this section and section IV.

C. Maternal and Paternal Grandparents: Is There a Difference?

As considered in section III.B, Nepali law and practice distinguish between maternal and paternal grandparents. In contrast to western countries, such as the UK, the daughter-in-law *belongs* to her husband's family. The marriage ceremony includes a ritual by which she is formally given by her parents to the husband's clan.[47] Hence paternal grandparents, *ipso facto*, have superior rights towards their grandchildren and maternal grandparents assume subordinate status.

---

[39] S Paudel, 'Women's concerns within Nepal's patriarchal justice system' (2011) 5(6) *Ethics in Action* 30, 30; Asha (n 29).

[40] M Dhungana, a lawyer for the Forum for Women Law and Development, in Global Press Institute, 'Rising awareness of legal rights doubles divorce rates in Nepal's capital' (4 May 2012) at news.trust.org/item/20120504144700-625zw/.

[41] Asha (n 29). See also H Masvie, 'The role of Tamang grandmothers in perinatal care, Makwanpur District, Nepal' in P Liamputtong, *Childrearing and Infant Care Issues: A cross-cultural perspective* (New York, Hauppauge, 2007) 167.

[42] See Sumina's story, who was forced by her mother-in-law to have a baby when she was only 16, in S Narang, 'The Teen Brides of Nepal' (24 February 2017) at deeply.thenewhumanitarian.org/womenandgirls/articles/2017/02/24/teen-brides-nepal-married-children-time.

[43] Jennings (n 38) 233.

[44] C Arnold et al, *Bringing up children in a changing world* (Save the Children, UNICEF, UN Children's Fund, 2000) 51.

[45] Paudel (n 39) 30.

[46] N Adhikari, 'Patriarchal Mind-set Impedes Women Empowerment' (3 October 2020) at risingnepaldaily.com/opinion/patriarchal-mind-set-impedes-women-empowerment.

[47] J Goddard, '15 Surprising Things About Parenting in Nepal' (10 September 2018) at www.cupofjo.com/2018/09/maggie-doyne-parenting-in-nepal/.

Maternal grandmothers tend to have the strongest, most frequent and, most often, positive effect on grandchildren's survival and health.[48] As discussed in chapter 2 of this volume, studies in the UK have also found that although there is no distinction in status in *law*, in practice maternal grandparents are usually in a stronger position socially.[49] Studies on grandparents in other patrilineal societies show that 'paternal grandmothers tend to be less commonly beneficial than maternal grandmothers'.[50] The main reason is identified as 'resource competition' or 'resource stress', where paternal grandparents may need to compete with their grandchildren given the limited/scarce resources within a joint family.[51] Yet social norms and laws in Nepal dictate that maternal grandparents are inferior to paternal grandparents; a concept that is non-existent in the UK law, where grandparents require leave from court to gain contact with their grandchildren,[52] regardless of their child's gender.

IV. Do Laws in Nepal Protect Grandparents' Rights?

In contrast to the position in French law, discussed in detail by Sauvé in chapter 9 of this volume, there is no direct legal protection afforded to grandparents in Nepal. There is, however, indirect protection provided by three pieces of legislation that will be considered in this section: the Act Relating to Children 2075 (2018); the Senior Citizens Act 2063 (2006); and the Civil Code 2074 (2017).

A. Act Relating to Children 2075 (2018)

Law is socially and historically constructed. '[L]aw both reflects and impacts culture, and how inequalities are reinforced through differential access to, and competence with, legal procedures and institutions.'[53] The gender hierarchy and joint family system, discussed in section III of this chapter, is prescribed by law under section 2(h), chapter 1 of the Act Relating to Children 2075 (2018) (ARC). The definition of 'family' puts the elder brother and younger brother before the elder and younger sisters, and although it includes 'grandfather or grandmother' and other relatives, it is qualified by the phrase 'living in an undivided family'.

---

[48] P Sheppard and R Sear, 'Do grandparents compete with or support their grandchildren? In Guatemala, paternal grandmothers may compete, and maternal grandmothers may cooperate' (2016) 3 *Royal Society Open Science* 1, 3.
[49] G Douglas and N Ferguson, 'The Role of Grandparents in Divorced Families' (2003) 17(1) *International Journal of Law, Policy and the Family* 41, 45, 51.
[50] Sheppard and Sear (n 48) 3.
[51] ibid.
[52] See chs 4, 5 and 7 of this volume for detailed discussion of the requirement for leave.
[53] Mather (n 10) 289.

An undivided family in this context is where the child(ren)'s parents are not divorced or separated and the grandparents live with them, making this a joint family arrangement. Therefore, grandfathers and/or grandmothers (whether they are single or together) have distinct rights towards their grandchildren, so long as they live with the children's parents who live together. Accordingly, any member who does not live in the same household does not fall with the definition of 'family'. Given the social (patrilocal) context, this omits maternal grandparents from 'family'.

For example, section 6(5) of the ARC states that if a child is in care or under guardianship, they have a right to meet their biological parents or families. This indirectly gives rights to grandparents to visit their grandchildren, but the narrow definition of 'family' withdraws any such indirect right if the grandparents do not live in an undivided family. Similarly, section 7(1) provides that every child has a right to obtain proper care, protection, maintenance, love and affection from their father, mother and other members of the family, yet it will only apply to grandparents who co-reside with the child's mother and father. The same applies under section 17(2)–(5), which emphasise the family's responsibility for the child's education, care and maintenance, guidance and so on. Put another way, paternal grandparents have indirect rights and responsibilities toward a grandchild if, and only if, they live in a joint family. Paradoxically, the Nepali law gives those grandparents' the right to contact and care for grandchildren when such rights need not be exercised because they live in the same household (except for circumstances under section 6(5)).

Maternal grandparents do not have even indirect rights, such as those afforded to co-resident paternal grandparents, discussed above. It is important to note that there are instances in Nepal where paternal grandparents pressurise their daughters-in-law to end contact with their families,[54] leaving maternal grandparents vulnerable to losing contact with their daughters and grandchildren. Women's lives in Nepal are constructed around the concepts of tolerance and devotion,[55] hence they do not easily recognise such behaviour by in-laws/husbands as a form of domestic abuse. Such circumstances in the UK are recognised in law as controlling and coercive behaviour that enables its victims to seek a legal remedy.[56] The Nepali law, as it stands, does not offer maternal grandparents any means of challenging/resolving such a situation to connect with their grandchildren.

B. Senior Citizens Act 2063 (2006)

The definition of a 'family member' under the Senior Citizens Act 2063 (2006) (SCA) complements the definition under the ARC set out in section IV.A, thereby

---

[54] Narang (n 42), see Rabina's story, a 15-year-old girl who was told to forget her maternal family if she wanted to be with her husband.

[55] Paudel (n 39) 31.

[56] Family Law Act 1996, s 42 (non-molestation orders); see also the Serious Crime Act 2015, s 76.

approving the higher status attributed to sons in Nepali society. The order of priority as set out in section 2(g) is as follows (emphasis added):

'Family Member' means the following relative of a senior citizen:

1. son, daughter-in-law, daughter, grand-son or grand-daughter *on the line of the son* living in a *joint family*;
2. in the absence of … (1) [the same as above but] living *separately*;
3. [if not] *any other* close relative.

The patrilineal culture is embedded within Nepali law and culture. The son and daughter-in-law, for instance, come before the unmarried daughter, and only the grandchildren 'on the line of the son' are considered to be direct family members. Furthermore, those living in a joint family come first, reflecting the traditional patrilocal norm. It can be reasonably inferred that 'any other close relative' may include married daughters and their children, but this is not explicitly stated. Including them under the label of 'close relatives' reinforces the perception that married daughters do not form a part of their parents' family, hence the importance of a relationship between grandchildren and their maternal grandparents is consistently ignored by the law.

Section 4(3) of the SCA confers negative rights on grandparents towards their grandchildren, providing that 'No one shall detach the senior citizen from the family or compel … [them to detach themselves against their will].' Although the grandparents may file a complaint, under section 5, if they are separated or uncared for, they do not have a positive right to seek contact with their grandchildren. Again, this negative right will apply only to paternal grandparents given the patrilocal living arrangement. There is thus a clear imbalance of power between maternal and paternal grandparents, which reflects the interplay between culture and the law in relation to grandparents in Nepal.

C. Civil Code 2074 (2017)

i. Child Arrangement Law

The current Nepali law places an enormous responsibility on 10-year-olds to choose between their parents. The law in England and Wales attempts to eliminate the risk of placing such burden on young children as child welfare is assessed through a report by the Children and Family Court Advisory and Support Service (CAFCASS),[57] which considers the child's best interests under the welfare checklist.[58] The judge then applies the welfare principle in court, in line with the report. No such safety net/system exists in Nepal to ensure that the best interests of children are upheld. The welfare checklist might be an effective

---

[57] Children Act 1989, s 7.
[58] ibid s 1(3).

tool to consider in Nepal, as it could assist judges in cases involving children, where the court's paramount consideration ought to be the child's best interests.

The rule under section 115 of the Civil Code is that if divorced/separated parents have not entered into a separate agreement, the court will decide child custody as follows:

Divorce (section 115(1)–(4))

(a) minor under 5 years of age – mother gets first preference as regards custody, irrespective of her marital status;

(b) minor above 5 years of age – mother gets first preference as regards custody, unless she remarries;

(c) in all other circumstances – the father gets custody (ie if the mother chooses not to take custody, or if she remarries when the minor is aged between 5 and 10 years).

When deciding custody for a minor above 10 years old, the minor's opinion *may* also be obtained.

Separation (section 115(5))

(a) minor below 5 years of age – the mother *shall* have custody;

(b) minor above 5 but below 10 years of age – the father *shall* have custody;

(c) minor above 10 years of age – the minor *shall* decide which parent should have custody.

It is peculiar that although child arrangements for divorced and separated couples are similar, the provision regarding the opinion of a minor older than 10 years old differs depending on whether the parents divorce or separate. Whilst divorced couples have some flexibility, separated couples fall under stricter child custody rules. Furthermore, the 5-year and 10-year rules are more prescriptive and less child-focused.[59] This could be inappropriate, as there may be individual factors in each case that give rise to unique needs and vulnerabilities of each child. Moreover, on what basis is a minor over 10 years of age considered capable of deciding with whom they should live if the parents are separated, but *may* only give their opinion if their parents are divorced? Such blanket rules, without due consideration to the individual child's welfare, make it problematic for grandparents to maintain their relationship with their grandchildren during different stages of their lives.

ii. Visitation Rules

In cases of divorce or separation of parents, section 117(1) of the Civil Code provides that the child can visit the non-resident parent from time to time or, with

---

[59] cf *Gillick* competence (English law), where weight is given to a competent child's opinion. This is dependent upon the sufficient intelligence and understanding of the child, which does not depend on a specific age but tends to be 12+. See *Gillick v West Norfolk and Wisbech AHA* [1985] UKHL 7.

the consent of the mother and father, 'stay with them for some time'. It is interesting to note that this is the first time the child's interests are mentioned in the legislation, albeit in negative wording:

> [I]f it appears that the interest of the minor is likely to be prejudiced ... the court may issue an order prohibiting such visit or stay.

The statute does not state how a child's best interests are to be determined under Nepali law, hence it is unclear how this decision is to be reached. These are merely commonsense factors at the judge's discretion. It also seems bizarre that the court can prohibit contact if it prejudices the child's interests under visitation rules, but in custody decisions, which are more sensitive and long-term, the child's best interests are not explicitly stated. Instead, there are rules depending on the child's age, which are insensitive to the long-term impact on an individual child.

Furthermore, visitation rights only extend to the non-resident parent, not grandparents (either maternal or paternal), whether divorced or separated. The reason behind this may be on the premise that the father or mother will be living with their respective families, hence the child will be able to maintain relationships with both sets of grandparents.[60] Chapter 2 of this volume describes this as 'reliance on the parental route', which is indicative of a legal hierarchy that does not reflect the strength of grandparent–grandchild relationships.[61] Such an assumption cannot be made by the law in a modern society if it is to be effective, because there may well be mothers and fathers who do not live with or maintain contact with their natal family for a variety of reasons[62] owing to social norms, for example the shame of divorce/separation and the fear of burdening the family, separation from joint family, remarriage, migration, etc. This issue could be remedied by extending the visitation right to grandparents (maternal and paternal) as a standalone right, notwithstanding how non-contact occurred. This would require thorough consideration, as even in the UK, grandparents do not have an automatic right to contact as they must first seek leave from court[63] to apply for a contact order. Should policy makers in Nepal extend visitation rights to grandparents, the welfare checklist would be a valuable tool to employ in determining whether this is the child's best interests.

iii. Guardianship: Grandparents

Section 131 of the Civil Code gives grandparents responsibility under the law as guardians of the child. This is different from having the right to contact and maintaining a relationship with their grandchildren; nonetheless, it is relevant to the

---

[60] See Douglas and Ferguson (n 49) 47–48.

[61] Bendall and Davey, ch 2 of this volume, section III.C.

[62] Douglas and Ferguson (n 49) 48, where in one family, the mother had remarried, 'left her past behind', and cut herself and her children off from her own parents as well as her former in-laws.

[63] Children Act 1989, s 10(9).

recurring theme, the distinction between maternal and paternal grandparents, in this chapter. This responsibility is only triggered if:

(a)   the mother and father have died or disappeared;
(b)   the mother remarried following the death of the father; or
(c)   the mother and father are of unsound mind.

There is clearly a high threshold to surpass for this responsibility to be triggered, but even if any such situation were to occur, the law prescribes an order of priority under section 136 of the Civil Code. The full list includes nine categories of possible guardians for an incompetent or quasi-competent person. However, for the purposes of section 131, the grandfather/grandmother is first on the list for a child, then any elder/younger brother or elder/younger sister, then the maternal grandfather/grandmother or maternal uncle/aunt. Section 136(2)(d) of the Civil Code provides that the maternal grandparents' rights will only be triggered once the parental grandparents and the elder/younger brother or elder/younger sister decline or cannot act in the capacity of a guardian, thereby directly discriminating against maternal grandparents.

Whilst maternal grandparents are described as 'grandfather or grandmother on the mother's parent side', paternal grandparents are simply 'grandfather or grandmother'. This implies that maternal grandparents must be differentiated because they are secondary, hence they should not be confused with the main grandparents – the paternal grandparents – with greater rights. The child can choose their guardian when they are 10 years old,[64] but the emotional turmoil and distress younger children may experience in Nepal during their formative years, because of the order of priority, should not be underestimated. The law ought not to make such distinctions between paternal and maternal grandparents, if it is to protect the child's best interests.

D. Maternal and Paternal Grandparents: Non-discrimination and Equality before the Law

Society, culture and the law are inextricably linked. In the three pieces of legislation discussed in section IV, married women are consistently discriminated against, as their natal family no longer qualifies as their family in society and, more importantly, in *law*. The Civil Code prohibits discrimination on grounds of, inter alia, religion, caste, sex, marital status, etc, yet only mothers lose custody of their children (above 5 years old) upon remarriage. Fathers' remarriages bear no relevance to child custody rights. Accordingly, paternal grandparents may see their grandchildren even if their son remarries, whereas maternal grandparents'

---

[64] Civil Code 2017, s 136(2)(b).

rights towards their grandchildren become a fiction, as they are irretrievably disconnected once their daughter moves to her new husband's house without her children. Such laws appear to be guided by 'outdated and orthodox social values'[65] that continue to perpetuate inequality and discrimination in Nepal. In effect, such a cultural impact on child arrangement laws in Nepal leaves maternal grandparents in the most vulnerable position. In stark contrast, child arrangement laws in the UK are primarily focused on children's welfare, through the Children Act 1989, as opposed to strict rules on custody dictated by their parents' gender or marital status.

Since the law in Nepal has enshrined male preference and patrilocal practices, it is no surprise that Nepali society is still subject to patriarchal values. The inequality that exists between maternal and paternal grandparents cannot be in the best interests of a child. As discussed in section III.C, maternal grandmothers in Nepal are often associated with having a closer bond with their grandchildren. A study in the UK found that maternal grandparents were more significant in grandchildren's lives, before and after divorce.[66] Nevertheless, in Nepal, indirect grandparents' rights only apply to paternal grandparents in a joint/undivided family. This reveals the law's lack of equality and inability to reflect current social norms.

Nevertheless, there have been several positive movements in the law towards empowering women, making it fertile ground for reform of patriarchal laws that overlook or discriminate against maternal grandparents in Nepal. In particular, the three pieces of legislation discussed above could follow the progressive movement demonstrated by the Gender Equality Act (2006), which removed discriminatory language and repealed several discriminatory provisions.[67] This Act provides a basis for addressing such discrimination when interpreted in conjunction with the other Acts. For example, the definition of 'family' under the ARC could remove the requirement to be 'living in an undivided family', and the SCA could remove the proviso 'on the line of the son living in a joint family'. As regards child custody under section 115(1)(b) of the Civil Code, the wording unless she remarries (see section IV.C.i) could be removed, as this unjustifiably discriminates against the mother, which simultaneously discriminates against maternal grandparents. More importantly, as to explicit discrimination against maternal grandparents in connection with guardianship, the phrase 'grandfather, grandmother on the mother's parent side' ought to be removed, as under section 136(1)(f), 'grandfather or grandmother' can include the rights of both maternal and paternal grandparents. Such scrutiny of the articulation of laws would ensure equality between maternal and paternal grandparents before the law.

---

[65] S Gaunle, 'Splitting up: Divorce cases are on the rise, and the law remains loaded against women' *Nepali Times* (19 January 2001) at www.archive.nepalitimes.com/news.php?id=8614#.YgBS8S2cbUp.
[66] Douglas and Ferguson (n 49) 45.
[67] Paudel (n 39) 32–33.

V. Is There a Case for Protecting Grandparents'
Rights in Nepal?

'Grandparents in every society can be the threads that hold cultural traditions, family histories and legacies together.'[68] In Nepal, traditionally, grandparents were so involved in their grandchildren's lives that their rights never came into question, but they do not possess legal rights, as already discussed. However, a gap in the law alone does not justify creation of new laws: there ought to be awareness and the need for it in the society. This section proposes to make a case for grandparents' rights to be protected in Nepal, particularly given the changes to the country's social fabric.

A. Why Preserve the Grandparent–Grandchild Relationship?

The special relationship between grandparents and their grandchildren is culturally recognised in most countries. It has recently been enshrined in international law[69] that a child clearly benefits from the inter-generational bonds with their wider family members.[70] Chapter 6 of this volume emphasises the child's right to learn about their ancestry and genetic origin, which is an approach adopted by the United Nations Convention on the Rights of the Child (UNCRC). Moreover, as working parents become the norm, grandparents are heavily involved in raising grandchildren.[71] A survey in the UK highlighted the prevalence of 'grannannying' in today's society, as it revealed that over 5 million grandparents provide regular childcare for their grandchildren.[72] A study found that Chinese-American grandparents assume their role is to 'help build moral character, teach social manners, support the grandchildren's aspirations, and applaud their achievements'.[73] In most countries around the world, grandparents are known to pass on a legacy:[74] they teach their native

---

[68] Hossain, Eisberg and Shwalb (n 1) 283.

[69] See, eg, Case C-335/17 *Valcheva v Babanarakis* (CJEU, 12 April 2018); *A and another v C* [2018] EWHC 2048 (Fam).

[70] K Res Pritchard and K Williams, 'The rights of grandparents and other family members in relation to children – from both a domestic and international perspective' (2018) 4 *International Family Law Journal* 281, 286.

[71] Hossain, Eisberg and Shwalb (n 1) 282. See also Kim (n 31) 1; P Kamnuansilpa and S Wongthanavasu, 'Grandparents' Relationships with Grandchildren in Thailand' (2005) 3(1) *Journal of Intergenerational Relationships* 49, 49.

[72] Age UK, '5 Million Grandparents take on Childcare Responsibilities' (29 September 2017) at www.ageuk.org.uk/latest-news/articles/2017/september/five-million-grandparents-take-on-childcare-responsibilities.

[73] C Cox, 'Cultural diversity among grandparent caregivers: Implications for interventions and policy' (2018) 8 *Educational Gerontology* 484, 487.

[74] Z Zeng and Y Xie, 'The Effects of Grandparents on Children's Schooling: Evidence from Rural China' (2014) 51 *Demography* 599, 601; see also V King and G Elder, 'The legacy of grandparenting: Childhood experiences with grandparents and current involvement with grandchildren' (1997) 59 *Journal of Marriage and the Family* 848.

language,[75] religious and cultural values,[76] family heritage and life skills to their grandchildren.[77] For these reasons, grandparents are often described as 'cultural transmitters, oral historians, and wisdom keepers'.[78] In Nepal, grandparents play a vital role in the transfer of knowledge, skills and traditions to their grandchildren.[79] This was recognised in 2014, by a project that focused on storytelling by grandparents to preserve endangered oral heritage.[80]

Although grandparent–grandchild relationships have recently gained more international attention, they are generally ignored by policy makers as these relationships appear to have been taken for granted in many societies,[81] including Nepal. Despite the collectivistic and close-knit family culture in Nepal, when relationships break down, grandparents have no legal recourse when denied contact by the parent(s).

B. Changes and Trends

Grandparents' relationship with their grandchildren can no longer be taken for granted because of social norms, religious beliefs and customary practices. The recent changes and trends in Nepal have brought grandparents' rights to the fore. These changes and trends can broadly be divided into two categories: first, the rise in the divorce rate (single parents may keep their children away from grandparents for various social/personal reasons); and, second, the decline in joint families (grandparents no longer spend unlimited time with their grandchildren from birth).

i. Growing Divorce Rates

'The rigid boundaries governing traditional Nepali life are starting to crumble and so is the notion of marriage.'[82] There was a dramatic rise in divorce rates between 2001 to 2011,[83] and the numbers almost doubled over just five years in

---

[75] C Kenner, R Mahera and J Jessel, 'Intergenerational learning between children and grandparents in East London' (2007) 5 *Journal of Early Childhood Research* 219.

[76] C Copen and M Silverstein, 'The transmission of religious beliefs across generations: Do grandparents matter?' (2008) 38 *Journal of Comparative Family Studies* 59.

[77] See generally Hossain, Eisberg and Shwalb (n 1) 280–81; Kenner, Mahera and Jessel (n 75).

[78] Cox (n 73) 487.

[79] DK Shrestha, 'Giving up on grannies' (September 2012) at www.archive.nepalitimes.com/news.php?id=19664#.Ye3bzi2cbUp.

[80] READ Nepal, 'My Grandparents' Stories, My Pictures, Nepal' (18 September 2015) at www.uil.unesco.org/case-study/effective-practices-database-litbase-0/my-grandparents-stories-my-pictures-nepal.

[81] Kamnuansilpa and Wongthanavasu (n 71) 49.

[82] Honourable Justice Sapana Pradhan-Malla, Supreme Court Nepal, in B Rai, 'Not so happily ever after' (July 2014) at www.archive.nepalitimes.com/article/nation/%20number-of-nepali-women-filing-for-divorce-rises,1513.

[83] Global Press (n 40).

the capital, Kathmandu, from 1,039 cases in 2009 to 1,824 by 2013.[84] Women are much less dependent on men than they were in the past, and financially independent women are 'less inclined to remain in an unhappy marriage'.[85] Whilst these may be progressive movements towards women empowerment,[86] divorces sever connections between grandparents and grandchildren.

Research suggests that grandparents 'might be able to provide stability and a sense of security for children'[87] who experience trauma from the breaking apart of their family. There is, however, always a danger that the resident parent might deny a child contact with the non-resident parent ('parental alienation'[88]) and grandparents due to hostility/bitterness[89] or stigmatisation. Pritchard and Williams pertinently encapsulate the child-centred approach in such circumstances:

> Familial relationships are usually central to a child's upbringing, therefore, should not necessarily end following the breakdown in an adult relationship, whether that is between parents or between a parent and grandparent.[90]

The current child arrangement laws in Nepal are inadequate, as discussed in section IV. The law clearly does not treat this area with the sensitivity and foresight it requires. It is far too simplistic for an area that has such a profound impact on a child's 'physical, emotional as well as social development'.[91] Perhaps that is why, in practice, when parents separate or divorce (or if one or both are deceased) in Nepal, child arrangements are determined by the local culture, the decision of the immediate parent, recommendations from relatives, neighbours

---

[84] Rai (n 82); for the trend around the world, see CL Wang and E Schofer, 'Coming Out of the Penumbras: World Culture and Cross-National Variation in Divorce Rates' (2018) 97(2) *Social Forces* 675.

[85] Acharya (n 33) 5.

[86] See, eg, Civil Code 2017, s 72 – marriage void if concluded without the consent of the man *or* the woman; marital rape criminalised (Country Penal Code 2017, s 219) and has been added as a valid ground for divorce for women (Civil Code 2017, s 95).

[87] Douglas and Ferguson (n 49) 41; see also E Marcus, 'Over the Hills and Through the Woods to Grandparents House We Go: Or do We, Post-Troxel?' (2001) 43 *Arizona Law Review* 751.

[88] See, eg, *Re A (Children) (Parental alienation)* [2019] EWFC B56.

[89] See, eg, *Re W (Contact: Application by grandparent)* [1997] 1 FLR 783 – mother stopped contact between the child and the grandmother. In this case the child's best interest only extended to indirect contact with the grandmother, due to the risk of his suffering emotional harm as a result of the hostility. However, the court recognised that grandparents play an important role in children's lives and that it 'would be nonsense in the long term for a child to be denied contact with his grandmother because of bitterness between the mother and the grandmother'; cf *Re K (Mother's Hostility to Grandmother's Contact)* [1996] CLY 565 – where the grandmother's application was refused and a prohibited steps order was made.

[90] Pritchard and Williams (n 70), 281: see, eg, *A and Another v C* [2018] EWHC 2048 (Fam), where the father stopped contact between the child and the maternal family. The maternal grandmother's and aunt's application for rights of access to the child were allowed as they were considered to be people with whom it was important that the child should maintain a personal relationship, pursuant to Art 21 of the Hague Convention on the Civil Aspects of International Child Abduction 1980.

[91] AM Guragain et al, 'Orphanhood and Living Arrangements of Children in Nepal' (2015) 11(12) *Asian Social Science* 84, 84.

and distant relatives.[92] Child arrangement laws in Nepal require nuanced consideration and amendment to pave the way for non-resident grandparents, paternal and maternal, to have contact with their grandchildren. Such rights could then be exercised by grandparents in court, even if a parent denies contact out of court.

ii. Modern Families: Diminishing Family Values and Migration

Grandparents were shown a lot of respect and [were] well-loved by families, but that culture has slowly faded away. We are so busy running after money and making a name for ourselves, we have forgotten some of our good social values.[93]

The 'prevailing religious belief systems and cultural ideals throughout South-East Asia stress filial respect and support for older-age parents as a moral obligation,[94] but despite filial support laws in Nepal,[95] thousands of senior citizens are orphaned at an old age.[96] Some grandparents have never even met their grandchildren.[97] Elderly Nepali citizens say that sons and daughters-in-law 'do not respect and obey their elderly fathers and mothers like they did in the old days', and that they separate to form their own households.[98] As social norms change rapidly,[99] joint families with grandparents, parents, uncles, aunts and cousins have become increasingly rare in Nepal.[100] This change in the Nepali family structure lends support to the contention of modernisation theorists that 'extended families break down under the impact of modernization leaving the nuclear family as the dominate family form'.[101]

Migration has a similar impact on grandparent–grandchild relationships. Challenges in securing employment for young adults in Nepal, in the absence of government support, has resulted in mass migration of the youth to cities and abroad,[102] whilst elderly parents are left behind.[103] Mishra states that, 'with the high rate of foreign employment and migration, the connection to family and wider kin has become brittle'.[104] The changing livelihoods coupled with urbanisation are

---

[92] ibid 84–85.
[93] Sociologist S Dhakal in Shrestha (n 79).
[94] Knodel and Nguyen (n 30) 1962.
[95] See Civil Code 2017, s 122(2); SCA, s 4(1).
[96] Recent findings suggest that young people in Asian societies are exhibiting increasingly negative attitudes towards their elders; see, eg, M North and S Fiske, 'Modern Attitudes Toward Older Adults in the Aging World: A Cross-Cultural Meta-Analysis' (2015) 141(5) *Psychological Bulletin* 993.
[97] Shrestha (n 79).
[98] See anecdotes from Nepali elderly citizens in Goldstein and Beall (n 35) 306–07.
[99] Jennings (n 38) 243.
[100] Shrestha (n 79); see also Guragain et al (n 91) 85.
[101] Goldstein and Beall (n 35) 307.
[102] Guragain et al (n 91) 89 – according to the Department of Foreign Employment of Nepal, more than 1.8 million males migrated abroad (excluding India) between 2008–14.
[103] RK Yadav, 'Aging population in Nepal: challenges and management' (2012) 2(1) *Academic Voices: A Multidisciplinary Journal* 48, 51.
[104] Sociologist Chaitanya Mishra in Rai (n 82).

leading to new dynamics of married couples in both urban and rural areas. These trends increase the likelihood of grandparent estrangement in Nepali society, which in turn calls for the protection of grandparents' rights in relation to their grandchildren.

Changes and trends in Nepal reveal that as women become more independent, and as modernisation[105] results in 'transformation from joint to nuclear family structure'[106] (a reflection of a trend throughout the world[107]), grandparents' rights become increasingly relevant. The state ought to consider prioritising policies that protect grandparents from the potential detriments of changing family structures. Such trends in the Nepali society, combined with the importance of preserving grandparent–grandchild relationships, provide a strong case for bringing grandparents' rights into focus. The law needs to evolve by catching up with the social changes in contemporary Nepal, as it is currently lagging behind.

VI. Addressing Grandparents' Rights: Possible Next Steps

A. Is Law the Answer?

> The power of law as well as its attraction and danger lie in its ability to create and impose social reality, meanings and values, and eventually to make them appear natural and self-evident and thus uncontested.[108]

Whilst section IV discussed the current laws and lack of grandparents' rights, the preceding section identified social grounds that present a case for that gap to be filled. However, an important consideration for legal anthropologists in Nepal is 'whether law ... will really solve the problems of unequal power relations and absence of genuine, egalitarian, inclusive multiculturalism'.[109] Another dimension to examine is the general respect for laws in a country. According to the World Bank, there is 'wide between-country variance in the extent to which residents have confidence in, and abide by, national legislation'.[110] As we have seen

---

[105] See Hossain, Eisberg and Shwalb (n 1) 277: 'Western values of economic competition, geographical mobility and individual gain has caused many Asians to re-evaluate their cultural assumptions of interdependency and collective lifestyles'; Acharya (n 33) 6: '[E]xtended family have been the [cause] of conflict and led [to] dissatisfaction among many modern couples.'

[106] Yadav (n 103) 48.

[107] Arnold et al (n 44) 101.

[108] R Pradhan, 'Negotiating Multiculturalism in Nepal: Law, Hegemony, Contestation and Paradox', *Conference on Constitutionalism and Diversity* (Kathmandu, Nepal, 2007) 4.

[109] ibid 2.

[110] R Serrano, R Saltman and M Yeh, 'Laws on Filial Support in Four Asian Countries' (2017) 95(11) *Bulletin of the World Health Organisation* 788, 790.

from section II, historical trauma, natural disaster and distrust in the state[111] continue to affect the way citizens respond to the law in Nepal. Families tend to protect each other from the state rather than expect support from allegedly corrupt leaders and human rights violators who govern the state. Discrimination and patriarchal values that still seep into the law are concerns that can deter the utilisation of rights.[112] Therefore, it is suggested that grass-root studies and research are pivotal; working with those affected and improving their social and legal inclusion will greatly benefit Nepali citizens.

Indeed, it is important to recognise that law may not be the answer to every social issue: 'Some issues cannot be resolved merely by changing a discriminatory law. Rampant poverty and illiteracy facilitate these harms.'[113] However, it may be rather restrictive to end on the premise that law cannot be the answer to grandparents' rights protection in Nepal, given the changes in modern society and the discussions throughout this chapter with regard to discrimination, which is at the heart of the problem. However, any state intervention must at first be exercised with great caution, as this is a novel and challenging task that cannot be undertaken in haste. Similarly, chapter 7 of this volume stresses the significant risks and inherent challenges of uncertainty within family law, which cannot be resolved by symbolic and expedient solutions. Deciphering the best method to protect grandparents' rights in Nepal requires expert and interdisciplinary research, empirical studies, effective consultation and dialogue among key actors. If the creation or amendment of laws are then found to be appropriate, they will need to be sensitive to the cultural norms and history of Nepal.

B. Interdisciplinary Research: Empirical Studies and Surveys

There is a lacuna of research on grandparent–grandchild relationships in Nepal. Such research would contribute to a broader understanding of Nepali grandparents' expectations and concerns in relation to their grandchildren. In particular, this topic would benefit from empirical studies that encompass diverse ethnicities, castes and religious differences in Nepal, which aim to include sufficient participants from separate categories to produce reliable results. 'It is about listening to people and having real conversations about their concerns ... Genuine respect and empathy is the key – and can't be packaged.'[114] Community surveys, interviews and group discussions are methods that have proved highly effective in exploring grandparents' relationships with grandchildren in other Asian countries.[115]

---

[111] See also Cox (n 73) 488.
[112] See generally ibid 489.
[113] Aiken (n 2) 411; see generally N Mascie-Taylor, 'Regional Dimensions of Poverty and Vulnerability in Nepal' (DFID Discussion Paper, May 2013) at assets.publishing.service.gov.uk/government/uploads/system/uploads/attachment_data/file/204015/Regional-Dimensions-Poverty-Nepal.pdf.
[114] Arnold et al (n 44) 157.
[115] Kamnuansilpa and Wongthanavasu (n 71) 51.

They result in qualitative data that can capture a rich and detailed picture of the grandparent–grandchild relationship, currently absent in Nepal. Such empirical studies would ask questions to gauge whether the lack of legal protection of grandparents' rights in Nepal is a problem or is likely to become a problem in the near future. They can also help organisations and individuals advocate for changes in policy or practice based on an understanding of the realities on the ground.[116]

Effective participatory methods would initiate fruitful discussions and dialogue on key issues for grandparents' rights. For example, 'Bringing up Children in a Changing World'[117] is a thorough report, including empirical studies among different localities, castes and ethnicities. This report is not only extremely informative, it also demonstrates effective participatory processes such as 'dialogue sessions',[118] which provide opportunities for local people to engage with researchers in greater detail. This report also found that plenty of work has yet to be done to 'develop appropriate training to overcome engrained hierarchical attitudes on the part of facilitators',[119] which should be borne in mind when conducting studies on grandparents' rights in Nepal.

Acharya's[120] field study on the analysis of divorce in Pokhara, Nepal, was conducted among different castes and ethnic groups. He made an especially important finding about cultural divorce cases in Nepal that are not found in the court record. This demonstrates cultural sensitivity and adds another layer of context to families in Nepal, which indicates that grandparents' rights are relevant not only in legally divorced households, but also in customary divorce cases. Acharya also makes a point that sociological and anthropological research is 'not dominant in Nepal'.[121] If this is true, it is time researchers took it upon themselves to employ interdisciplinary and holistic approaches to empirical studies in Nepal, to explore grandparents' rights from multiple perspectives. Such interdisciplinary work has been globally more common in the recent years.[122] An approach including legal experts, anthropologists, historians and sociologists could make the policy makers' task in Nepal more constructive and successful, by assisting them in considering this topic in a concrete manner and finding diverse solutions for the current lack of protection of grandparents' rights.

i. Research Trends on Grandparents Around the World

Due to the of lack research and academic discussion on grandparent–grandchild relationships in Nepal, several studies from around the world, particularly Asia,

---

[116] Arnold et al (n 44) 170.
[117] Arnold et al (n 44).
[118] ibid 146.
[119] ibid.
[120] Acharya (n 33).
[121] ibid 1.
[122] Mather (n 10) 290.

have been utilised in this chapter. Further examples may provide some useful research guidance in Nepal.

Researchers have suggested it is important to gather grandchildren's experiences and views towards their grandparents, 'since grandparents have such a profound impact on grandchildren's lives across the globe'.[123] Though research in this area is very limited in general, anecdotal data have found that grandchildren in South Asia see their grandparents as an additional set of parents.[124] In North East Thailand, a substantial number of grandparents serve as surrogate or substitute parents.[125] Research show that grandparents are seen as a source of moral guidance and strong authority in Chinese, South Asian and Middle Eastern families,[126] whilst across Latino and African cultures, grandchildren perceive grandparents as a source of positive socialisation and economic support.[127]

Chaudhary writes that in India, grandparents express more love and affection towards their grandchildren than to their own children.[128] This is bound to be the case in Nepal, which shares many social norms with India. It would be beneficial to have concrete evidence of the positive relationship shared between grandparents and grandchildren in Nepal to foster awareness and support for grandparents' rights protection.

Most research across the globe focuses on the role of grandmothers,[129] as they are generally more enthusiastic about and involved with their grandchildren's upbringing than grandfathers.[130] However, grandfathers should not be overlooked amidst issues surrounding patriarchy in Nepal. Just as maternal grandparents' rights need to be protected as much as paternal ones, it is vital to ensure that grandfathers are not left behind, because 'both grandmothers and grandfathers contribute to their grandchildren's development'.[131]

Another group of under-represented people in the grandparenting literature are grandparents whose children and grandchildren have migrated to cities and abroad. This is a particularly pressing social phenomenon in Nepal, as most of the young population go abroad for work and/or studies. How should grandparents'

---

[123] Hossain, Eisberg and Shwalb (n 1) 282.

[124] ibid 282–83.

[125] Kamnuansilpa and Wongthanavasu (n 71) 49.

[126] See generally M Emam, Y Abdelazim and M El-Keshky, 'Grandparents in the Middle East and North Africa: Changes in identity and trajectory' in D Shwalb and Z Hossain (eds), *Grandparents in Cultural Context* (New York, Routledge, 2018) 223; X Li and M Lamb, 'Fathering in Chinese culture: Traditions and transitions' in J Roopnarine (ed), *Fathers Across Cultures: The importance, roles, and diverse practices of dads* (Santa Barbara, CA, Praeger, 2015) 273.

[127] Hossain, Eisberg and Shwalb (n 1) 283; Cox (n 73) 485–86.

[128] N Chaudhary, 'The father's role in the Indian family: A Story That Must Be Told' in D Shwalb, B Shwalb and M Lamb (eds), *Fathers in Cultural Context* (New York, Routledge, 2012) 68–94.

[129] See, eg, Sheppard and Sear (n 48); E Voland, A Chasiotis and W Schiefenhövel (eds), *Grandmotherhood: The evolutionary significance of the second half of female life* (New Brunswick, NJ, Rutgers University Press, 2007); Masvie (n 41).

[130] Douglas and Ferguson (n 49) 45, 49.

[131] Hossain, Eisberg and Shwalb (n 1) 283.

rights be protected in a country where geographical separation from their grand-children is the social norm? It would be helpful to have empirical research on grandparents' and grandchildren's perspectives on the social/legal landscape and the impact of separation on grandparent–grandchild relationships.[132] This would be an interesting and relevant topic area for research in Nepal, which would allow academics, practitioners and law makers to consider ways of confronting this issue. Simply starting this conversation and recognising the social dilemma would be a worthy start.

C. Key Actors: Dialogue, Consultation and Reports

Research and studies in Nepal, as suggested, will help understand grandparents' rights in context. Findings from such studies can assist key actors, that is, policy makers, family law practitioners and other stakeholders, to start a dialogue on this social phenomenon.

Thereafter, the state may consider running a formal consultation, targeted at those with a clear interest in the policy question. This can allow policy makers to make informed decisions on ways of addressing grandparents' rights in Nepal. Such an exercise would need to be accessible and 'flexibly adapted to the needs and interests of specific families and communities'.[133] A post-consultation summary report on grandparents' rights would be an invaluable document, as it would expand policy makers' vision and help them design practical and effective solutions. In addition, the report would attract streamlined academic and research interest, increase public knowledge and encourage public engagement on grandparents' rights.

Since there are over 100 ethnic and caste groups that speak 129 recognised languages[134] and practise a variety of religions in Nepal, new systems and changes to policy will require key state actors to appreciate that 'competency of professional personnel is a prerequisite for their effectiveness'.[135] Unfortunately in Nepal, implementation of new policies and provisions by men in the past have created overwhelming obstacles for women and their families.[136] Perhaps culturally/gender-sensitive policies should require female officials and officials from diverse ethnic/caste backgrounds to be included in the process. This may help tackle the long-standing patriarchal and hierarchical practices[137] that impede progress.

---

[132] See, eg, L Drew and P Smith, 'The impact of parental separation/divorce on grandparents–grandchild relationships' (1999) 48 *International Journal of Aging & Human Development* 191.

[133] Arnold et al (n 44) 156.

[134] 'Six new languages added to the list of languages spoken in Nepal' (5 November 2019) at english. khabarhub.com/2019/05/53137/.

[135] Cox (n 73), 485, 489.

[136] Paudel (n 39) 32.

[137] Mawby and Applebaum (n 11) 16; see generally The Equal Rights Trust Report, *My Children's Future Ending Gender Discrimination in Nationality Laws* (UK, Stroma Ltd, 2015) 9–11.

These are ongoing concerns in Nepal that would benefit from a wider dialogue among key actors.

D. Changes in Laws and Alternative Dispute Resolution

> The diversity among these grandparents mandates that policies and programs serving them be sensitive to culture, traditions, and histories which may impact their resources, well-being and functioning ...[138]

Laws cannot be effective if they are 'ignorant or insensitive to cultural expectations and values or to historical or current events that may make specific populations reluctant to seek support'.[139] Any changes in laws to protect grandparents' rights in Nepal must be considerate and sensitive towards the country's historical, social and cultural context, discussed in the early sections of this chapter. This area requires robust research in Nepal. Proposing new and detailed laws to protect grandparents in Nepal, in the absence of much-needed empirical data at this primitive stage, would be overreaching the boundaries of this chapter. In any case, attempting such a task from the UK, with a bird's-eye view of Nepal, could well be inapt. Fundamental questions posed by Aiken[140] are incredibly relevant: 'How do we step outside ourselves and imagine something that grows out of a culture so different from our own? How do we fight the urge to replicate what we know?' That is not to say that the suggestions made throughout this chapter, particularly in section IV, based on laws in the UK are redundant, but simply replicating British laws may not be the answer given Nepal's unique context.

A general observation/recommendation on law, however, may be of some value. As society changes and evolves, so too do the family structures; merely addressing the grandparents' issue would be piecemeal. While it is beyond the scope of this chapter, more comprehensive reform is needed as the rise in family proceedings indicates a need for Nepal to develop its family procedure rules. It may be advantageous for family law to be recognised as a distinct area of law, with its own 'Family Procedure Rules', as in the UK, rather than its being appended to the all-encompassing Civil Code under part 3. This would allow for a focused approach in dealing with family law reforms, including, and not limited to, grandparents' rights.

Further down that line, provided grandparents' rights are accommodated by the law, the 'alternative dispute resolution' route might assist in Nepal. It is well established in the UK that the cost of legal proceedings is clearly a deterrent to

---

[138] Cox (n 73) 484.
[139] ibid 485.
[140] Aiken (n 2) 411.

grandparents' pursuit of their rights.[141] Therefore, a grandparent is required to attend a compulsory family mediation information and assessment meeting (MIAM) before applying for contact with their grandchildren.[142] In Nepal's context, social stigma,[143] shame/disgrace[144] and potential loss of 'reputation'[145] could prevent many women and their maternal families from accessing justice when the traditional joint families fall apart. The added legal expense and delays of the court system[146] will no doubt act as further obstacles. Chapter 2 of this volume, which discusses the pros and cons of mediation in detail, highlights that while courts impose a solution on parties, mediation offers support to parties in finding their own solutions that are agreeable to all. In light of this, MIAM or voluntary mediation in grandparents' contact cases could potentially increase accessibility to and utilisation of the law, as the matter could be resolved before reaching the courts, which would protect grandparents from the cost and distress around making their family issues public.

VII. Conclusion

The need to protect grandparents' rights to maintain their relationship with their grandchildren in Nepal is now relevant more than ever:

> [S]ocial and cultural complexities, mobility for job, impact of secularism, global impact of capitalism, emerging legal grounds, of industrialization and urbanization, changing attitudes on traditional norms and value system [are] causing disintegration of marital [and familial] relations.[147]

The state has a central role in the shaping of 'the Nepali family' and 'Nepali culture' through its laws.[148] However, in Nepal, the battle appears to be with the patriarchal society, culture and laws that perpetuate unequal and ancient practices.[149] It will take a long time for such entrenched social norms to change, but there is always the 'ability to change if we change our assumptions'.[150] If the law can lead the way,[151] at least citizens can realise their legal rights and have the opportunity

---

[141] Douglas and Ferguson (n 49) 48.

[142] Children and Families Act 2014, s 10; Family Procedure Rules 2010, pt 3, r 3.6 and Practice Direction 3A.

[143] Jennings (n 38) 230.

[144] See Shanta's story in Aiken (n 2) 409–10.

[145] Paudel (n 39) 32.

[146] Rai (n 82); see Usha's story, where she settled out of court (despite being entitled to some property) to avoid the legal expense and years of battle that the court process would involve.

[147] Acharya (n 33) 2.

[148] Tamang (n 16) 127.

[149] See generally Paudel (n 39).

[150] Aiken (n 2) 413.

[151] Y Dror, 'Law as a Tool of Directed Social Change: A Framework for Policy Making' (1970) 13(4) *American Behavioural Scientist* 553, 558.

to exercise them in court. Incrementally, liberal judgments will set a precedent in the community, which will require deep-rooted social norms to adjust. Progressive laws will help contemporary Nepali families, who simply do not fit into the patrilinear definition of a family.

The rights of grandparents to spend time with their grandchildren is an issue that has only recently attracted judicial and ministerial attention in the international context.[152] Hence, it is understandable that a developing, collectivistic country such as Nepal, in contrast to the UK, is far from discussing the issue. Nevertheless, it is a problem lurking on the horizon, given the changes in society, and one that needs to be recognised and addressed in Nepal.

Contextualised thus, I end with the central purpose of this chapter, which is to unwrap the topic judiciously and identify whether it is of relevance in Nepali society. This aim has been achieved by discussing the context and lack of legal protection for grandparents' rights at length in sections II, III and IV, and by making a case for that gap to be filled in section V. The recommendations made in this chapter are by no means comprehensive. Many suitable avenues and solutions will come out of interdisciplinary research around grandparents' rights, which is identified in section VI as the first step in the process. The next steps need to be taken cautiously and considerately. This is an 'entry point' contribution on grandparents' rights in Nepal, which aims to bring grandparents' rights to public consciousness and, more importantly, to the policy makers' consciousness, so that the country can prepare before it becomes a problem without a remedy. This is the right time for progressive dialogues to commence in Nepal, as it is in a state of transition and its laws are still under construction (post-conflict, post-disaster). It seems apt to conclude on an optimistic note:

> Nepal is at a crossroads. This is a defining moment for addressing the challenges of Nepali society, governance, and community relationships.[153]

---

[152] Pritchard and Williams (n 70) 286.
[153] Mawby and Applebaum (n 11) Foreword.

INDEX

9 781509 953417